Sports Illustrated

The Football Book

1981 | MEAN JOE GREENE'S STEELERS HELMET

COURTESY PRO FOOTBALL HALL OF FAME

SAMMY BAUGH
Washington Redskins | QB
1938
Photograph by CARL M. MYDANS

BRETT FAVRE
Green Bay Packers | QB
2002
Photograph by WALTER IOOSS JR.

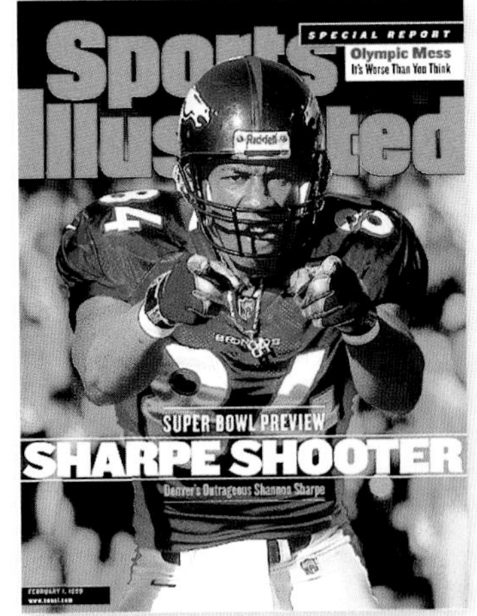

The Football Book

ROB FLEDER
Editor

STEVEN HOFFMAN
Designer

BOB ROE / MARK GODICH *Senior Editors*

HEATHER BROWN *Photo Editor* JOSH DENKIN *Associate Designer*

KEVIN KERR *Copy Editor* ANDREA WOO *Reporter*

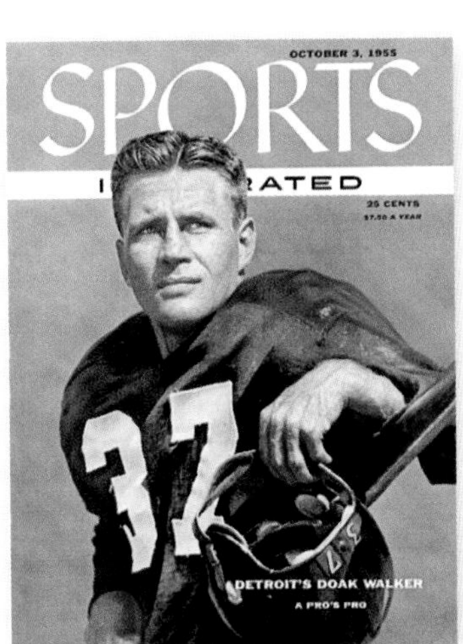

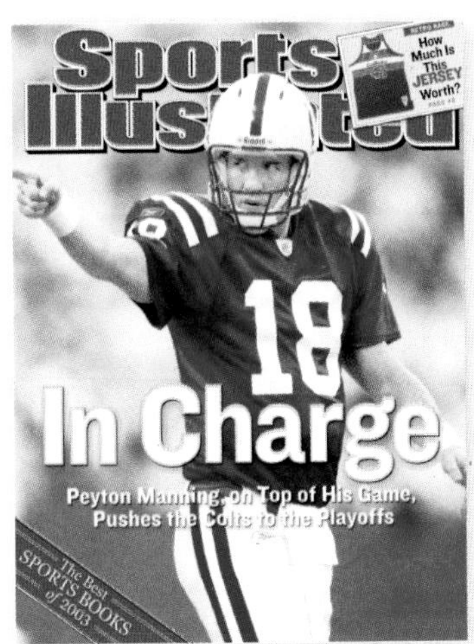

Sports Illustrated

Contents

 • ISBN: 1-932994-74-2 • LIBRARY OF CONGRESS CONTROL NUMBER: 2005906437

Y.A. TITTLE'S SHOULDER PADS
(worn throughout his NFL career)

1950–1964

Photograph by DAVID N. BERKWITZ

COURTESY OF THE PRO FOOTBALL HALL OF FAME

NFL STARTING QUARTERBACKS

1961

Photograph by RALPH MORSE

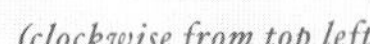

(clockwise from top left)

MILT PLUM • 16
Cleveland Browns

BOBBY LAYNE • 22
Pittsburgh Steelers

SAM ETCHEVERRY • 14
St. Louis Cardinals

BILL WADE • 9
Chicago Bears

DON MEREDITH • 17
Dallas Cowboys

FRAN TARKENTON • 10
Minnesota Vikings

JIM NINOWSKI • 15
Detroit Lions

(clockwise from top left)

BART STARR • 15
Green Bay Packers

JOHNNY UNITAS • 19
Baltimore Colts

NORM SNEAD • 16
Washington Redskins

ZEKE BRATKOWSKI • 12
Los Angeles Rams

Y.A. TITTLE • 14
New York Giants

SONNY JURGENSEN • 9
Philadelphia Eagles

JOHN BRODIE • 12
San Francisco 49ers

THE KICKOFF
The Colts' Steve Myhra put the boot to The Duke againts the Bears in Baltimore's Memorial Stadium
1960
Photograph by GEORGE SILK

INTRODUCTION

{BY RICK REILLY}

YEAH, YEAH, YEAH.

EVERYBODY CELEBRATES PRO FOOTBALL BY TALKING ABOUT THE FAMOUS PLAYS, TOUCHDOWNS, COACHES, STADIUMS, UNI'S AND *GREATEST HITS* VIDEOS. ❧ BUT WHAT ABOUT THE ADS? ❧ REALLY, WHERE WOULD AMERICAN CULTURE BE WITHOUT JOE NAMATH'S PANTYHOSE?

1973 | JOE NAMATH was a pioneer when it came to cashing in on his celebrity in commercials, including this stunt for Schick.

c. 1960 | OTTO GRAHAM cheerfully kicked off a tea campaign.

1962 | FRANK GIFFORD lit up again when he got his check.

Mean Joe Greene's gullet? Peyton Manning's meat?

Nowhere is right. So isn't it time we looked at NFL players only through their ads?

In these pages, we celebrate pro football during the 50-plus years that SPORTS ILLUSTRATED has been covering it—and beyond. But without the ads in SI starring NFL players, the magazine might've folded 49 years ago.

The most famous NFL ad of all—one of the most controversial in Madison Avenue history—was very nearly not an ad at all. In 1974, Joe Namath was in a car with his agent, Jimmy Walsh, on his way to tape an a TV spot for Beautymist pantyhose.

"Uh, Joe, you'll have to shave your legs for this," Walsh reportedly said. Namath looked like somebody had served him his own liver on a plate.

"I'm not doing it," Namath said.

But Namath finally did do it—the money was too good to leave on the table—and people are *still* talking about it. The spot opened with a shot of a pair of shapely feet, panned up a pair of shapely legs in pantyhose, past a pair of green Jets shorts and then up a Jets jersey to the face that made women's knees go weak. And then Namath said, "If Beautymist can make *my* legs look good, imagine what they'll do for yours."

And then a gorgeous model came into the shot and planted a big kiss on Namath, lest anybody doubt which "team" he played for.

The ad only ran for three months, but some people think it helped bring millions of women to the game. Some people think Namath did that all by himself.

Until Namath, ads starring pro football players were almost exclusively for men. In fact, at the beginning, they were mostly for men who *played* football. The only ad featuring a football player in the first SI in 1954 was one that included the great Otto Graham, pitching his signature model Wilson football.

Things were different then. The NFL didn't regulate what players could endorse. (Now: no alcohol, tobacco, forbidden supplements or gambling, not even those "What happens in Las Vegas, stays in Las Vegas" ads.) Back then, football players like Frank Gifford could shill for Lucky Strike cigarettes. Graham did an ad for the tea industry. "Tea is the lively, refreshing cup that brings out the best in a man . . . snaps him back, refreshes him—keeps him hitting on all eight."

Some ideas were dumb: One time, when New York quarterback Y.A. Tittle was a star for the Giants, an advertising agency asked if he would do an ad for a hair tonic. One little problem: Tittle was bald. It was sort of like the time Bowman's Dairy paid Chicago Bears back Ray Nolting to endorse its milk in 1938. "It tastes better!" Nolting says in the newspaper ads, in full uni, holding up a bottle of milk.

TEA COUNCIL OF THE U.S.A. INC. (GRAHAM); A.T. CO. (GIFFORD)

1968 | RAY NITSCHKE had a secret weapon for goal line stands.

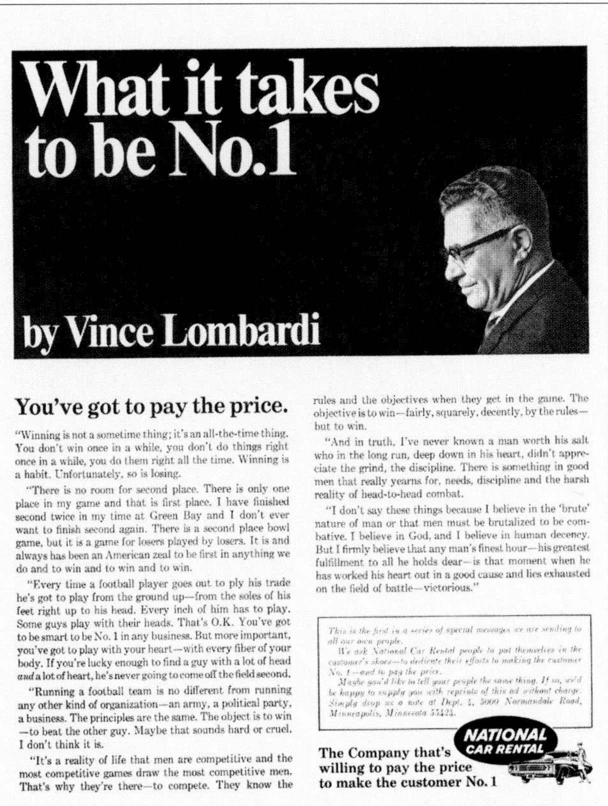

1968 | VINCE LOMBARDI: Run to daylight in a convertible?

But how would Nolting have known? He was allergic to the stuff.

And some ideas were just weird: The Packers' nasty linebacker Ray Nitschke was shown in his uniform, on a football field in front of a goalpost, holding up his favorite chainsaw—the Stihl 041AV. No wonder guys didn't want to come over the middle.

Even Vince Lombardi did a few ads—his way. In a 1968 National Car Rental print ad, Lombardi never said a word about renting or cars. Instead, the ad quoted Lombardi ranting hither and yon about his philosophy of winning and life. "I firmly believe that any man's finest hour is that moment when he has worked his heart out in a good cause," Lombardi declared at the end of a page-long speech, "and lies exhausted on the field of battle—victorious." Maybe the ad was subliminal. Maybe you were supposed to understand that when you were lying there, sprawled out on the field, you should call National—'cause *they'll pick you up!* O.K., wrong company. So sue.

Anyway, then came Broadway Joe.

"Man, my mom talked about Joe Namath a lot," says New England's Tom Brady, the hottest quarterback in the league today and winner of three of the first four Super Bowls since the turn of the millennium. "She really liked him. He owned a bar, right? I don't think I could pull something like that off. No way."

Terminally shy, Brady turns down nearly everything, which is probably a good impulse because he gets offered all kinds of crazy ideas. Like Namath before him, a razor company offered the disgustingly handsome Brady many, many dollars to shave before every game with a Gillette razor, since Gillette has its name on the stadium Brady plays in. Brady said no. "I'd rather keep what I got on my face, thanks."

He's no Namath. Namath started getting paid the moment he woke up in the morning. He was once even paid to shave his face. See, after the Jets fell short of the AFL playoffs in 1967, the players vowed not to shave their mustaches and beards until they made it to the postseason. But AFL president Milt Woodard decreed: "Off with their whiskers!" Namath got $20,000 to shave off his moustache with a Schick razor for a TV spot. Pretty good money since he had to do it anyway.

So what's Brady's problem? He needs to join the bunch of NFL superstars who will shill for every possible trinket and bob they can get their famous mugs next to. Terry Bradshaw, formerly or the Steelers, now of Fox, may be the alltime champ. He was known for having absolutely no restrictions on what he'd endorse, including the Qaylar toupee. His worst gig may have been an ad for the stupidest fitness gizmo ever perpetrated on the American public—the Jog & Lift.

The Jog & Lift allowed you to lift weights and jump rope *at the same time!* It was a kind of steel barbell with a jump rope attached to it. This

Take it from Terry Bradshaw
'Jog & Lift™
your way into shape with the perfect exercise'

main bar and hand sleeves are made of durable stainless steel
JOG & LIFT
weight is adjustable from 4½ lbs. to 12 lbs.
eight basic adjustable hand positions
"the best workout I ever had..."
Rope is adjustable to suit your height
Portable. Easy to assemble or dismantle.
"When I played football for the Pittsburgh Steelers, I HAD to be in shape. Now that I'm retired, I WANT to be in shape. Jog & Lift does it for me."
Patent Pending

JOG & LIFT Skipping rope and lifting weights simultaneously

JOG & LIFT A complete workout . . . moving the gym into the convenience of your home.

Use 8 basic hand positions for 2½ minutes each, 20 minutes a day to help you:

- Reduce your weight
- Stimulate your cardio-vascular system
- Add strength and firmness
- Improve your body tone
- Coordinate your body

CALL 800-245-LIFT Toll Free
800-235-LIFT PA residents only
Or send in this coupon

SEND TO Jog & Lift
P. O. Box 1269
Johnstown, PA 15907
JOG & LIFT™

☐ YES! I want the perfect exercise! Please send me ___ Jog & Lift exercisers at $99.95 (Postage and Handling included) each so I can begin my home workout!
Name
Street Address
City State Zip
☐ Check or money order enclosed
Bill my ☐ MasterCard ☐ VISA
Card #
My card expires Signature
PA residents add 6% Sales Tax for each order

1985 | TERRY BRADSHAW had an indomitable will to shill.

1978 | O.J. SIMPSON was a long-running hit for Hertz.

was a very important step forward in scientific achievement because there are not enough injuries in jump-roping and weightlifting by themselves. Let's double the carnage! And all for only $99.95! (Comes with free *How to Care for Your Hernia* videotape.)

It matters not whether a guy can spell kat or enjoys biting the heads off pigeons for lunch. When it comes to endorsements, fans tend to swallow them whole, and football stars are not just good pitchmen, they are often the *best* pitchmen, athlete or nonathlete. Three guesses who was named by *Advertising Age* magazine as its Spokesman of the Year in 1976? Wrong! The answer: O.J. Simpson.

That year, O.J. was unstoppable, especially in airports. In one survey, 100% of those surveyed recognized the name and 90% knew he pitched for Hertz.

Every company wanted Simpson in its driver's seat. Handsome, well-spoken, TV star, Heisman winner, budding movie actor. How's that *possibly* going to go south?

The golden age of muscles was here. One spot featuring NFL stars kicked off one of the longest running campaign in history: Miller Lite's *Tastes Great, Less Filling* ads, which started with Jets' running back Matt Snell and didn't end until 20 years later. In between, football rogues became its divas: John Madden, Bubba Smith and Dick Butkus, especially. Smith stood in front of the camera with a Miller Lite in his hands. "I like Miller Lite because it tastes great and it's less filling," he declared. "I also like the easy-opening can." Then Smith ripped off the top with his bare hands. What nobody knew is that he opened a five-inch gash in his hand taping the spot (the can wasn't rigged right by the prop dept.). Like the true football stud that he was, he continued taping between blood soppages.

(Hundred-point bonus question: Can you name the two SI writers who appeared in Miller Lite ads 20 years apart, one of whom was lauded for being a groundbreaker and the other ripped for not being able to act? Answer: Frank Deford and Yours Truly.)

One ad became a made-for-TV-movie, if you can believe that. Of course, they should've stopped at the one-minute version. It's 1979 and Mean Joe Greene is limping down the tunnel, carrying his jersey, after what looks like a devastating loss when a kid comes up to him and says, "Mr. Greene? D'you need help?"

O.K., now, right off, you know NFL life has changed in the last 25 years. Do you know what they'd do now to a kid who got into the tunnel and accosted a player? He'd be swept up by a SWAT team and taken to Guantánamo for questioning, with a note sent to his fifth-grade teacher: *Billy will be out of school indefinitely. Don't ask.*

So Greene just grunts "uh, uh" to the kid, but the boy gets up the

JOG & LIFT (BRADSHAW); HERTZ SYSTEM INC (SIMPSON)

1978 | BUBBA SMITH was a soldier in the Miller Lite army.

1979 | JOE GREENE didn't seem so mean if you gave him a Coke.

courage to say, "I think you're the best ever," and hands him a Coke. Greene chugs the whole thing down without a breath. (He chugged 18 during that two-day taping, at a little stadium in Mount Vernon, N.Y.) Then Greene and the kid start to walk away in opposite directions, until Greene says, "Here . . . catch" and throws him the jersey. Not a bad deal, considering that jersey today would cost a kid about $350 at any retro shop.

The ad won a Clio and was once named by *USA Today* as the best Super Bowl ad ever. That's pretty good for a guy like Greene, who was so scared during a school play once that he quit the night of the dress rehearsal. The made-for-TV movie? Don't ask.

One ad changed someone's life. It was 1984, and Joe Montana was shooting an ad for Schick razors. (Are you sensing a theme here?) The model was Jennifer Wallace, and she was supposed to be the sheriff in town, demanding a shave from the unkempt stranger. Montana, Mr. Cool when he had 300-pound lineman moving in, became Mr. Freeze when he had a line to deliver. He was so nervous that Jennifer pinched him in the butt to relax him. Must've worked. Montana ended up marrying her. They live today with their four kids on a huge ranch north of the Napa Valley.

Right now, the 800-pound gorilla of the NFL ad game is Indianapolis quarterback Peyton Manning, who has the big three: 1) football stardom; 2) likability; and 3) the ability to actually act. He is far and away the money-leader among active players in ads, and Brady says he can have it. "I just don't want to do hardly any of them," he says. "It's like, 'You want me to wear *what*? You want me to say *what*?' So I usually turn most everything down because, well, you see some guys in some commercials, and other players rag them on the field. Like with Peyton, he's out there trying to call audibles and our guys are yelling, 'Cut . . . that . . . meat! Cut . . . that . . . meat!' I'm *so* glad I didn't do that one."

"That's true," Manning admits sheepishly. "Seems like every team we play does that to me. That was the only part of that ad I didn't really want to do. [The director] begged me to do it. *Begged* me. So I finally did it. And I'll never hear the end of it." At least Manning hasn't gone to the complete dark side of NFL ads, the place where no self-respecting athlete should go, and yet so many do—erectile dysfunction.

Even though Levitra is an official "partner" of the NFL, no active players are doing ads for it. But you do have former Chicago Bears tough guy Iron Mike Ditka proudly discussing his penile dysfunctions for all to see.

Can you imagine Red Grange letting them put his face up on a 50-foot billboard, with the huge line: "Hi! I'm Red Grange! And I need help getting an erection!"

Sigh.

May Mike Ditka's next Christmas present be the Jog & Lift.

MILLER BREWING CO. (SMITH); THE COCA-COLA CO. (GREENE)

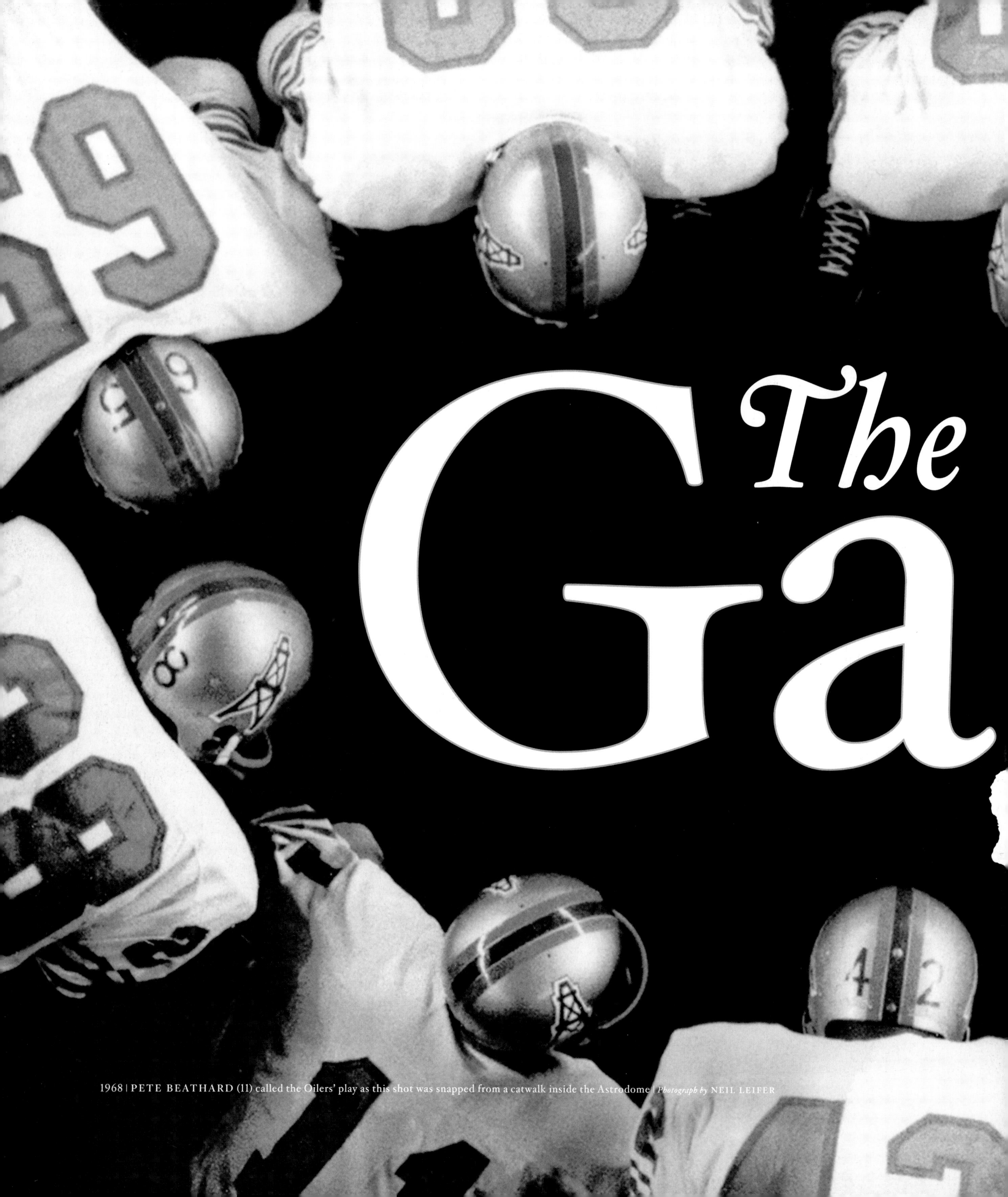

The Ga

1968 | PETE BEATHARD (11) called the Oilers' play as this shot was snapped from a catwalk inside the Astrodome | *Photograph by* NEIL LEIFER

me

1994 | DAN MARINO had to contend with the Patriots' rush and a ravaged field in Miami | *Photograph by* GEORGE TIEDEMANN

73

1976 | STEELERS WIDEOUT Lynn Swann laid out the Cowboys in Super Bowl X in Miami, and was the game's MVP | *Photograph by* HEINZ KLUETMEIER

1982 | DWIGHT CLARK'S last-minute catch beat the Cowboys and put the 49ers in the Super Bowl | *Photograph by* WALTER IOOSS JR.

58
49
61

c.1960 | PACKERS TACKLE Forrest Gregg, whom Vince Lombardi called "the best player I ever coached" | *Photograph by* VERNON BIEVER

1960 | JIM TAYLOR could grind out yardage for Green Bay even when the tundra wasn't frozen | *Photograph by* HY PESKIN

1973 | O.J. SIMPSON broke Jim Brown's single-season rushing record with this carry, and ended the season with 2,003 yards | *Photograph by* NEIL LEIFER

1972 | LARRY CSONKA (39) was the battering ram for a Miami team that won back-to-back Super Bowls | *Photograph by* NEIL LEIFER

COURTESY OF THE PRO FOOTBALL HALL OF FAME

1970 | TOM DEMPSEY, though born with half his right foot missing, set an NFL record with this 63-yard field goal; his kicking shoe is in the Hall of Fame | *Photograph by* AP *(right)*

19
45

1994 | THE COWBOYS' Emmitt Smith ran into heavy traffic while the Giants' Lawrence Taylor tried to run into Smith | *Photograph by* JOHN IACONO

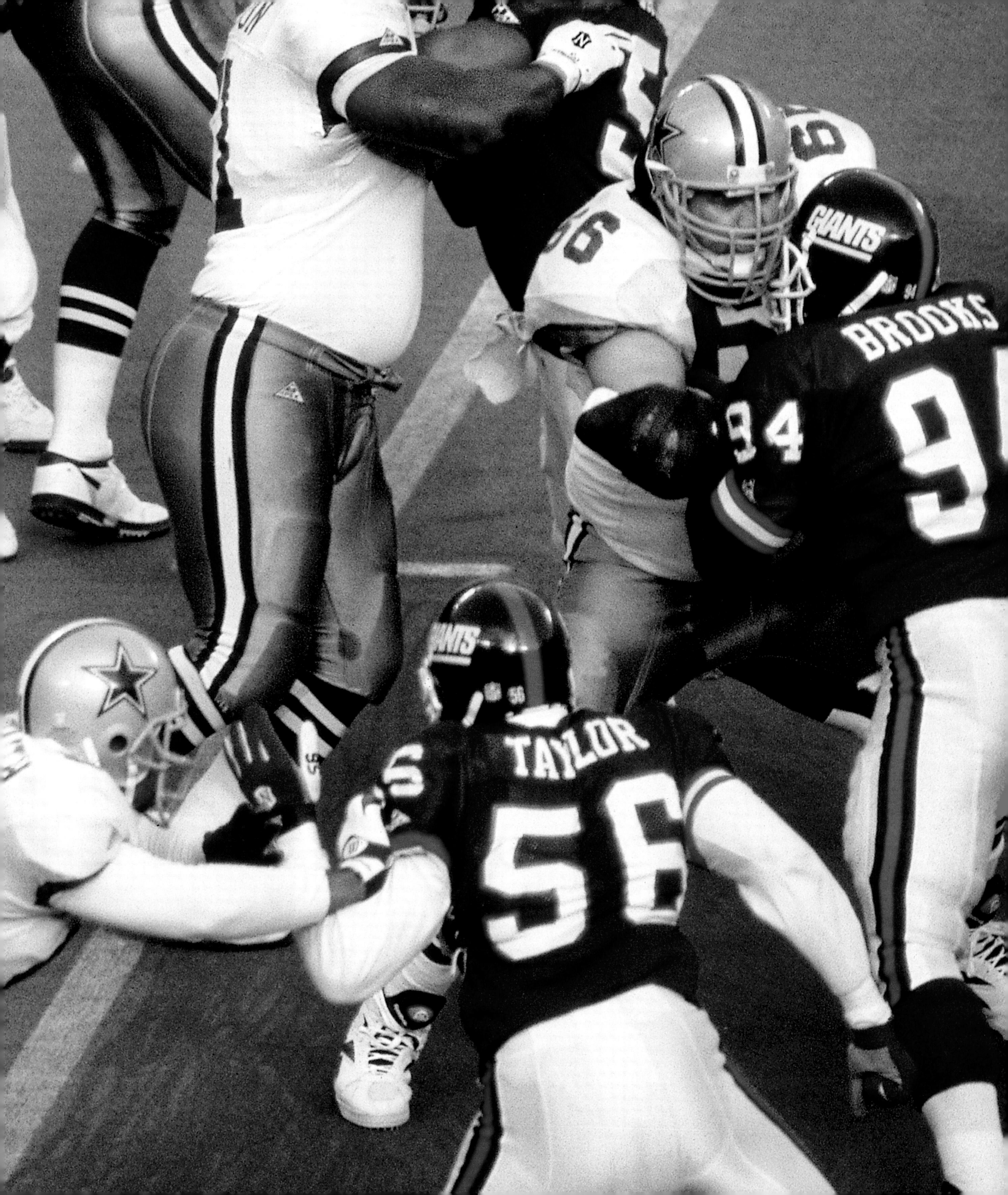
GIANTS
BROOKS
94
TAYLOR
56

THE GAME THAT WAS

BY MYRON COPE

Some of the NFL's pioneers recall, in their own words, the league's wild and uncertain early days, when one team promoted its New York games by having players ride horses down Broadway and a $1 investment could yield $1.5 million.—from SI, OCTOBER 13 & 20, 1969

INDIAN JOE GUYON

(1919–1927: Canton Bulldogs, Cleveland Indians, Oorang Indians, Rock Island Independents, Kansas City Cowboys, New York Giants)

The late Ralph McGill, the distinguished Atlanta newspaper publisher and author, once wrote, "There is no argument about the identity of the greatest football player who ever performed in Dixie. There is a grand argument about second place, but for first place there is Joe Guyon, the Chippewa brave."

I PLAYED halfback on offense, and on defense I played sideback, which I suppose is what they later started calling defensive halfback. I had more damn tricks and, brother, I could hit you. Elbows, knees or whatchamacallit—boy, I could use 'em. Yes, and it's true that I used to laugh like the dickens when I saw other players get injured. Self-protection is the first thing they should have learned. You take care of yourself, you know. I think it's a sin if you don't. It's a rough game, so you've got to *equip* yourself and know what to do.

The games that were real scraps were the ones in Chicago. George Halas was a brawler. There'd be a fight every time we met those sons of biscuits. Halas knew that I was the key man. He knew that getting me out of there would make a difference. I was playing defense one time, and I saw him coming after me from a long ways off. I was always alert. But I pretended I didn't see him. When he got close I wheeled around the nailed him, goddam. Broke three of his ribs. And as they carried him off I said to him, "What the hell, Halas. Don't you know you can't sneak up on an Indian?"

ED HEALEY

(1920–1927: Rock Island Independents, Chicago Bears)

IN 1922 the Rock Island Independents sold me to the Chicago Bears following a game that I remember as clearly as if it were just played today. We had a great team! We had lost just once. And on the Sunday prior to Thanksgiving we played the Bears at Wrigley Field.

Now understand, in Chicago the officialdom was such that on occasion it made it a little difficult for the outsider to win. On this day the game was really a tight one. In fact, it was going along 0–0. George Halas, who along with Dutch Sternaman owned the Bears and played for them, was at right end, the opponent for myself, who was the left tackle. Halas had a habit of grabbing ahold of my jersey, see? My sleeve. That would throw me a little off my balance. It would twist me just enough so that my head wasn't going where I was going.

I didn't enjoy being the victim with reference to this holding, so I forewarned him of what I intended to do about it. Likewise it was necessary for me to forewarn the head linesman, whose name was Roy. I said, "Now, Roy, I understand to start with that you're on the payroll of the Bears. I know that your eyesight must be failing you, because this man Halas is holding me on occasion and it is completely destroying all the things that I'm designed to do." I said, "Roy, in the event that Halas holds me again I am going to commit mayhem."

Now bear in mind, please, that we had a squad of about 15 or 16 men. Neither Duke Slater, our right tackle, nor I had a substitute on the bench. So I said, "Roy, you can't put me out of the game, because we don't have another tackle. And I can't really afford to be put out of this ball game because of your failure to call Halas's holding. I have notified him, and now I am about to commit mayhem."

Well, the condition of the field was muddy and slippery—a very unsafe field. Halas pulled his little trick once more, and I come across with a right, because his head was going to my right. Fortunately for him he slipped, and my fist went whizzing straight into the terra firma, which was soft and mucky. My fist was buried. When I pulled it out it was with an effort like a suction pump.

This was on a Sunday, and on the following Tuesday, I believe it was, I was told to report to the Bears. George Halas had bought me for $100.

Three years later, on a Saturday prior to Thanksgiving 1925 Red Grange performed in his last game for Illinois. He played against Ohio State at Columbus, then took the sleeper to Chicago and the next day he joined the Bears. And then, with Grange as the main attraction, we set out on a trip and exploded the Eastern Coast, playing by day and hopping to the next city by overnight sleeper. Of course, we did not always play up to our capability, because the human body can stand just so much. But the Redhead broke away in Philadel-

RED GRANGE brought the credibility of the college game to the pros when he signed with the Bears in 1925.

CULVER PICTURES

phia on a Saturday. He broke away in New York on Sunday.

With Red Grange, a gentleman and a scholar, we exploded not only the Eastern Coast but likewise the Western Coast and the South with the introduction of professional football. . . .

RED GRANGE

(1925–1934: Chicago Bears, New York Yankees)

Alone among all the players of the pro football decades that preceded television, Grange earned from football the six-figure income that stars of the 1960s were to realize. Behind his early financial success was that unique operator, C.C. (Cash & Carry) Pyle, probably the first players' agent known to football. It was the Roaring Twenties, the Golden Age of Sport, and with Pyle calling the shots Grange became the plutocrat of football. He fondly remembers Cash & Carry.

CHARLIE PYLE was about 44 years old when I met him. He was the most dapper man I have ever seen. He went to the barbershop every day of his life. He had a little mustache that he'd have trimmed, and he would have a manicure and he'd have his hair trimmed up a little, and every day he would get a rubdown. He wore a derby and spats and carried a cane, and believe me, he was a handsome guy. The greatest ladies' man that ever lived.

Money was of no consequence to Charlie.

At this particular time he owned three movie theaters—two in Champaign, Ill. and one in Kokomo, Ind. One night during my senior year at Illinois I went down to the Virginia Theater in Champaign and one of the ushers told me, "Mr. Pyle wants to see you in his office." Well, the first words Charlie Pyle said to me were, "Red, how would you like to make $100,000?" I couldn't figure what he was talking about. But he said, "I have a plan. I will go out and set up about 10 or 12 football games throughout the United States."

Of course I was flabbergasted. But Charlie made good his word. He lined it up for me to play with the Bears and then went out on the road and set up the whole program.

I'll never forget the game we played in Coral Gables outside of Miami, at a time when Florida was swinging. In 1925 everybody there was selling real estate and building things. Three days before the game we looked around, and there was no place to play a football game, so we said, "Where are we going to play?" The people told us, "Out here in this field." Well, there wasn't anything there except a field. But two days before the game they put 200 carpenters to work and built a wooden stadium that seated 25,000. They sold tickets ranging up to $20 apiece, and the next day they tore down the stadium. You'd never know a ball game had taken place there.

One thing about Charlie was that he always thought pro football had a future. I didn't. When I played, outside of the franchise towns nobody knew anything about pro ball. A U.S. Senator took me to the White House once and introduced me to Calvin Coolidge and said, "Mr. President, I want you to meet Red Grange. He's with the Chicago Bears." I remember the President's reply very well. He said, "Well, Mr. Grange, I'm glad to meet you. I have always liked animal acts."

OLE HAUGSRUD

(1926–1927: Owner, Duluth Eskimos)

Originally the Duluth club was a fine semipro outfit called the Kelley-Duluths, having been named for the Kelley-Duluth Hardware Store. The Kelley-Duluths' opposition came largely from teams in nearby towns in the iron-ore range. But in 1923, in order to obtain a professional schedule, Dan Williams and three others—the trainer and two players—put up $250 apiece and bought a National Football League franchise for $1,000. Even then, the renamed Duluth Eskimos were able to arrange no more than seven, and sometimes as few as five, league games a season. Bills piled up. Finally the four owners offered to make a gift of the franchise to Ole Haugsrud, the club's secretary-treasurer. To make the transaction legal, Haugsrud handed them a dollar, which the four men immediately squandered drinking nickel beer. The dollar they paid for those 20 beers would be one Dan Williams and his colleagues would never forget.

The year was 1926, and the struggling NFL was fighting for its life. C.C. Pyle had Red Grange under contract and with Grange as his box-office attraction was formulating his new nine-team league, to be known as the American Football League. Pyle spread the word that he also had signed the celebrated All-America back, Ernie Nevers, a handsome blond who, though just emerging from Stanford, had captured the nation's fancy. The NFL knew Nevers to be the only big name with whom the league could salvage its slim prestige, but NFL club owners took Pyle at his word, and they made no effort to sign Nevers.

Alone, Ole Haugsrud, a mild-looking little Swede, was skeptical. He had been a high-school classmate of Ernie Nevers in Superior, Wis. When he paid a dollar for the Duluth franchise he had it in the back of his mind to travel to St. Louis, where Nevers was pitching for the St. Louis Browns, to see for himself if Pyle actually had Nevers under contract.

ERNIE WAS very glad to see me, and I was glad to see him. I met with him and his wife at their apartment, and Ernie showed me a letter he had from C.C. Pyle. Ernie told me,

JOE GUYON, who starred on both sides of the ball for the Canton Bulldogs, liked to play rough and didn't apologize for that.

PRO FOOTBALL HALL OF FAME/WIREIMAGE

"Ole, if you can meet the terms Pyle is offering in this letter, it's O.K. with me. I'll play for Duluth." And, really, that's all there was to it. I would have to pay Ernie $15,000 plus a percentage of the larger gates. I didn't pay him five cents to sign. Oh, maybe I gave him a dollar to make it legal, but really a handshake was all Ernie wanted. A handshake with an old friend was good enough for Ernie.

The league meeting was at the Morrison Hotel, and it was getting on close to August, I believe. See, they didn't hold meetings way ahead of the season, because a lot of teams didn't know if they could operate for another year, and they had to get some funds behind them before they could go to a meeting.

In Chicago the first fellows I got hold of were Tim Mara of the New York Giants and George Halas of the Bears. I had called Tim Mara prior to that, and he was really the only one who knew about the contract I had with Ernie Nevers.

This was kind of a historic point for the National League, because here everybody was, with the threat that Pyle had hanging over them, and the league really didn't know if it was going to operate again. So Mara said to me, "Wait till I highball you, and then you go up to the league president with your option on Nevers." Well, I waited and watched Mara, and when he signaled I took the option up to Joe Carr, who was being paid $500 to be league president. He read that little document and then looked up and said: "Gentlemen, I got a surprise for you!" He read the option paper aloud, and some of them out front got up and yelled like a bunch of kids. Carr said to me, "You've saved the league!"

There was almost a celebration right there. But Tim Mara said, "Gentlemen, we got to make a league out of this, so we'll start all over by first rehiring the president and paying him a salary that means something."

Then Mara said, "Now let's start over and get a new schedule. "Well, we started putting down that 1926 schedule, and now everybody wanted to play me. I had 19 league games as fast as I could write them down. Before I got back to Duluth I had 10 exhibition games, too, which made a total of 29. And all because I had Nevers.

Mr. Mara got up and said, "What we've got to do is to fill the ball parks in the big cities. So we've got to make road teams out of the Duluth Eskimos and the Kansas City Cowboys." He knew we would draw the big-city crowds with Ernie, and the Kansas City Cowboys were good at drawing crowds because they had a gimmick. When they arrived in a town they'd borrow a lot of horses and ride them down the main street. They rode horseback down Broadway and drew 39,000 people in New York.

So we had only two home games—one in Duluth and one over in Superior, where the ball park had railroad tracks on both sides. The railroad men would leave boxcars lined up there. We drew 3,000 or 4,000 at the box office in Superior, but there were just as many standing on the boxcars watching free.

I believe it was September 6th that we hit the road, and we didn't get back until February 5th. We traveled by train and occasionally by bus, and one time we took a boat from New York to Providence. During one stretch we played five games in eight days, with a squad of 17 men.

After that '27 season, I put the club in mothballs, and then I sold the franchise for $2,000. . . .

But I didn't do so bad by selling. You see, we negotiated the deal at a league meeting in Cleveland, and the fellows from the other clubs were anxious to see it settled and get away, because they didn't always have money enough to stay three, four days in a high-priced hotel. I wanted $3,000 but the fellow wanted to give me $2,000. The others said to me, "Come on, Swede. We got to get going home."

So I said, "All right, but with one stipulation. The next time a franchise is granted in the state of Minnesota I will have the first opportunity to bid for it."

In 1961, when the Minnesota Vikings were created, I got 10% of the stock. The franchise cost $600,000, and I paid $60,000. Since then we've had offers of between $12 million and $15 million for the franchise. So I guess you would have to say that as result of originally buying a franchise for a dollar, and later investing $60,000, I now own stock that is worth about a million and a half.

BULLDOG TURNER

(1940–1952: Chicago Bears)

In 1941, only a year after he had turned pro with the Chicago Bears, he became the first man in nine years to unseat the great Mel Hein of the New York Giants as the NFL's All-League center. Men who played against Turner say that among his virtuosities must be included exquisite stealth in the art of holding.

HERE WAS George Halas's method of operation in practice. First he'd say, "Give me a center!" Then he'd say, "Bausch!" He'd say, "Give me two guards!" Then he'd say, "Fortmann and Musso!" Well, the first time I heard Halas say, "Give me a center!" I didn't wait for nothing more and ran out there and got over the ball. I noticed he looked kind of funny at me, but I didn't think anything about it. I found out later that Pete Bausch was the center—a big, broad, mean ol' ballplayer, a real nice German

PAPA BEAR George Halas was a pioneer in the NFL, first as a scrappy player and then as the often flinty owner of the Chicago Bears.

BETTMANN/CORBIS

from Kansas. But all I knew was George had drafted me No. 1 and I had signed a contract to play center, and I thought when it come time to line up I should *be* at center. From the beginning I was overendowed with self-confidence. I feared no man. So I just went out there and got over that ball, and I was there ever since. They didn't need Pete no more.

I was such a good blocker that the men they put in front of me—and some of them were stars that were supposed to be making a lot of tackles—they would have their coaches saying, "Why ain't you making any tackles?" They'd say, "That bum Turner is holding!" Well, that wasn't true. I held a few, but I was blocking them too. I used to think I could handle anybody that they'd put in front of me.

One guy I remember was big Ed Neal. There in the late 1940s he played at Green Bay, and by this time they had put in the 5–4 defense. They put the biggest, toughest guy they had right in front of the center, and I was expected to block him either way. Well, Ed Neal weighed 303 pounds stripped. His arms was as big as my leg and just as hard as that table. He could tell when I was going to center the ball, and he'd get right over it and hit me in the face. You didn't have a face guard then, and so Ed Neal broke my nose seven times. Yes, that's right. No—he broke my nose *five* times. I got it broke seven times, but five times *he* broke it.

Anyway, I got where I'd center that ball and duck my head, so then he started hitting me on top of the headgear. He would beat hell out of my head. We had those headgears that were made out of composition of some kind—some sort of fiber—and I used to take three of them to Green Bay. These headgears would just crack when he'd hit 'em—they'd just ripple across there like lightening had struck them. So there one day, every time Neal went by me I'd grab him by the leg, and I began to get him worried. He said, "You s.o.b., quit holding me!" I said, "If you'll quit hitting me on the head, I'll quit holding you." And Neal said, "That's a deal, 'cause I ain't making no tackles." So the second half of that game we got along good, and later I got Halas to trade for him.

I don't know if you want to put this in your book, and I don't care if you do, but I originated the draw play, along with a lot of other plays. I discovered the draw play because Buckets Goldenberg, who played for Green Bay, could read our quarterback, Sid Luckman, real well. Somehow he could tell when Sid was going to pass. As soon as that ball was snapped, Buckets Goldenberg would pull back and start covering the pass. So I said, "Let's fake a pass and give the ball to the fullback and let him come right up here where I am, 'cause there's nobody here but me." The next year we put that play in, and it averaged 33 yards a try. The fullback would run plumb to the safety man before they knew he had the ball.

I also originated a play that got me even with Ed Neal for beating my head off. I said to Halas one day, "You can run somebody right through there, 'cause Ed Neal is busy whupping my head." I suggested that we put in a sucker play—we called it the 32 sucker—where we double-teamed both of their tackles and I would just relax and let Neal knock me on my back and fall all over me. It'd make a hole from here to that fireplace. Man, you could really run through it, and we did all day. Later Ralph Jones, who had once been a Bears coach and was coaching a little college team, told me he brought his whole team down to watch the Bears play the Packers that day, and he told them, "Boys, I want you to see the greatest football player that ever lived, Bulldog Turner. I want you to watch this man on every play and see how he handles those guys." But ol' Ralph didn't know about that sucker play, and later he said to me, "Damn if you wasn't flat on your back all day!"

BULLDOG TURNER, who signed his first pro contract in 1940, played linebacker and was a perennial All-NFL center for the Bears.

ART ROONEY

(1933– : Owner, Pittsburgh Steelers)

The down-to-earth, ward-loving, last-hurrah millionaire president of the Pittsburgh Steelers, Arthur J. Rooney is one of the supreme contradictions in sport. Perhaps the most successful horseplayer America has ever known—he is said to have won a quarter of a million dollars in a single day—he is professional football's champion loser. In 35 years his team has never earned so much as a divisional title.

Like George Halas, Rooney once played as a pro himself. His team was called Hope-Harvey. He founded it, owned it, coached it and even halfbacked it against the likes of Jim Thorpe and the Canton Bulldogs. Sometimes he was a winner in his Hope-Harvey days, but then. . . .

IN 1933 I paid $2,500 for a National Football League franchise, which I named the Pirates because the Pittsburgh baseball team was called the Pirates. It wasn't until 1940, when we held a contest for a new name, that we became the Steelers. Joe Carr's girlfriend won the contest. There were people who said, "That contest don't look like it was on the level."

I bought the franchise because I figured it would be good to have a league schedule and that eventually professional football would be a big sport. The reason I bought at that particular time was that we knew Pennsylvania was going to repeal some of its blue laws, which had prevented Sunday football.

The laws were changed, but a couple of days before our opening game the mayor phoned me and said, "I got a complaint here from a preacher that this game should not be allowed. The blue-law repeal hasn't been ratified yet by the city council."

The mayor told me he didn't know what I could do about it, but that I should go see a fellow named Harmar Denny, who was director of public safety and over the police department.

But this Denny was pretty much of a straitlaced guy. All he would say was that he was going away for the weekend. "Good," I told him. "You go away." Then I went to see the superintendent of police, a man named McQuade, and told him my problem.

"Oh, that there's ridiculous," he said. "Give me a couple of tickets and I'll go to the game Sunday. That'll be the last place they'll look for me if they want me to stop the thing." So McQuade hid out at the game, and Pittsburgh got started in the NFL.

The biggest mistake I've made was that, although I understood the football business as well as anybody, I didn't pay the attention to it that some of the other owners did.

I still believe that John Blood could have been a tremendous coach if he would have just paid attention. We once played a game in Los Angeles and John missed the train home. John was known to enjoy a good time, of course, so we didn't see him the whole week. On Sunday he stopped off in Chicago to see his old team, the Green Bay Packers, play the Bears. The newspaper guys asked him, "How come you're not with your team?" And John said, "Oh, we're not playing this week." Well, no sooner did he get those words out of his mouth than the guy on the loudspeaker announced a score. Philadelphia 14, Pittsburgh 7. You really couldn't depend on John a whole lot.

We've had a lot of great ballplayers, you know. Just think of the quarterbacks. We've had Sid Luckman, Earl Morrall, Len Dawson, Jackie Kemp, Bill Nelsen. I'd say we were experts on quarterbacks at Pittsburgh. We had them all, and we got rid of every one of them. We had Johnny Unitas in for a tryout, but our coach then, Walter Kiesling, let him go. Kies said, "He can't remember the plays. He's dumb." You had to know Kies. He was a great coach, but he thought a lot of ballplayers were dumb. We were arguing about a guy one day, and I said, "I don't care how dumb he is. He can run and he can pass and he can block. If he can do those three things, he don't have to be a Rhodes scholar." But all Kies said to that was, "He's dumb."

SAMMY BAUGH

(1937–1952: Washington Redskins)

Starting in 1937, he lasted 16 years and is held by many to have been the finest passer of his or any other time. In one season ('45) he completed 70.3% of his passes. In addition, his leg was as potent as his arm; he holds almost every punting record in the book. But above all, he gave to pro football a radical concept that he had learned from his college coach at Texas Christian, Dutch Meyer—namely, that the forward pass could be more than just a surprise weapon or a desperation tactic. Sammy Baugh made the pass a routine scrimmage play.

THE THING that hurt when I first came into pro football in 1937 was that the rules didn't give any protection to passers. Those linemen could hit the passer until the whistle blew. If you completed a pass out there and somebody's running 50 yards with the ball, well, that bunch could still hit you. In other words, a passer had to learn to throw and *move*. You would never see him just throw and stand there looking. You had to throw and start protecting yourself, because those linemen were going to lay you flatter than the ground every time.

If you were a good ballplayer—a passer or whatever—they tried to hurt you and get you out of there. We had only 22 or 23 men on a squad, and your ballplayers were playing both ways—offense and defense—so if you lost two good ones, you were dead. Well, every now and then they'd run what they called a "bootsie" play, and everybody'd hit one man and just try to tear him to pieces. The object was to get him out of there. I don't mean they ran this kind of play very often, but if they came up against a guy that was giving them a lot of trouble, along would come the bootsie.

I guess it was my third year, 1939, that we finally got the rule protecting the passer. Pro football was changing by then. Back in the '30s it was more of a defensive game. In other words, when you picked your starters, they usually had to be good on defense first. Take the New York Giants. They had such a good defensive ball club that they wouldn't mind punting to you on third down from practically anywhere. They'd kick the ball to you 'cause they didn't think you were ever going to move it.

The fact is, most men played pro football in those days because they liked football. A lot of players today say they only play for the money, but even now, it's not all money. I don't care if salaries went back down, they'd still play. Of course, nobody was making a lot of money out of football in the '30s. That's why I'll always think a lot of George Marshall and George Halas and Art Rooney and those kind of people—they stayed in there when it was rough. They made a great game out of it. . . .

ERNIE NEVERS, the star running back out of Stanford, was the big draw that saved the fledgling NFL after Grange started his own league in 1926.

UNDERWOOD & UNDERWOOD

1994 | THE BEARS' Chris Zorich felt the chill of 15° weather in December, in Green Bay | *Photograph by* JOHN BIEVER

1997 | BRYAN COX didn't lose his head as a linebacker for the Bears. One reason: his massive neck pad | *Photograph by* DAVID LIAM KYLE

B. COX
52
BEARS

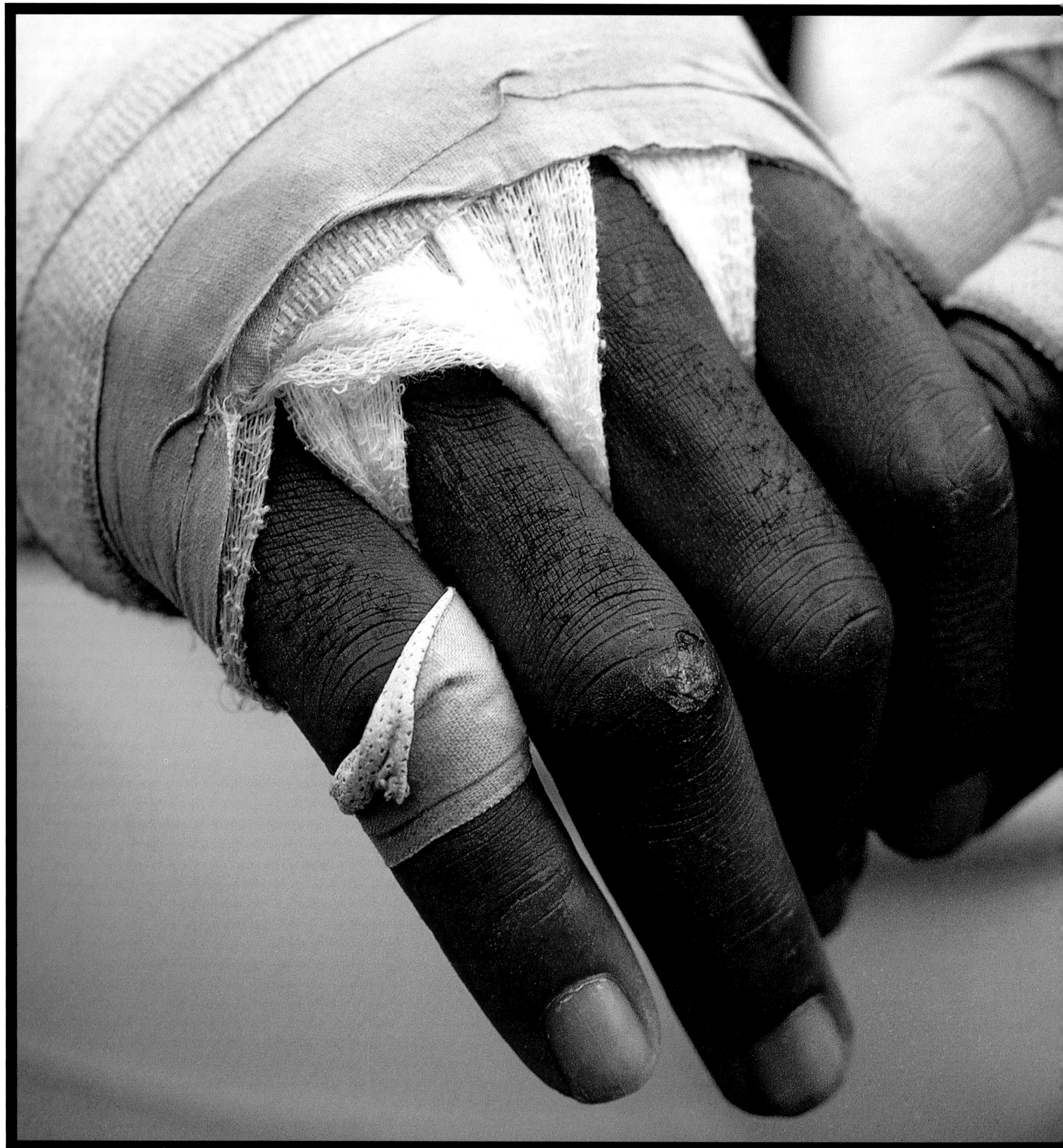

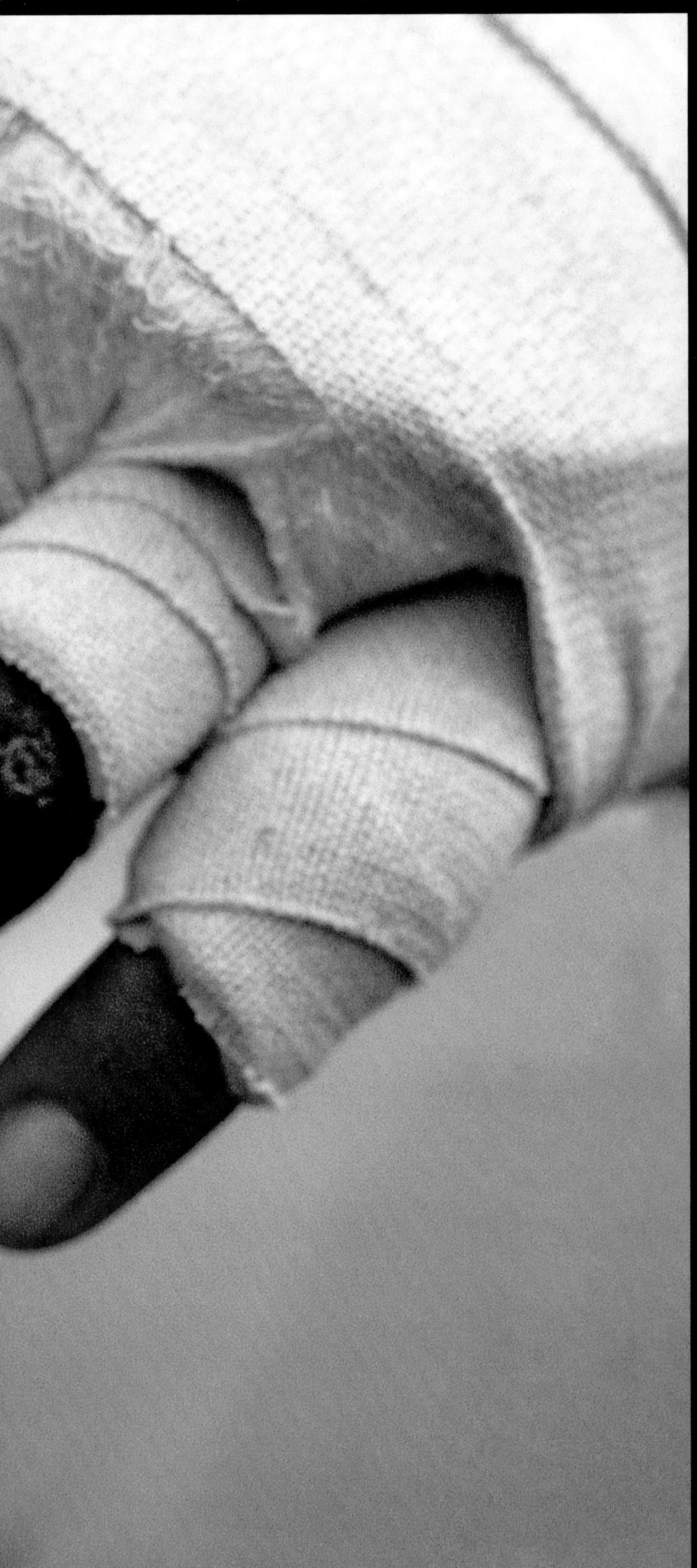

from HOW DOES IT REALLY FEEL? | BY ROY BLOUNT JR.
SI August 12, 1974

ONE AFTERNOON DURING practice I was watching the linemen pound away at each other—*wump, clack.* Guard Bruce Van Dyke paused to say, "What are you doing?" ❧ "Trying to get a feel for this," I said. ❧ "If you really want to get a feel for it you should put on some pads and get out here and get blocked," he said.

"Well," I said, "I thought I would get a feel for it by asking *you* how it feels."

"I try not to notice how it feels," he said. "If you felt it, you wouldn't do it."

I admired coach Chuck Noll's response when a reporter came up to him after the Steelers' loss to Cincinnati and asked, "How do you feel?"

"It hasn't changed," said Noll. "I still feel with my hands."

So I thought I might try treating the question of how football feels by asking players about their hands. One conclusion I was led to from that line of questioning was that football feels terrible. On the backs of their hands and on their knuckles many of the players had wounds of a kind I have never seen on anyone else: fairly deep digs and gouges that were not scabbed over so much as dried. They looked a little like old sores on horses. The body must have given up trying to refill those gouges and just rinded them over and accepted them.

I've never broken a finger," said Mean Joe Greene. "I had 'em stepped on, twisted, but not broken. One time I grabbed at Jim Plunkett and my little finger caught in a twist of his jersey and he ran for a ways dragging me that way, by my little finger. That turned my little finger around, but it didn't break it."

In '72 L.C. Greenwood looked down in the midst of a play to see his middle finger twisted around backward and crossed over the ring finger. "I couldn't figure out what had happened." He had it splinted and played with the splint on, and now that finger sticks out at a grotesque angle. He said he would get it straightened after he was out of football; no point doing it until then.

Most of the defensive linemen had broken *many* fingers. "You can't play football, I don't care what position, without hands," said Dwight White. "I use 'em to pull, knock down, grab. Hands are as important as eyes." He glanced down at his. "See this fanger?" he said. "I got it jammed five years ago, and it's just started to straighten out. See that fanger? Can't wear a ring on it. I got some of the ugliest fangers in the world." . . .

1973 | THE MAYHEM of football took a toll on the hands of L.C. Greenwood.
Photograph by WALTER IOOSS JR.

LJ
130

2003 | CHARGERS QUARTERBACK Drew Brees had no margin for error after catching a 21-yard TD pass from LaDainian Tomlinson | *Photograph by* JOHN W. MCDONOUGH

> Artifacts

Crown Jewels

Before there were Super Bowl rings for every player to covet, there were all manner of other precious mementoes awarded to championship teams as tokens of their victory

1922 | CANTON BULLDOGS CHARM

1941 | CHICAGO BEARS CHARM

1954 | CLEVELAND BROWNS WATCH

1948 | CLEVELAND BROWNS TIE-CLIP

1905 | THE CANTON BULLDOGS, the pro game's first dynasty, won titles in their first two NFL seasons, 1922 and '23

COURTESY OF THE PRO FOOTBALL HALL OF FAME; HOF/WIREIMAGE

C
S

2003 | THE JETS' Curtis Martin (28) needed four-wheel drive to make headway against the Steelers in New Jersey | *Photograph by* DAVID BERGMAN

GILDON

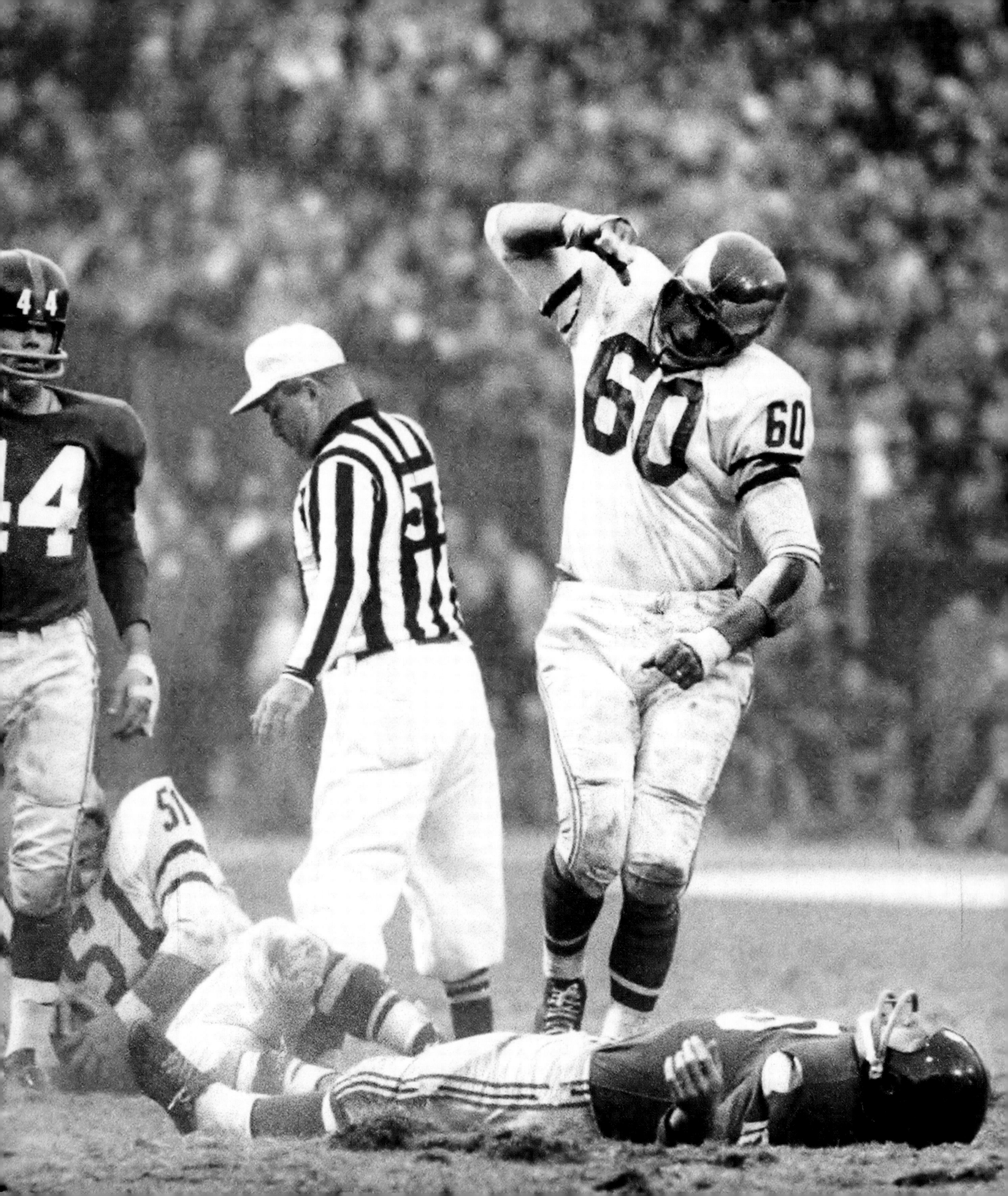
44
44
60
60
51

CONCRETE CHARLIE

BY JOHN SCHULIAN

Chuck Bednarik, the last of the 60-minute men, was a stalwart at both linebacker and center but will be known forever for one play, the Tackle. — *from* SI, SEPTEMBER 6, 1993

THE PASS WAS BEHIND Gifford. It was a bad delivery under the best of circumstances, life-threatening where he was now, crossing over the middle. But Gifford was too much the pro not to reach back and grab the ball. He tucked it under his arm and turned back in the right direction, all in the same motion—and then Chuck Bednarik hit him like a lifetime supply of bad news.

Thirty-three years later there are still people reeling from the Tackle, none of them named Gifford or Bednarik. In New York somebody always seems to be coming up to old number 16 of the Giants and telling him they were there the day he got starched in the Polo Grounds. (It was Yankee Stadium.) Other times they say that everything could have been avoided if Charlie Conerly had thrown the ball where he was supposed to. (George Shaw was the guilty Giant quarterback.) And then there was Howard Cosell, who sat beside Gifford on *Monday Night Football* for 14 years and seemed to bring up Bednarik whenever he was stuck for something to say. One week Cosell would accuse Bednarik of blindsiding Gifford, the next he would blame Bednarik for knocking Gifford out of football. Both were classic examples of telling it like it wasn't. But it is too late to undo any of the above, for the Tackle has taken on a life of its own. So Gifford plays along by telling what sounds like an apocryphal story about one of his early dates with the woman who would become his third wife. "Kathie Lee," he told her, "one word you're going to hear a lot of around me is Bednarik." And Kathie Lee supposedly said, "What's that, a pasta?"

For all the laughing Gifford does when he spins that yarn, there was nothing funny about Nov. 20, 1960, the day Bednarik handed him his lunch. The Eagles, who complemented Concrete Charlie and Hall of Fame quarterback Norm Van Brocklin with a roster full of tough, resourceful John Does, blew into New York intent on knocking the Giants on their media-fed reputation. Philadelphia was leading 17–10 with under two minutes to play, but the Giants kept slashing and pounding, smelling one of those comeback victories that were supposed to be the Eagles' specialty. Then Gifford caught that pass. "I ran through him right up here," Bednarik says, slapping himself on the chest hard enough to break something. "*Right here.*" And this time he pops a visiting reporter on the chest. "It was like when you hit a home run; you say, 'Jeez, I didn't even feel it hit the bat.' "

Giants linebacker Sam Huff would later call it "the greatest tackle I've ever seen," but at the time it happened Huff's emotion was utter despair. Gifford fell backward, the ball flew forward. When Eagles linebacker Chuck Weber pounced on it, Bednarik started dancing as if St. Vitus had taken possession of him. And as he danced, he yelled at Gifford, "This game is over!" But Gifford couldn't hear him. "He didn't hurt me," Gifford insists. "When he hit me, I landed on my ass and then my head snapped back. That was what put me out—the whiplash, not Bednarik." Whatever the cause, Gifford looked like he was past tense as he lay there motionless. A funereal silence fell over the crowd, and Bednarik rejoiced no more. He has never been given to regret, but in that moment he almost changed his ways. Maybe he actually would have repented if he had been next to the first Mrs. Gifford after her husband had been carried off on a stretcher. She was standing outside the Giants' dressing room when the team physician stuck his head out the door and said, "I'm afraid he's dead." Only after she stopped wobbling did Mrs. Gifford learn that the doctor was talking about a security guard who had suffered a heart attack during the game.

Even so, Gifford didn't get off lightly. He had a concussion that kept him out for the rest of the season and all of 1961. But in '62 he returned as a flanker and played with honor for three more seasons. He would also have the good grace to invite Bednarik to play golf with him, and he would never, ever whine about the Tackle. "It was perfectly legal," Gifford says. "If I'd had the chance, I would have done the same thing to Chuck." . . .

BEDNARIK knocked Gifford out of the game . . . and the following season.

JOHN G. ZIMMERMAN; HERB SCHARFMAN (CIGAR)

1996 | CHIEFS CORNERBACK Dale Carter was stretched to the limit when he broke up this pass to Packers wideout Don Beebe | *Photograph by* DAMIAN STROHMEYER

> Artifacts

Cardboard Heroes

Beginning with college stars in the 1890s, football players have been featured on trading cards—including these from the NFL of the 1940s, '50s and '60s—encouraging little boys to dream big

COURTESY OF THE PRO FOOTBALL HALL OF FAME

DAN EDWARDS

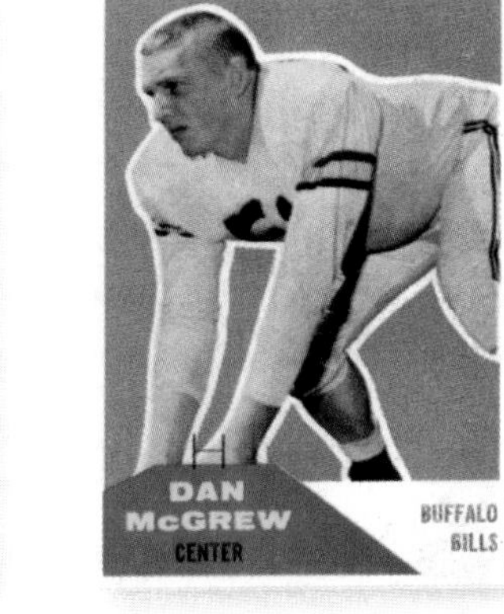
DAN
McGREW
CENTER
BUFFALO
BILLS

81
GEORGE CONNOR

48
THURMAN MC GRAW

31
BILLY
KINARD
HALFBACK
BUFFALO
BILLS

DON MAYNARD
NEW YORK JETS
FLANKER

BUFFALO
PAUL MAGUIRE linebacker

ROGER
ELLIS
CENTER
NEW YORK
TITANS

BILL DUDLEY

DOAK WALKER
37

SAN DIEGO
RON MIX tackle

55
RAY
MOSS
LINEBACKER
BUFFALO
BILLS

BUFFALO
JACK KEMP quarterback

TOM
DIMITROFF
QUARTERBACK
NEW YORK
TITANS

CONFESSIONS OF A PRO WHO PLAYED SIX POSITIONS IN 10 YEARS (AND DID NONE OF THEM JUSTICE)

BY ALEX HAWKINS WITH MYRON COPE

Or: How I went from "fleet breakaway threat" to "hard-running blond" to "fun-loving off the field." — *from* SI, NOVEMBER 16, 1970

A FEW MORE WEEKS AND it would be time to report to training camp—time to get ready for the 1969 season—but something was telling me that I faced a decision. I had awakened with a case of the hives. Whenever I get the hives I know it's time for a change. Usually I solve the problem by going off on a fishing trip or flying up to Baltimore to have a few drinks with my fans (mostly bartenders, petty hoodlums and worthless newspapermen), but lately I had been brooding about my career. Mind you, I had no illusions—I had not expected great things of myself. It's true that the first year a thumbnail sketch of me appeared in the Baltimore Colts' press book, I was described as a "fleet breakaway threat," but, of course, publicity men write press books grimly determined to find a compliment for every player. In my case it was a terrible struggle. Becoming less of a threat each year, I was demoted to "the hard-running blond," then to "the solid-socking blond." Finally, publicist Jim Walker reached the bottom of the barrel. He put down that I was "loose and fun-loving off the field" and let it go at that.

But no, it was not my station that I brooded about. Actually, you could say my career had been unique. I mean, how many football players can you name who in 10 years in the National Football League played six positions—cornerback, halfback, fullback, split end, flanker and tight end—and did none of them justice?

Although I would be 32 in just a few days, I wasn't worried about being able to take the football grind for another year. On practice days our coach, Don Shula, used to say to me, "Well, Hawk, what are you going to do today?" I'd say, "I think I'll warm up the quarterbacks and later I'll go over and bat the breeze with the kickers." Shula would say, "Good. Just stay out of everybody's way." It was a routine I could live with.

Nor was I worried that I might not be able to retain my position as the number 6 man in the Colts' six-man corps of receivers. Having risen to the captaincy of the suicide squad, I commanded a certain amount of prestige, and while it's true that Shula's better judgement often told him to release me, he always managed to rationalize his way out of the decision by noting that I knew the plays at six positions and that if I happened to turn up in the right saloon at the right time I usually could talk Lou Michaels out of a fight before the cops arrived. No, Shula wouldn't cut me. But for reasons I'll get to presently, I had become dissatisfied with life as a pro football player. The hives were telling me to take stock. Their message was clear. I decided to quit while I was still on the bottom.

From my home in Atlanta I telephoned Baltimore and called a press conference. The *club* was damn well not going to, but I still had a little Super Bowl money left that would pay for a nice luncheon, so I booked the back room at the Golden Arm, which is owned by John Unitas and Bobby Boyd, and leaked the word that I intended to announce my retirement. The turnout was huge and, I might say, enthusiastic. Shula showed up, and so did a number of my teammates. The newspapermen already were charging drinks to my tab before I arrived. Also, there were bellboys and bookies and thieves and even a few thirsty priests. If I shock you by admitting that while playing pro football I associated with hoodlums, let me explain that in Baltimore there is no such thing as a clever hoodlum. One of my good friends, for example, made his getaway from a bank robbery by hailing a cab. After traveling five blocks he was caught, owing to the fact that he had neglected to tell the driver he had robbed a bank and the driver had stopped for a red light.

The speeches were terrific. Bert Bell Jr., the son of the late NFL commissioner, got up and said, "I think the Colts ought to retire the Hawk's jersey. Ball clubs are always retiring the stars' jerseys, but they never do anything for a stiff."

Gussie the Bookie got up and said, "Does anybody know who won the second at Monmouth?"

The sight of all my old pals so touched me that I arose and said, "I can't go through with it. I'm not going to quit." Shula threw down his napkin and stalked out of the room.

When the shouting died away and my resolve to remain active had been vetoed, the celebration began in earnest.

HAWKINS ANNOUNCED his retirement in 1969, but then changed his mind, much to the disappointment of his coaches.

WALTER IOOSS JR.

The luncheon ended at 9:30 the next morning, at which time I awoke on the barroom floor, knowing that I had gone out in style.

Actually, I quit for two reasons. One was that my teammate Tom Matte had made the Pro Bowl the previous season. I hold no personal grudge against Tom, but the more I thought about his selection, the more I wondered what the game had come to. The way Tom got to be a star, you see, was that the newspapermen ran out of questions for John Unitas. So they looked around the room one day and there was Matte.

Tom makes few mistakes, he hardly ever fumbles, but he lacks one quality that you sort of expect in a star. Ability. Tom has no illusions about himself, I'm certain of that, but the sportswriters needed a new Colt star and Tom was not about to contradict them.

But Tom in the Pro Bowl? That bothered me, it really did, because having had a 10-year ticket on the 50 and having been able to enjoy pro football with few interruptions by coaches wanting me to get in there, I had developed a great romance with the game. I'm one of those purists, meaning that I love football for the sport itself. I hate anything I see that detracts from the sport, and that includes my own performances. Unlike Matte, however, I never grew sufficiently important in the scheme of things to expose the sport to ridicule. What's more, they've already put a piece of his equipment in the Hall of Fame. You may recall that in 1965 all the Colt quarterbacks were injured, so Tom played quarterback in the final game of the season and again in a playoff against Green Bay for the Western Conference title. He read the plays from a wristband he was wearing, a wristband that is now on display at the Pro Football Hall of Fame, believe it or not. Last year I visited the Hall and I heard that another visitor shortly before had suffered a heart attack there and had dropped dead. I cannot swear to it because I was not there at the time, but the information I was given is that the poor man was stricken when he came upon Tom Matte's wristband.

But as I said, there were *two* reasons why I decided to get out. The second was that football was no longer fun. The feeling that the fun was ebbing began to creep up on me in 1965, when John Unitas and I fell to reflecting on our training camp that year. We agreed that for the first time the place had no zest. You had to search high and low for a poker game. Players sat around checking their investment portfolios. In the past, if the coach gave the team the weekend off, 30 players would get together for a party, but now, with a free weekend starting, you would see them scattering like quail. The briefcase carriers had taken over. We were now a team during working hours only.

If I seem to be saying that in order to play pro football properly it's necessary that large groups of players hang out in bars, you read me perfectly. Regardless of what the Fellowship of Christian Athletes says, true pro football teams accomplished half of their pregame preparation in bars. Each team had its favorite after-practice hangout, a hangout being any bar where, let's say, six or more players gathered. By the third round of drinks you actually could see men getting themselves up for Sunday's game. For no apparent reason, except that we talked football (and girls) endlessly, you would suddenly hear a lineman say, "I'm going to block that son of a bitch all over the field!" Having been immersed in the football talk, he was bringing his own little battle into focus and committing himself.

Confrontations took place at those hangouts. "When the hell are you going to start doing a better job?" a player would demand of another. Players were taken apart point-blank by their equals, and the team was the better for it. Today if you confront a teammate, he becomes highly indignant. When a few players occasionally get together, they talk about their Dairy Queen franchises. If more than two players meet after practice for a beer, the odds are heavy that at least one wife will phone to say, "Now you be sure to be home on time because we're going over to Green Spring Inn with the Braases." I'm not saying it's a crime. I'm saying it's civil. Pro football was not designed to be played by sane or civil men.

The first day I reported to the Colts, in 1959, Bert Rechichar held out his hand and said, "I'm 44. What's your name?" He never thought of himself as Bert Rechichar. Had he been introducing himself to the President, he would have said, "I'm 44." He carried a cigar in the corner of his mouth and, being blind in one eye, which remained closed as he studied me with

MATTE (41) NEEDED a crib sheet on his wristband to remember the plays when he was pressed into action at quarterback.

WALTER IOOSS JR

his good eye, he gave me the feeling that if I hadn't met him in the Colts' dressing room I would have guessed his occupation as hangman.

He was a mystery man. While no one had ever been inside Raymond Berry's house, no one even knew where Rechichar lived. He carried his entire savings in his pocket, which caused players to refer to him as the First National Bank of Rechichar. In line at the $10 window at Pimlico, our general manager, the late Don Kellett, would find it irritating to see Bert at the $100 window.

A mean football player? He was meaner than hell at high noon. He had played quarterback, fullback, receiver, safety (where he made All-Pro) and linebacker. He was an Alex Hawkins with ability. In his first year at Baltimore, I was told, Bert fooled around in practice, kicking long field goals, although he wasn't the club's regular field goal man. In a game against the Chicago Bears the Colts had the ball on the Bears' 49 with four seconds left in the first half. Bert had started walking to the dressing room when an assistant coach, Otis Douglas, said, "I wonder if Bert can kick a field goal from back there." Then he yelled, "Hey, Bert! Go in there and try a field goal!" Bert shrugged and said, "Why the hell not?" He walked back into the game and, without bothering to hook up his chin strap, booted a line drive that sailed 56 yards through the uprights. Until last week, when Tom Dempsey of New Orleans kicked a 63-yarder, it was a professional record.

When Weeb Ewbank coached the Colts, Bert would walk up to him every now and then and stare down at him with his good eye and say, "Don't you ever trade me." When at last Ewbank released him, Bert asked me to give him a lift in my car—he had to pick up his belongings. I thought I would finally learn where he lived, but instead Bert had me stop at half a dozen places at least—back alleys and side streets where I had never been. He would disappear into a doorway and return a few minutes later with a pair of pants and a jacket. At the next stop he would come out with a couple of shirts and maybe a pair of shoes. I drove him around for an hour before he said, "O.K., that's it." Would you say that Bert Rechichar was a totally sane man?

I'm not saying every pro football player has to be abnormal to perform well at the sport, but if you are it helps.

JUST SMELLING security has destroyed brilliant careers. Jim Taylor, the Green Bay fullback, was my idea of a perfect pro football player, which is to say half man, half animal. I knew him briefly at Green Bay, where I spent a few months as a rookie. It seemed to me that Taylor enjoyed talking to himself. This impression was confirmed years later when John Unitas returned from the Pro Bowl and said to me, "I was in the huddle, starting to call a play, when I heard that guy Taylor muttering. I said, 'What's wrong, Jim?' He said, "Don't pay no attention to me. I'm talking to myself." Like Bert Rechichar, Taylor never, to my knowledge, referred to himself by his Christian name. Sometimes he called himself Roy and at other times he called himself Doody. I have no idea why. He called other people Doody, too.

But when I say that Jim Taylor was right for pro football I'm thinking mostly of an incident related to me by an old Baltimore teammate, Wendell Harris. Wendell had played at Louisiana State, where Taylor had played a bit earlier, and one day in the off-season Wendell was exercising a weak knee by running up and down an aisle in the LSU stadium. He thought the stadium was empty, but then he looked down to the field and saw Taylor working out. Taylor was beating his backside against the stadium wall. "Jim!" yelled Wendell. "What are you doing?"

Taylor turned halfway around and patted himself on the backside. "I got the toughest ass in the business!" he barked, and with that he walked proudly out of the stadium.

He was all football player, Jim Taylor was, but then, as the gold began to flow on all sides, he started thinking about security. He played out his option at Green Bay. Vince Lombardi said, "The hell with him." Taylor went to New Orleans on a fat contract, but you'll notice that he instantly turned into a shadow of the player he had been.

Be that as it may, one day toward the end of my career in the NFL, Don Shula was moved to point out just how far *I* had come. "You know, I saw you play for South Carolina," he told me, "and I put you down as a surefire pro prospect. I told myself, 'Can't miss, offensively or defensively.' " Shula stroked his chin for a few moments and then said, "Hawk, it just goes to show you how wrong a guy can be." . . .

JIM TAYLOR (31) was the kind of player Hawkins admired: extremely tough and a little crazy.

WALTER IOOSS JR.

> SI's TOP 25 *The Running Backs*

EARL CAMPBELL
Photograph by HEINZ KLUETMEIER

BRONKO NAGURSKI
Photograph by AP

FRANCO HARRIS
Photograph by JOHN IACONO

HUGH McELHENNY
Photograph by CAL PICTURES

ERIC DICKERSON
Photograph by RONALD C. MODRA

GALE SAYERS
Photograph by KEN REGAN

TONY DORSETT
Photograph by AL MESSERSCHMIDT

O.J. SIMPSON
Photograph by ERIC SCHWEIKARDT

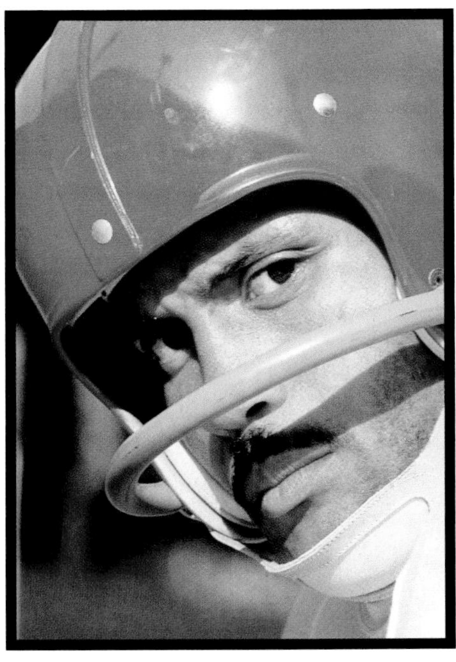
OLLIE MATSON
Photograph by JOHN G. ZIMMERMAN

MARSHALL FAULK
Photograph by TODD ROSENBERG

MARCUS ALLEN
JEROME BETTIS
JIM BROWN
EARL CAMPBELL
LARRY CSONKA
ERIC DICKERSON
TONY DORSETT
MARSHALL FAULK
RED GRANGE
FRANCO HARRIS
PAUL HORNUNG
CURTIS MARTIN
OLLIE MATSON
HUGH MCELHENNY
MARION MOTLEY
BRONKO NAGURSKI
ERNIE NEVERS
WALTER PAYTON
JOHN RIGGINS
BARRY SANDERS
GALE SAYERS
O.J. SIMPSON
EMMITT SMITH
JIM TAYLOR
JIM THORPE

2001 | ALAN FANECA and his helmet got caught in the riptide as Vikings converged on Steelers running back Chris Fuamatu-Ma'afala | *Photograph by* AL TIELEMANS

2001 | ALL HANDS were on deck—and on Aaron Brooks (2)—as the Giants' defense scuttled the Saints' quarterback | *Photograph by* JOHN IACONO

1962 | THE GIANTS didn't need anyone to light a fire under them for a December game against Green Bay in Yankee Stadium | *Photograph by* NEIL LEIFER

ny
ny
ny

20
Reebok
BELL

THE LION KING

BY PAUL ZIMMERMAN

Barry Sanders ran circles around NFL defenses with an electrifying style unlike anything the league had seen

— *from* SI, DECEMBER 8, 1997

BARRY SANDERS IS WHAT people in the NFL call a "freak runner." Defensive coaches can't draw up a scheme to stop him because his style follows no predictable pattern. It's all improvisation, genius, eyes that see more than other people's do, legs that seem to operate as disjointed entities, intuition, awareness of where the danger is—all performed in a churning, thrashing heartbeat.

The coaches will say things like "surround him," "cut off his escape angles" and "make sure you maintain your backside lanes," all the stuff they have been preaching since the days of Red Grange. For a while this might work, and there will be a neat little collection of one- and minus-two-yard runs in Sanders's pile. Then perhaps someone will get a little tired or misjudge an angle, and it's *whoosh*, there he goes!

It doesn't matter where the play is blocked; he'll find his own soft spot. It doesn't matter if he's running with a fullback in front of him or from a double-tight-end set or out of the old three- and four-wideout Silver Streak offense that the Detroit Lions used to employ. "What a waste," we used to say. "Four wideouts and Barry. Give him a fullback like Moose Johnston, put him behind a Dallas-caliber All Pro line, and he'd get his double G-note in yardage every season."

Well, this year the Lions gave him a blocking fullback and a fairly conventional offense, and after Sanders ran for 53 yards on 25 carries in his first two games, we all said, "Look what they've done. They've ruined him." Since then he has reeled off 11 straight games of 100 yards or more rushing.

The point is, the scheme doesn't seem to matter with Sanders. He can run from any alignment. While other people are stuck with joints, he seems to have ball bearings in his legs that give him a mechanical advantage. But there are drawbacks: He's not a goal line or short-yardage runner, though he's staying in the game more than he used to in those situations. When you need someone to smack in there for a tough yard, you can't take a chance with a guy who can lose three as easily as he gains 30. (During his nine-year career, he has been dumped for losses on 336 carries, almost 14% of his total rushing attempts, for 952 yards.) For this reason I believe he is behind Jim Brown on the alltime list of great running backs. Brown had that extra dimension of short-yardage muscle.

When you look at some of the great runners of the past—Grange, Bill Dudley, Ollie Matson, Gale Sayers—that's what you see, great running through a broken field, a field in which there's space to maneuver. Sanders's finest runs often occur when he takes the handoff and, with a couple of moves, turns the line of scrimmage into a broken field. Walter Payton ran with fury and attacked tacklers. O.J. Simpson and Eric Dickerson were instinctive runners who glided into the line and sliced through it with a burst, but nobody has ever created such turmoil at the point of attack as Sanders has.

Freak runners usually burn out quickly. One injury, one glitch in the stop-and-start mechanism, and the whole equation breaks down. But Sanders has missed only seven games because of injury, one in his rookie season, one in 1991 and five in '93. Knock on wood, he seems indestructible. . . .

SANDERS WAS just 1,457 yards short of Walter Payton's NFL career rushing record when he walked away from the Lions in 1998.

JOHN BIEVER; RONALD C. MODRA (RIGHT)

1974 | THE PACKERS' Mike Donohoe was about to have his number, if not his good name, dragged through the mud by the Bears' Don Rives | *Photograph by* JOHN BIEVER

1998 | DOLPHINS CORNERBACK Jerry Wilson made a splash after making a tackle on Pittsburgh running back Fred McAfee | *Photograph by* BILL FRAKES

> Artifacts

Ball and Change

The old pigskin has varied in size, shape and even color, but there's always been one constant: funny bounces

c. 1895 | Oldest ball in the Pro Football Hall of Fame

COURTESY OF THE PRO FOOTBALL HALL OF FAME

1911 | Game ball used by Columbus Panhandles, an early pro team

1935 | Ball used in championship game and signed by the winners, the Detroit Lions

c. 1950 | White balls were approved for use in NFL games from 1931 until 1953

1958 | Sudden-death championship game ball from Baltimore Colts' win over New York Giants

1967 | Game ball used on offense in Super Bowl I by the AFL team, the Chiefs

1973 | Ball used in Super Bowl VII to complete the Dolphins' 17–0 season

from PASSING MARKS | BY MICHAEL SILVER
SI December 20, 2004

DOWNSTAIRS IN PEYTON Manning's house, where the world's hottest quarterback regularly hosts parties for teammates after Indianapolis Colts home games, it's tough to take two steps without stumbling upon an exceptionally cool memento. Near the bar there's the large wicker basket overflowing with game balls; the *Caddyshack* poster signed by the film's stars is in the home theater (used exclusively, alas, for watching game video); and in the weight room, a wall is lined with framed photographs of the proprietor schmoozing with some of football's most recognizable faces.

"It's my Quarterback Wall," Manning proudly explained as he surveyed a cast of majestic passers that includes Johnny Unitas, Brett Favre and Michael Vick. Then, pointing to a shot of his father, Archie, the longtime New Orleans Saint, standing next to a young, excessively tan and bushy-haired Dan Marino in a Miami Dolphins uniform, Peyton lowered his voice to a reverential tone and added, "This one right here's my favorite. My dad, of course, was my idol, but when he retired in 1984, I needed a new favorite player, and Marino kind of took over." The photo was snapped hours before a 1986 game between the Dolphins and the Saints at the Superdome when Archie, then a radio broadcaster for the home team, walked onto the field with his second-oldest son to say hello to Dan the Man. Peyton, who was 10, remembers everything about the interaction, most notably the "big ol' Skoal can Marino was holding."

Now chew on this: No NFL passer, not even the great Marino, has had as productive a season as Manning's magical 2004 campaign seems destined to be. On Sunday, Manning threw a pair of first-quarter touchdown passes to lead Indianapolis to a 23–14 victory over the Houston Texans, giving him 46 for the year—two shy of the single-season record Marino set two decades ago. With their sixth consecutive victory the Colts clinched a second straight AFC South title, meaning the most suspenseful storyline heading into their home game against the Baltimore Ravens this Sunday night is if and when one of football's most hallowed milestones will be surpassed. . . .

2004 | MANNING FOLLOWED a playoff win over the Chiefs (right) with a season in which he threw for 49 TDs | *Photograph by* BILL FRAKES

Riddell
18

2003 | BENGALS WIDEOUT Chad Johnson was down before he was out on this TD catch against the Chargers in San Diego | *Photograph by* DONALD MIRALLE

2004 | RANDY MOSS made a two-point landing in the back of the end zone for six against the Jaguars | *Photograph by* JOHN BIEVER

20
37

19
19

1964 | Y.A. TITTLE of the Giants operated undercover against the Browns in the mud of Yankee Stadium | *Photograph by* NEIL LEIFER

1964 | JOHNNY UNITAS's magic wasn't enough to get the Colts past the Browns in the NFL Championship game | *Photograph by* NEIL LEIFER

THE LAST ANGRY MEN

BY RICK TELANDER

Running backs beware: All the best linebackers play with a chip on their shoulders. — *from* SI, SEPTEMBER 6, 1993

LINEBACKERS RISE OUT of the football ooze in a curious twist on Darwin: While the primitive stayed below, groveling on all fours, the *more* primitive ascended to the upright position. Of course in the beginning there were no linebackers at all in football. Because there was no forward pass, there was no need on defense for anything other than seven or eight down linemen who rooted like pigs and three or four defensive backs who could run down any ballcarrier who got past the swine. With the dawn of the pass in professional football in 1906, defensive principles slowly evolved. "Roving centers" started to pop up, and by 1920 something like a modern-day NFL middle linebacker had emerged. His name was George Trafton, and he played for the Decatur Staleys, who became the Bears. There is some dispute as to whether Trafton was the first true linebacker, but he was definitely the first Butkus-like personality in the NFL. Nicknamed the Brute, Trafton was as nasty as they come, despised by rival teams and their fans. In a Rock Island (Ill.) *Argus* account of a Staley game in 1920, Trafton was described as "sliding across the face of the rival center." Against the Independents in Rock Island that same year, Trafton took umbrage at a rumor that an opponent, a halfback named Fred Chicken, was out to get him. The Brute promptly knocked Chicken out with a hit that broke his leg. On the final play Staleys' coach George Halas sent Trafton running for the exit and a waiting taxi. Angry Rock Island fans mobbed the taxi, and Trafton had to hitch a ride with a passing motorist to get himself safely out of town. According to Bob Carroll, the executive director of the Professional Football Researchers Association, the first outside linebacker in the NFL was 6' 4" John Alexander, who played for the Milwaukee Badgers. Normally a tackle, one day in 1922 Alexander "stood up, took a step back, two steps out and became an outside linebacker," says Carroll. "He wondered why, as tall as he was, he was always getting down on the ground where he couldn't see." Alexander set the evolutionary clock moving, and 60 years later it brought us to LT.

Some people think that modern outside linebackers, blitz specialists primarily, aren't really linebackers at all, but gussied-up defensive ends. Some people say that inside linebackers, whether in tandem in a 3–4 alignment or standing alone in the increasingly rare 4–3 (wasn't a big part of Dick Butkus's dark majesty that aloneness?), are the only true linebackers today. But linebacking is really about responsibilities and attitude, not formations. Pain is the thing that separates linebackers from everyone else on the field—both dishing it out and receiving it. Linebackers dish out pain because it intimidates opponents. Says Butkus, "In college I figured punishing the ballcarrier wouldn't intimidate anybody, but it did. Then, in the pros, I thought I'd meet guys like me, but there were still guys who were chickens---, guys with big yellow streaks."

Linebackers see the game as superseding all guidelines on basic empathy for one's fellow man. "You want to punish the running backs," says Steelers Pro Bowl linebacker Greg Lloyd. "You like to kick them and, when they get down, kick them again. Until they wave the white flag." Or as Sam Huff of the Giants said to TIME magazine in 1959, "We try to hurt everybody."

Even themselves at times. The euphoria that linebackers experience afield comes during the white flash of great collisions—enlightenment literally being a blow to the head. Lloyd split two blockers in a game against the Cleveland Browns last year and then met runner Kevin Mack head-on. The ensuing crash overwhelmed Lloyd. "I was dizzy, my head was hurting and my eyes were watering," he says. "It felt good."

Where does such lunacy come from? "Off the field I'm quiet, laid-back, relaxed," says Eagles star Seth Joyner. "On the field I talk all kinds of garbage. I think it's a way to vent your anger."

Anger over what? Butkus struggles with the question. It's not really anger, he says. It's more a desire to set things right, to prove, as he says, "you don't get something for nothing." Violence can resolve ambivalence and uncertainty. And who doesn't crave certainty in life, a reward for the good, punishment for the bad? Things are so simple when you're a linebacker. One afternoon while Butkus was practicing with his high school team, he noticed four boys in a car harassing his girlfriend, Helen Essenberg, who was across the street. Without hesitation Butkus ran off the field, chased the car, dived through the open front window on the passenger side and, in full uniform, thrashed each of the passengers. Then he climbed out of the car and walked back to the field. He never said a word to Helen, who is now his wife. He had done what needed to be done, and it was over. "They could have been her friends, for all I knew," he says. . . .

RAY NITSCHKE was, according to Bart Starr, a "classic" Jekyll and Hyde type—a sweetheart off the field, a savage demon on it.

JOHN G. ZIMMERMAN

66

1969 | VIKINGS BACK Dave Osborn took a lick from the Rams' Deacon Jones (75) but still scored | *Photograph by* NEIL LEIFER

> SI's TOP 25 *The Receivers*

DON HUTSON
Photograph by AP

JERRY RICE
Photograph by ALLEN KEE

LANCE ALWORTH
Photograph by JOHN G. ZIMMERMAN

KELLEN WINSLOW
Photograph by PETER READ MILLER

CRIS CARTER
Photograph by TOM DIPACE

PAUL WARFIELD
Photograph by TONY TOMSIC

LYNN SWANN
Photograph by AP

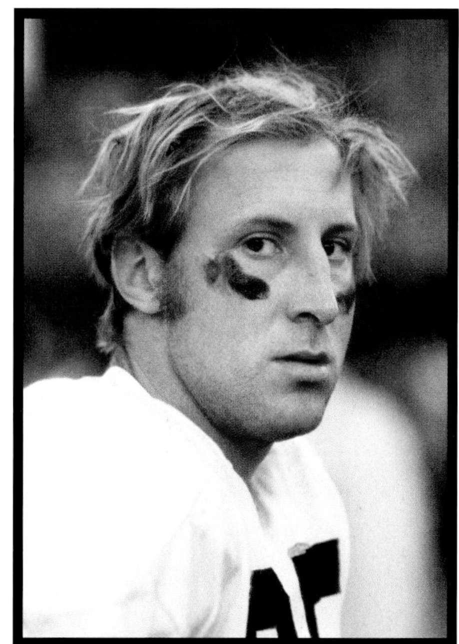

FRED BILETNIKOFF
Photograph by RICH CLARKSON

SHANNON SHARPE
Photograph by ALBERT DICKSON

MARVIN HARRISON
Photograph by TOM DIPACE

LANCE ALWORTH

RAYMOND BERRY

FRED BILETNIKOFF

TIM BROWN

CRIS CARTER

DAVE CASPER

MIKE DITKA

MARVIN HARRISON

ELROY (CRAZY LEGS) HIRSCH

DON HUTSON

CHARLIE JOINER

STEVE LARGENT

DANTE LAVELLI

JAMES LOFTON

JOHN MACKEY

DON MAYNARD

BOBBY MITCHELL

RANDY MOSS

OZZIE NEWSOME

JERRY RICE

SHANNON SHARPE

LYNN SWANN

CHARLEY TAYLOR

PAUL WARFIELD

KELLEN WINSLOW

THE SWEET LIFE OF SWINGING JOE

BY DAN JENKINS

Joe Namath quickly became the King of New York on the field and off, proving that he was equally adept under the microscope of the big-city media and the bright lights of Manhattan nightlife. —*from* SI, OCTOBER 17, 1966

STOOP-SHOULDERED AND sinisterly handsome, he slouches against the wall of the saloon, a filter cigarette in his teeth, collar open, perfectly happy and self-assured, gazing through the uneven darkness to sort out the winners from the losers. As the girls come by wearing their miniskirts, net stockings, big false eyelashes, long pressed hair and soulless expressions, he grins approvingly and says, "Hey, hold it, man—foxes." It is Joe Willie Namath at play. Relaxing. Nighttiming. The boss mover studying the defensive tendencies of New York's off-duty secretaries, stewardesses, dancers, nurses, bunnies, actresses, shopgirls—all of the people who make life stimulating for a bachelor who can throw one of the best passes in pro football. He poses a question for us all: Would you rather be young, single, rich, famous, talented, energetic and happy—or President?

Joe Willie Namath is not to be fully understood by most of us, of course. We are ancient, being over 23, and perhaps a bit arthritic, seeing as how we can't do the Duck. We aren't comfortably tuned in to the Mamas and the Uncles—or whatever their names are. We have cuffs on our trousers and, freakiest of all, we have pockets we can get our hands into. But Joe is not pleading to be understood. He is youth, success, the clothes, the car, the penthouse, the big town, the girls, the autographs and the games on Sundays. He simply *is*, man. The best we can do is catch a slight glimpse of him as he speeds by us in this life, and hope that he will in some way help prepare us for the day when we elect public officials who wear beanies and have term themes to write.

Right now, this moment, whatever Joe means to himself behind his wisecracks, his dark, rugged good looks, and his flashy tailoring, he is mostly one thing—a big celebrity in a celebrity-conscious town. This adds up to a lot of things, some desirable, some not. It means a stack of autographs everywhere he goes ("Hey, Joe, for a friend of mine who's a priest, a little somethin' on the napkin, huh?"), a lot of TV and radio stuff, a lot of photography stills for ads and news, and continual interviews with the press. Such things he handles with beautiful nonchalance, friendliness—and lip.

Then comes the good part. It means he gets to sit at one of those key tables in Toots Shor's—1 and 1A, the joke goes—the ones just beyond the partition from the big circular bar where everyone from Des Moines can watch him eat his prime rib. It means that when he hits P.J. Clarke's the maitre d' in the crowded back room, Frankie Ribando, will always find a place for him, while out front, waiter Tommy Joyce, one of New York's best celebrity-spotters, will tell everyone, "Joe's inside." It means he can crawl into the Pussy Cat during the late hours when the Copa girls and the bunnies are there having their after-work snacks, even though the line at the door may stretch from Second Avenue to the Triborough Bridge. It means he can get in just as easily at two of his other predawn haunts, Mister Laffs and Dudes 'n Dolls, places long ago ruled impenetrable by the earth people, or nonmembers of the Youth Cult.

Easing into the clubs and restaurants that he frequents, Joe Willie handles his role well. "Don't overdo it, man," he says. "I can hang around till 3 or 4 and still grab my seven or eight." He sits, he eats, he sips, he smokes, he talks, he looks, and maybe he scares up a female companion and maybe he doesn't. "I don't like to date so much as I just like to kind of, you know, run into somethin', man," he says.

Namath is unlike all of the super sports celebrities who came before him in New York—Babe Ruth, Joe DiMaggio and Sugar Ray Robinson, to name three of the more obvious. They were *grown men* when they achieved the status he now enjoys. Might even be wearing hats. They were less hip to their times and more or less aloof from the crowd. Joe thrusts himself into the middle of it. Their fame came more slowly—with the years of earning it. Joe Willie Namath was a happening.

Now as he goes about the business of proving that he is worth every cent of his $400,000 contract, he is becoming the quarterback that Jets owner Sonny Werblin gambled he would be—a throwing artist who may eventually rank with the best—and he is still a swinger. Namath may be Johnny Unitas and Paul Hornung rolled into one; he may, in fact, be pro football's very own Beatle. . . .

EVEN WHEN he was sitting on the Jets' bench, injured, Broadway Joe had a knack for attracting attention.

1972 | JOE NAMATH was known for his flashy wardrobe off the field; on the field, his signature look included white shoes and a heavy knee brace that today looks medieval | *Photograph by* NEIL LEIFER *(right)*

Jets

1987 | JOE MONTANA and his 49ers took a 49–3 beating from the Giants in the playoffs | *Photograph by* JACQUELINE DUVOISIN

GIANTS
BURT
16

PAYTON
56

from FURY ON THE FIELD | BY PAUL ZIMMERMAN
SI November 8, 1999

FEW NFL PLAYERS HAVE POSSESSED the fire that burned inside Walter Payton. ❧ How could this have happened to Walter Payton—a man defined by his great, passionate bursts of life? Waiting nine months for a transplant that could have saved him, slowly sinking, gradually slipping away. ❧ He played football in a frenzy, attacking tacklers with a fury that almost seemed personal. He got stronger as the game went on. Defenses tired, he attacked them.

In 1982, near the height of a remarkable career in which he rushed for more yards (16,726) than any man in history, I interviewed him at the Chicago Bears' training camp in Lake Forest, Ill. We were sitting in the lobby of the players' dorm. He had brought his motorcycle in and leaned it against a wall. Twilight was approaching but the lights in the lobby hadn't been turned on yet, and as we talked, he kept bouncing to his feet to emphasize some point—he couldn't sit still. His eyes sparkled in that half light, and I got this weird feeling that there was a glow around him, that he was giving off sparks, that there was some kind of fire burning inside, lighting him up. It was the fire of pure energy.

He told me about his off-season workouts, how he'd run up and down the steep levees near his home in Mississippi, how he'd burn out anyone foolish enough to try to keep up with him. He played in 186 straight games to finish his 13-year NFL career. All of them played at a furious pace.

"A little bundle of dynamite," Dallas Cowboys safety Cliff Harris once called him. This was after the 1977 Bears-Cowboys playoff game, and Harris, one of the more vicious hitters in NFL history, described a knockout shot he had laid on Payton. "As he caught a pass and turned upfield, I caught him just right, one of the hardest hits I ever delivered," Harris said. "He just bounced up and patted me on the behind and ran back to the huddle. I'd heard that you could never keep him on the ground. Now I know for sure."

Now, at 45, he's gone. It's hard to imagine. . . .

1981 | PAYTON WENT around, through and sometimes over the defense to pick up precious yards. | *Photograph by* RONALD C. MODRA

1971 | THE COLTS' margin of victory over the Cowboys in Super Bowl V was provided by Jim O'Brien (80) on this field goal | *Photograph by* NEIL LEIFER

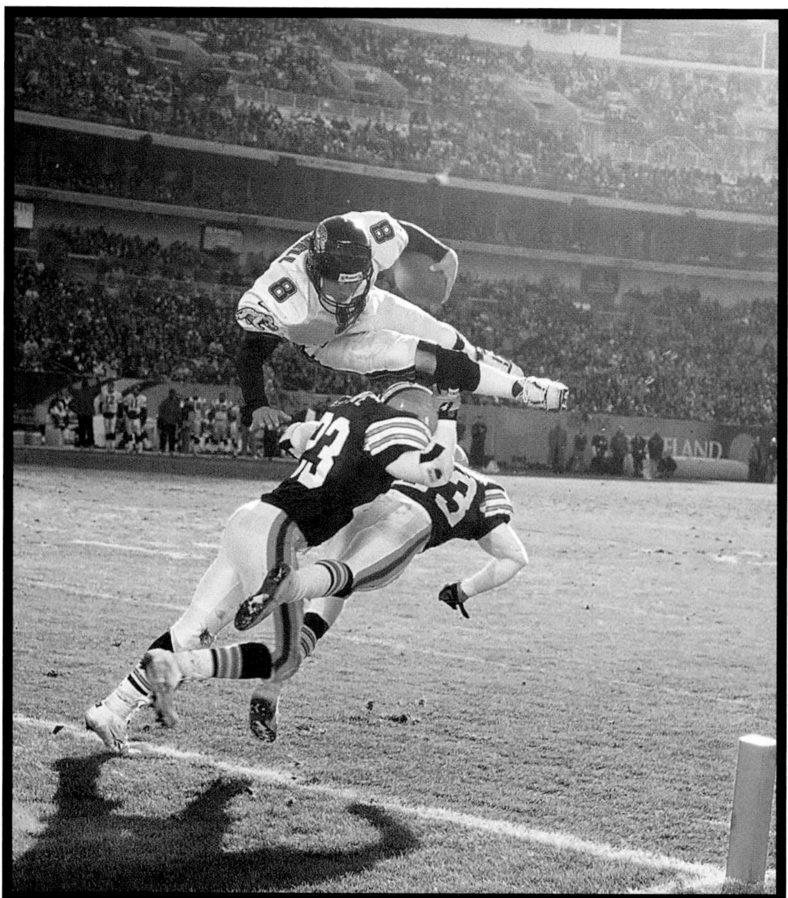

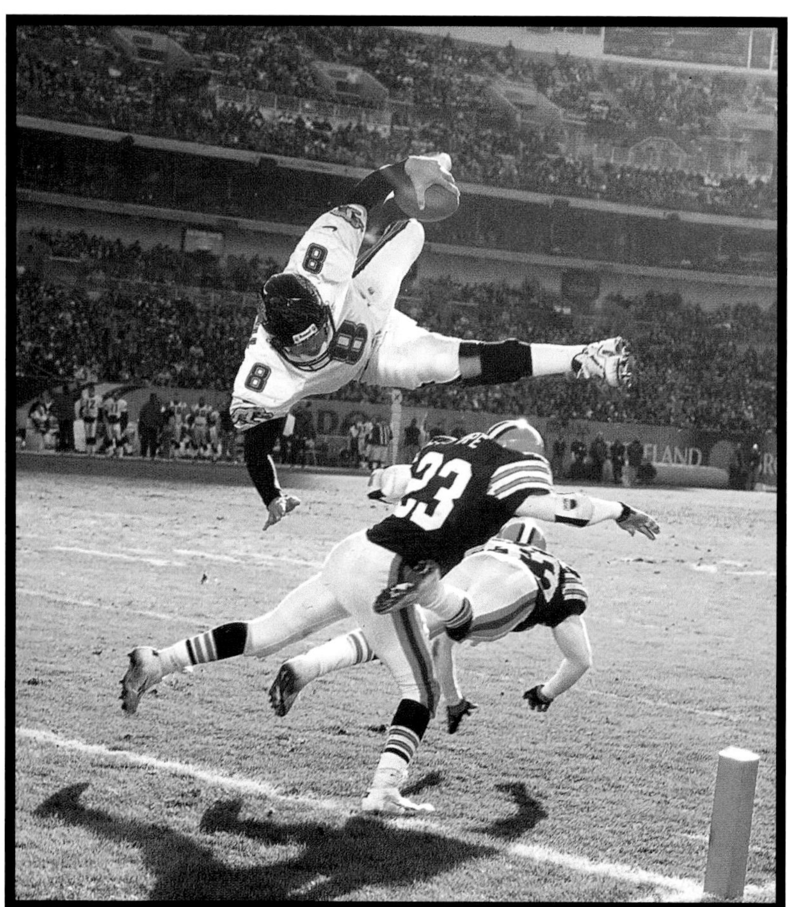

1999 | JAGUARS QUARTERBACK Mark Brunell went up (top, left) and over two Browns to reach the end zone in Cleveland | *Photographs by* JOHN BIEVER

ELAND
23

from FROZEN IN TIME | BY JOHNETTE HOWARD
SI January 13, 1997

THERE WAS A TIME WHEN PROfessional football franchises routinely settled in small towns like Canton and Kenosha and Green Bay. A time when Lambeau Field was not a quaint anomaly, when everyone played football on grass and there were no Teflon roofs to shut out the midday sun or hermetically sealed domes to block the winter wind. In 1961, when coach Vince Lombardi's players hoisted him into the air for his first NFL title ride, only God's gray sky hung overhead, just as it had at all football games back then.

The Packers were a league power in that era, and Lambeau Field was the NFL's answer to Boston Garden and Yankee Stadium—hallowed ground where dynasties were born. During Lombardi's nine-year stint as coach of the Packers, they won five league championships, including the first two Super Bowls. And no matter how many winters have passed since then, within the magical space of Lambeau Field it still seems to be 1967. "Forget Dallas," says Fuzzy Thurston, who played guard for Green Bay from 1959 to '67. "The Green Bay Packers are America's Team."

The more things change in the rest of pro sports, the more things remain blissfully the same in Green Bay.

People go out of their way to stop at Lambeau, even when they have no tickets—even when the stadium is empty. Immediately after Green Bay defeated the Carolina Panthers to take the NFC championship on Jan. 12, 1997, the gates of the stadium were thrown open so that fans could watch the awards ceremony. Visitors ask to be shown the spot in the south end zone where, in the 1967 NFL championship game—the Ice Bowl—Bart Starr plunged into the end zone from the one-yard line to give the Pack a 21–17 win over the Dallas Cowboys. It's as if setting foot on the sacred ground gives life to the grainy black-and-white film that shows Starr burrowing across the goal line with 13 seconds to play, his arms hugging the football in the -46° windchill as if he were protecting a newborn from the cold. "With Lombardi it was never cold here," says Thurston. "Before games he'd just say something like, 'Men, it's a little blustery out there today.' Blustery, see? Then he'd say, 'It's our kind of day. Now get out there and strut around like it's the middle of July.' " . . .

1967 | PLAYERS AND FANS at Lambeau Field endured the -46° windchill at the Ice Bowl. | *Photograph by* BETTMANN

14
88

1962 | NOTHING WAS a snap for the diminutive Cowboys quarterback Eddie LeBaron, not even the Cardinals | *Photograph by* MARVIN E. NEWMAN

THE DAY WORLD WAR II KICKED OFF

BY S.L. PRICE

On Dec. 7, 1941, the Redskins and the Eagles played football, not knowing that the U.S. had joined the rest of the world at war.
—from SI, NOVEMBER 29, 1999

EVERYONE IN WASHINGTON, D.C.'s Griffith Stadium that day knew his role. The wives walked in together, chattering like a flock of birds. The 27,102 fans shoved through the turnstiles, ready to shout and clap, to watch and feel. The press box filled with reporters prepared to scribble their notes. On the field the players tried to keep warm. Some were stars, some weren't. It was the final pro football game of the season for the Washington Redskins and the Philadelphia Eagles. It was quite cold. People stamped their feet. They could see their breath.

Kickoff was at 2 p.m.—9 a.m. in Hawaii. Bombs had already fallen on the U.S. fleet, men had died, war had come. In the stands, no one knew: The game was still everything. Philadelphia had taken a 7–0 lead on its first drive. Announcements began to pour out of the P.A. system. *Admiral Bland is asked to report to his office. . . . Captain H.X. Fenn is asked to report. . . . The resident commissioner of the Philippines is urged to report. . . .* "We didn't know what the hell was going on," says Sammy Baugh, the Redskins' quarterback that day. "I had never heard that many announcements one right after another. We felt something was up, but we just kept playing."

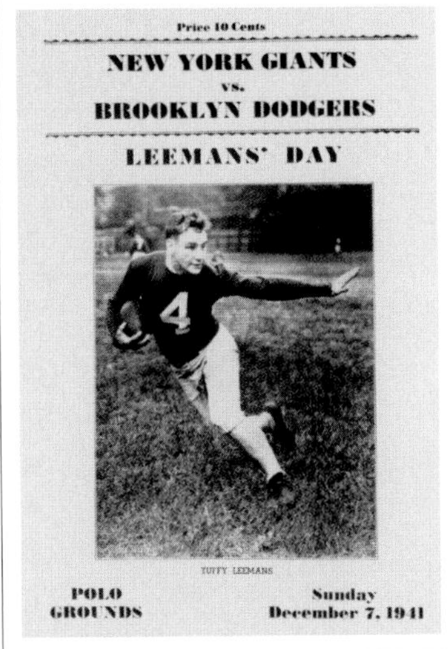

Only the boys in the press box had any idea. Just before kickoff an Associated Press reporter named Pat O'Brien got a message ordering him to keep his story short. When O'Brien complained, another message flashed: *The Japanese have kicked off. War now!* But Redskins president George Marshall wouldn't allow an announcement of Japan's attack during the game, explaining that it would distract the fans. That made Griffith Stadium one of the last outposts of an era that had already slipped away.

The crowd oohed and cheered. When the game—and season—ended with Washington a 20–14 winner, a few hundred fans rushed the goalposts. No one took much notice of Eagles rookie halfback Nick Basca. He hadn't played much all year, making his mark mostly as a kicker and punter, and on this day he'd converted just two extra points. Baugh, with three touchdown passes, was the game's hero.

Then everyone walked out of the stadium: the wives, the future Hall of Famer, the crowd. Outside, newsboys hawked the news. The world tilted; football lost all importance; roles shifted. Women began fearing for their men. Reporters and fans would be soldiers soon. The world would not be divided into players and spectators again for a very long time. "Everybody could feel it," Baugh says.

Baugh went home to Texas and waited for a call from his draft board that never came; he was granted a deferment to stay on his ranch and raise beef cattle. During the war he flew in on the weekends for games.

Nick Basca, meanwhile, had played his final game. A native of tiny Phoenixville, Pa., and a standout at Villanova, Basca enlisted in the Army three days after Pearl Harbor with his younger brother Stephen, who left Europe with three Purple Hearts. Nick was piloting a tank in Gen. George Patton's celebrated Fourth Armored Division in France when, on Nov. 11, 1944, the tank hit a mine and was blown apart.

In later years no one talked much about Nick's short pro football career. Then, in 1991, 50 years after events had rendered it meaningless, that game between Philadelphia and Washington became everything again. Stephen Basca Jr. says, "My father was lying 60 miles away in a hospital bed when Nick was killed. They recorded on his chart that he had gotten up screaming about the time Nick's tank blew up. [In 1991] my father and I were sitting watching TV, and they showed a clip of that old game. My dad froze in his chair. It was the first time I'd ever seen him cry." . . .

COURTESY OF THE PRO FOOTBALL HALL OF FAME

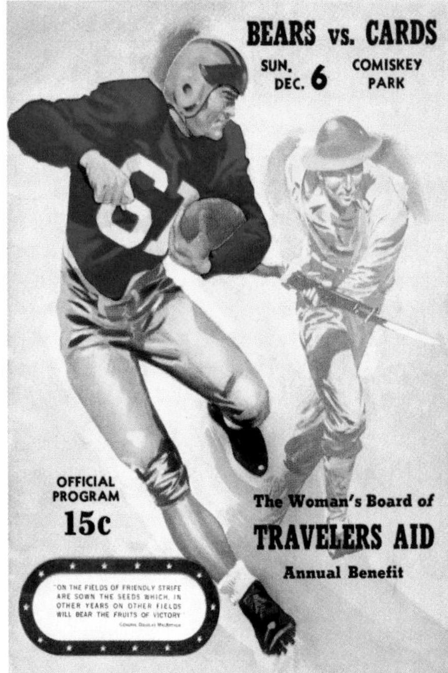

THE PATRIOTISM of the war years was reflected on NFL programs after news of Pearl Harbor spread on that December Sunday *(opposite)*.

1998 | VIKINGS DEFENSIVE tackle John Randle didn't spare the eye-black when he put his game face on | *Photograph by* WALTER IOOSS JR.

1958 | COLTS FANS got carried away, and so did fullback Alan Ameche after his overtime touchdown beat the Giants for the NFL title | *Photograph by* NEIL LEIFER

THE BEST THERE EVER WAS

BY FRANK DEFORD

Johnny Unitas was more than just a boyhood hero for a Baltimore native. He was an inspiration for the entire city.

—*from* SI, SEPTEMBER 23, 2002

SOMETIMES, EVEN IF IT WAS only yesterday, or even if it just feels like it was only yesterday. . . . ❧ Sometimes, no matter how detailed the historical accounts, no matter how many the eyewitnesses, no matter how complete the statistics, no matter how vivid the film. . . . ❧ Sometimes, I'm sorry, but. . . . ❧ Sometimes, you just had to be there. ❧ That was the way it was with Johnny Unitas in the prime of his life, when he played for the Baltimore Colts and changed a team and a city and a league. Johnny U was an American original, a piece of work like none other, excepting maybe Paul Bunyan or Horatio Alger.

Part of it was that he came out of nowhere, like Athena springing forth full-grown from the brow of Zeus, or like Shoeless Joe Hardy from Hannibal, Mo., magically joining the Senators, compliments of the devil. But that was myth, and that was fiction. Johnny U was real, before our eyes.

Nowadays, of course, flesh peddlers and scouting services identify the best athletes when they are still in junior high. Prospects are not allowed to sneak up on us. But back then, 1956, was a quaint time when we still could be pleasantly surprised. Unitas just surfaced there on the roster, showing up one day after a tryout. The new number 19 was identified as "YOU-ni-tass" when he first appeared in an exhibition, and only later did we learn that he had played, somewhere between obscurity and anonymity, at Louisville and then, for six bucks a game, on the dusty Pittsburgh sandlots. His was a story out of legend, if not, indeed, out of religious tradition: the unlikely savior come out of nowhere.

The quarterback for the Colts then was George Shaw, the very first pick in the NFL draft the year before, the man ordained to lead a team that was coalescing into a contender. Didn't we wish, in Baltimore! Didn't we dream! The Colts had Alan (the Horse) Ameche and Lenny (Spats) Moore and L.G. (Long Gone) Dupre to carry the ball and Raymond Berry and Jim Mutscheller to catch it and Artie Donovan and Big Daddy Lipscomb and Gino Marchetti to manhandle the other fellows when they had the pigskin. Then one day, as it is written, Shaw got hurt in a game, and YOU-ni-tass came in, hunched of shoulder, trotting kind of funny. He looked *crooked*, is how I always thought of him. Jagged. Sort of a gridiron Abraham Lincoln.

And on the first play the rookie threw a pass that went for a long touchdown. Only it was an interception; the touchdown went the other way.

For those of us in Baltimore, this seemed like the cruelest fate (however likely). Finally Baltimore was going to amount to something, and then, wouldn't you know it, Shaw gets taken from us. It seemed so terribly unfair, if perhaps exactly what we could expect for our workingman's town, where the swells passed through, without stopping, on their way to Washington or New York.

But then, there couldn't have been a mother's son anywhere who knew exactly what Unitas had in store for us. Marchetti, apparently, was the first one to understand. It was a couple of weeks later, and he was lying on the training table when the equipment manager, Fred Schubach, wondered out loud when Shaw might come back. Marchetti raised up a bit and said, "It doesn't matter. Unitas is the quarterback now."

Evidently all the other Colts nodded; they'd just been waiting for someone to dare express what they were beginning to sense. Marchetti had fought in the Battle of the Bulge when he was a teenager and thus, apparently, had developed a keen appreciation for things larger than life.

Of course, no matter whom John Constantine Unitas had played football for, it would've been Katie-bar-the-door. But perhaps greatness has never found such a fitting address. It wasn't only that Baltimore had such an inferiority complex, an awareness that all that the stuck-up outlanders knew of our fair city was that we had crabs and white marble steps in profusion and a dandy red-light district, the Block. Since H.L. Mencken (he who had declared, "I hate all sports as rabidly as a person who likes sports hates common sense") had died, the most famous Baltimorean was a stripper, Blaze Starr. The city hadn't had a winner since the Old Orioles of a century past. For that matter, until very recently Baltimore hadn't even *had*

TONY TOMSIC

a major league team in the 1900s. Before the Colts arrived in 1947, the best athlete in town was a woman duckpin bowler named Toots Barger. Football? The biggest games in Baltimore had been when Johns Hopkins took on Susquehanna or Franklin & Marshall at homecoming.

But no mother ever took her children to her breast as old Bawlmer, Merlin (as we pronounced it), embraced the Colts. It wasn't just that they played on Sundays and thus finally made us "big league" in the eyes of the rest of a republic that was rapidly becoming coaxial-cabled together. No, the Colts were just folks, all around town, at crab feasts and bull roasts and what-have-you. Why, I knew I could go a few blocks to Moses' Sunoco station on York Road and see a bunch of Colts there, hanging out, kicking tires. If I'd had a good enough fake I.D., I could've even gotten into Sweeney's, up Greenmount Avenue and drunk beer with them. The Colts were real people, so we loved them even more as they went on their merry way to becoming champions of the world.

With each passing game, though, Unitas elevated above the others until, on Dec. 28, 1958, he entered the pantheon of gods. 'Twas then, of course, in Yankee Stadium itself, that he led us from behind to an overtime victory over the despised New Yorkers in the Greatest Game Ever Played. Yet even as we deified him, we still had it on the best authority that he remained one of the boys. Just because he was quarterback, he wasn't some glamour-puss.

Certainly he didn't look the part of a hero. This is how his teammate Alex Hawkins described Unitas when Hawkins first saw him in the locker room: "Here was a total mystery. [Unitas] was from Pennsylvania, but he looked so much like a Mississippi farmhand that I looked around for a mule. He had stooped shoulders, a chicken breast, thin bowed legs and long, dangling arms with crooked, mangled fingers."

Unitas didn't even have a quarterback's name. All by himself he redrew the profile of the quarterback. Always, before, it had been men of Old Stock who qualified to lead the pros. Baugh and Albert and Van Brocklin and Layne and Graham. (All right, Luckman was a Jew, but he was schooled in the WASP-y Ivy League.) Unitas was some hardscrabble Lithuanian, so what he did made a difference, because even if we'd never met a Lithuanian before, we knew that he was as smart a sonuvabitch as he was tough. Dammit, he was *our* Lithuanian.

They didn't have coaches with headphones and Polaroids and fax machines then, sitting on high, telling quarterbacks what plays to call. In those halcyon days, quarterbacks were field generals, not field lieutenants. And there was Unitas after he called a play (and probably checked off and called another play when he saw what the ruffians across the line were up to), shuffling back into the pocket, unfazed by the violent turbulence all around him, standing there in his hightops, waiting, looking, poised. I never saw war, so that is still my vision of manhood: Unitas standing courageously in the pocket, his left arm flung out in a diagonal to the upper deck, his right cocked for the business of passing, down amidst the mortals. Lock and load.

There, to Berry at the sideline. Or Moore. Or Jimmy Orr real long. Lenny Lyles. John Mackey. Hawkins. Ameche out of the backfield. My boyhood memory tells me Johnny U never threw an incompletion, let alone an interception, after that single debut mistake. Spoilsports who keep the numbers dispute that recollection, but they also assure me that he threw touchdown passes in 47 straight games. That figure has been threatened less seriously than even DiMaggio's sacred 56. Yes, I know there've been wonderful quarterbacks since Unitas hung up his hightops. I admit I'm prejudiced. But the best quarterback ever? The best player? Let me put it this way: If there were one game scheduled, Earth versus the Klingons, with the fate of the universe on the line, any person with his wits about him would have Johnny U calling the signals in the huddle, up under the center, back in the pocket.

I'VE ALWAYS WONDERED HOW people in olden times connected back to their childhoods. After all, we have hooks with the past. When most of us from the 20th century reminisce about growing up, we right away remember the songs and the athletes of any particular moment. Right?

A few years ago I saw Danny and the Juniors performing at a club, and all anybody wanted them to sing was *At the Hop*, which was their No. 1 smash back in 1958, the year Unitas led the Colts to that first, fabled championship. About a year after I saw Danny, I read that he had committed suicide. I always assumed it was because no matter how many years had passed, nobody would let him escape from singing *At the Hop*, exactly as he did in 1958.

Unlike songs, athletes, inconveniently, get on. They grow old. Johnny U couldn't keep on throwing passes. He aged. He even let his crew cut grow out. Luckily for me, after I grew up (as it were) and became a sportswriter, I never covered him. Oh, I went to his restaurant, and I saw him on TV, and I surely never forgot him. Whenever Walter Iooss, the photographer, and I would get together, we would talk about Johnny U the way most men talk about caressing beautiful women. But I never had anything to do with Unitas professionally. That was good. I could keep my boy's memories unsullied.

Then, about five years ago, I finally met him at a party. When we were introduced he said, "It's nice to meet you, Mr. Deford." That threw me into a tailspin. *No, no, no. Don't you understand? I'm not Mr. Deford. You're Mr. Unitas. You're Johnny U. You're my boyhood idol. I can't ever be Mr. Deford with you, because you have to always be number 19, so I can always be a kid.* But I didn't explain that to him. I was afraid he would think I was too sappy. I just said, "It's nice to meet you, too, Mr. Unitas," and shook his crippled hand.

A couple of years later I went down to Baltimore and gave a speech for a charity. What they gave me as a thank-you present was a football, autographed by Himself. When you're not a child anymore and you write about athletes, you tend to take 'em as run-of-the-mill human beings. Anyway, I do. I have only one other athlete's autograph, from Bill Russell, who, along with Unitas, is the other great star of the '50s who changed his sport all by himself.

After I got that autographed Unitas football, every now and then I'd pick it up and fondle it. I still do, too, even though Johnny Unitas is dead now, and I can't be a boy anymore. Ultimately, you see, what he conveyed to his teammates and to Baltimore and to a wider world was the utter faith that he could do it. He could make it work. Somehow, he could win. He *would* win. It almost didn't matter when he actually couldn't. The point was that with Johnny U, it always seemed possible. You so very seldom get that, even with the best of them. Johnny U's talents were his own. The belief he gave us was his gift. . . .

UNITAS STOOD tall in a 45–17 win over the Redskins in 1964, one of the three seasons in which he was the NFL's player of the year.

NEIL LEIFER

1962 | THE BROWNS' Bernie Parrish climbed the ladder on an extra-point attempt by the Giants in Cleveland | *Photograph by* TONY TOMSIC

1996 | COWBOYS CORNERBACK Deion Sanders was also an offensive threat against the Steelers in Super Bowl XXX | *Photograph by* RICHARD MACKSON

1962 | THE COLTS' Jimmy Orr beat tight coverage for a touchdown catch against the 49ers | *Photograph by* WALTER IOOSS JR.

> Artifacts

Bling of Truth

Super Bowl rings don't lie: The only people entitled to wear them are NFL champions

SUPER BOWL I
Packers 35, Chiefs 10

SUPER BOWL III
Jets 16, Colts 7

SUPER BOWL IV
Chiefs 23, Vikings 7

SUPER BOWL V
Colts 16, Cowboys 13

SUPER BOWL VI
Cowboys 24, Dolphins 3

SUPER BOWL VIII
Dolphins 24, Vikings 7

SUPER BOWL X
Steelers 21, Cowboys 17

SUPER BOWL XVIII
Raiders 38, Redskins 9

SUPER BOWL XXI
Giants 39, Broncos 20

SUPER BOWL XXIV
49ers 55, Broncos 10

SUPER BOWL XXVI
Redskins 37, Bills 24

SUPER BOWL XXXIII
Broncos 34, Falcons 19

SUPER BOWL XXXIV
Rams 23, Titans 16

SUPER BOWL XXXVI
Patriots 20, Rams 17

DAVID N. BERKWITZ; JOSTEN'S (PATRIOTS)

SUPER BOWL XXIX

49ers 49, Chargers 26

76
SPUR
11

1976 | STEELERS TACKLE Ernie Holmes shed a blocker as he pressured Roger Staubach in Super Bowl X | *Photograph by* JOHN BIEVER

1972 | PACKERS TACKLE Mike McCoy had mayhem in mind but couldn't reach 49ers QB Steve Spurrier before he let fly | *Photograph by* JOHN BIEVER

33

from THE TOUGHEST JOB IN SPORTS | BY PETER KING
SI August 17, 1998

IN 1948 CHICAGO BEARS COACH George Halas traded disappointing rookie Bobby Layne, who eventually became one of the NFL's top quarterbacks with the Detroit Lions. In the late '50s the Pittsburgh Steelers gave up on young signal-callers John Unitas and Jack Kemp, and kept, among others, Vic Eaton and Jack Scarbath. Warren Moon wasn't among the 334 players selected in the '78 draft. The following year Joe Montana was a third-round pick. In '83 the Lions felt so good about incumbent Eric Hipple that they passed on Jim Kelly and Dan Marino. In '91 at least 10 teams had Browning Nagle rated higher than Brett Favre.

Of the 10 quarterbacks selected among the top 10 picks in the regular or supplemental draft during the 1990s, only the New England Patriots' Drew Bledsoe has performed at a Pro Bowl–caliber level. Seven have struggled mightily (Dave Brown, Rick Mirer, Heath Shuler, Trent Dilfer, Kerry Collins) or been abject failures (Andre Ware, David Klingler).

Twelve of the 30 projected starting quarterbacks this fall were selected in the third round or later, and two more were undrafted. The quest for a quarterback who may one day lead a team to a Super Bowl is getting more and more like the lottery: Take your best shot, then cross your fingers.

Why is it so hard to unearth a good quarterback? Let's start with this premise: Quarterback is the most complex position in sports. A pitcher has to be precise in his pitch location and outwit the hitter; a point guard must direct his teammates and adjust on the fly to make a play work; a hockey goalie must be athletic and fearless. A quarterback has to be able to do and be all of those things. "I'd say quarterback's the toughest position," says Phoenix Suns coach Danny Ainge, a former all-state high school quarterback, major league shortstop and All-Star NBA guard. "A quarterback has to be a leader, have good vision, be physically and mentally tough and be athletic. He has to be able to read defenses and figure out what the other team's giving him."

"Every fall Sunday, you're the nerve center for a city, a county, a state, a region," says Boomer Esiason, who played quarterback for 14 NFL seasons. "You step behind center, and millions of people watch to see what you'll do next. The pressure kills some guys. There's no other job like it in sports." . . .

1942 | REDSKINS QUARTERBACK Sammy Baugh held most of the NFL's passing records when he retired in 1952 | *Photograph by* AP

> SI's TOP 25 The Quarterbacks

JOHN ELWAY
Photograph by TIM DEFRISCO

FRAN TARKENTON
Photograph by NEIL LEIFER

BOBBY LAYNE
Photograph by NFL

TERRY BRADSHAW
Photograph by NEIL LEIFER

SONNY JURGENSEN
Photograph by FRED ROE

BRETT FAVRE
Photograph by DARREN HAUCK

JOE MONTANA
Photograph by ANDY HAYT

TROY AIKMAN
Photograph by ROB TRINGALI

FRITZ POLLARD
Photograph by BROWN UNIVERSITY ARCHIVES

DAN MARINO
Photograph by BOB ROSATO

TROY AIKMAN
SAMMY BAUGH
TERRY BRADSHAW
TOM BRADY
LEN DAWSON
JOHN ELWAY
BRETT FAVRE
DAN FOUTS
BENNY FRIEDMAN
OTTO GRAHAM
BOB GRIESE
SONNY JURGENSEN
JIM KELLY
BOBBY LAYNE
SID LUCKMAN
PEYTON MANNING
DAN MARINO
JOE MONTANA
JOE NAMATH
FRITZ POLLARD
BART STARR
ROGER STAUBACH
FRAN TARKENTON
JOHNNY UNITAS
STEVE YOUNG

J.JOHNSON
20
33

1990 | JERRY RICE searched for an escape route as the Vikings closed in on him during the NFC playoffs | *Photograph by* WALTER IOOSS JR.

1986 | TONY DORSETT was looking past the Rams in this playoff game, but his Cowboys lost, 20–0 | *Photograph by* RICHARD MACKSON

76
74
63

1962 | THE TOE, Lou Groza, was a Hall of Fame tackle for the Browns for 12 years, and their stalwart kicker for 21 | *Photograph by* TONY TOMSIC

THE ULTIMATE WINNER

BY PAUL ZIMMERMAN

Heading an offense tailored to his unique skills, San Francisco's Joe Montana enjoyed unparalleled success as a quarterback, including victories in four Super Bowls. —*from* SI, AUGUST 13, 1990

WHEN SAN FRANCISCO 49ers coach Bill Walsh talks about offensive football, he eventually mentions the "quick, slashing strokes" of attack. He'll use analogies with tennis and boxing, even warfare, which was why he was so taken with quarterback Joe Montana's nimble feet. A quick, slashing attack needs a quick-footed quarterback. The statuesque quarterback who can throw the ball 60 yards downfield has never been Walsh's type. And when he refined his offense to blend with Montana's skills, Walsh introduced the X factor, which was the great escape talent of his quarterback—elusiveness, body control, the ability to throw while in the grasp of an opponent.

"A lot of our offense was play-action," Walsh says, "and I learned through my experience that on a play-pass you have to expect an unblocked man just when you're trying to throw the ball. If you can throw and take the hit—TD. If you can avoid him, so much the better. We were on the cutting edge of Joe's ability. He was gifted at avoiding and throwing. We practiced the scrambling, off-balance throw. It was a carefully practiced thing"

Finally it all came into focus in the '81 postseason, in one momentous play, the last-minute touchdown pass to wideout Dwight Clark that buried the Dallas Cowboys in the NFC Championship Game. The play will always be known as The Catch—Montana scrambling to his right, with three Cowboys clutching at him; the off-balance throw; and finally Clark, on a breakoff route, ducking inside, then cutting back—just the way he and Joe had practiced on their own so many times in camp.

The Super Bowl was an anticlimax. The 49ers beat the Bengals 26–21, with Montana taking MVP honors. In each of the 49ers' next two Super Bowls, he again was matched with a consensus All-Pro, Dan Marino of the Miami Dolphins in '85 and Boomer Esiason of Cincinnati in '89. Montana had gone in as the second-best quarterback each time and won. By the time of the 49ers' fourth Super Bowl, in '90, everyone had learned, and the question was only how badly would Montana and the 49ers beat John Elway and the Denver Broncos?

The first talk of Montana being the greatest of all came in Bay Area circles after the '82 Super Bowl, as put forth by a couple of old 49ers quarterbacks. John Brodie said it, flat out, and people laughed. Frankie Albert said, "At 25, he's ahead of Unitas, Van Brocklin, Waterfield . . . all the immortals."

Based on the NFL quarterback rating system, Montana's '89 season was the best anyone has ever had—the highest rating (112.4) and third-highest completion percentage (70.2) in history. But those are just numbers. The 49ers swept through the playoffs and the Super Bowl like a broom, trouncing Denver 55–10 to repeat as NFL champions. Their efficiency was frightening, and Montana was the master.

If you want to highlight one game during the season, try the game in Philadelphia on Sept. 24. Some people call it the finest Montana has ever played. For three quarters the 49ers' offense was falling apart. Montana had been sacked seven times, with one more to come. He had tripped twice while setting up and had fallen in the end zone for a safety. The Eagles were coming at him like crazy, and the 49ers were down 21–10 with 10 seconds gone in the fourth quarter. Then Montana threw four touchdown passes into the teeth of the Eagles' rush to pull out a 38–28 victory. His fourth-quarter stats read 11 completions in 12 attempts for 227 yards, and he scrambled for 19 more.

"Worried? Oh, hell, yes, we were worried," 49ers tackle Harris Barton says of the Eagles' assault on Montana. "Joe gets that glazed look in his eyes, and you know he's been shellacked. It wasn't a good situation to be in. We'd get to the sideline and Joe would say, 'O.K., let's get this thing settled down.' I was just amazed that he could line up at all after getting smacked in the head by Reggie White."

If you want to make a case for Montana as the greatest quarterback who ever played the game, there it is. Toughness. The great ones all had it—Unitas, Graham, Baugh, Waterfield, Tittle, Bradshaw. When you add Montana's finesse, the sensuous and fluid qualities that Walsh saw at the beginning, plus his uncanny accuracy—no one has ever thrown the short crossing pattern with a better touch—you've got a special package. . . .

JOE COOL was an apt nickname for Montana, who engineered 31 fourth-quarter come-from-behind wins.

JOHN IACONO

SF
16

1974 | FIVE-TIME Pro Bowler Len Hauss anchored the center of the Redskins' offensive line | *Photograph by* NEIL LEIFER

2003 | THE RAIDERS' Barret Robbins had his own signals to call before he snapped the ball to Rich Gannon | *Photograph by* RON SCHWANE

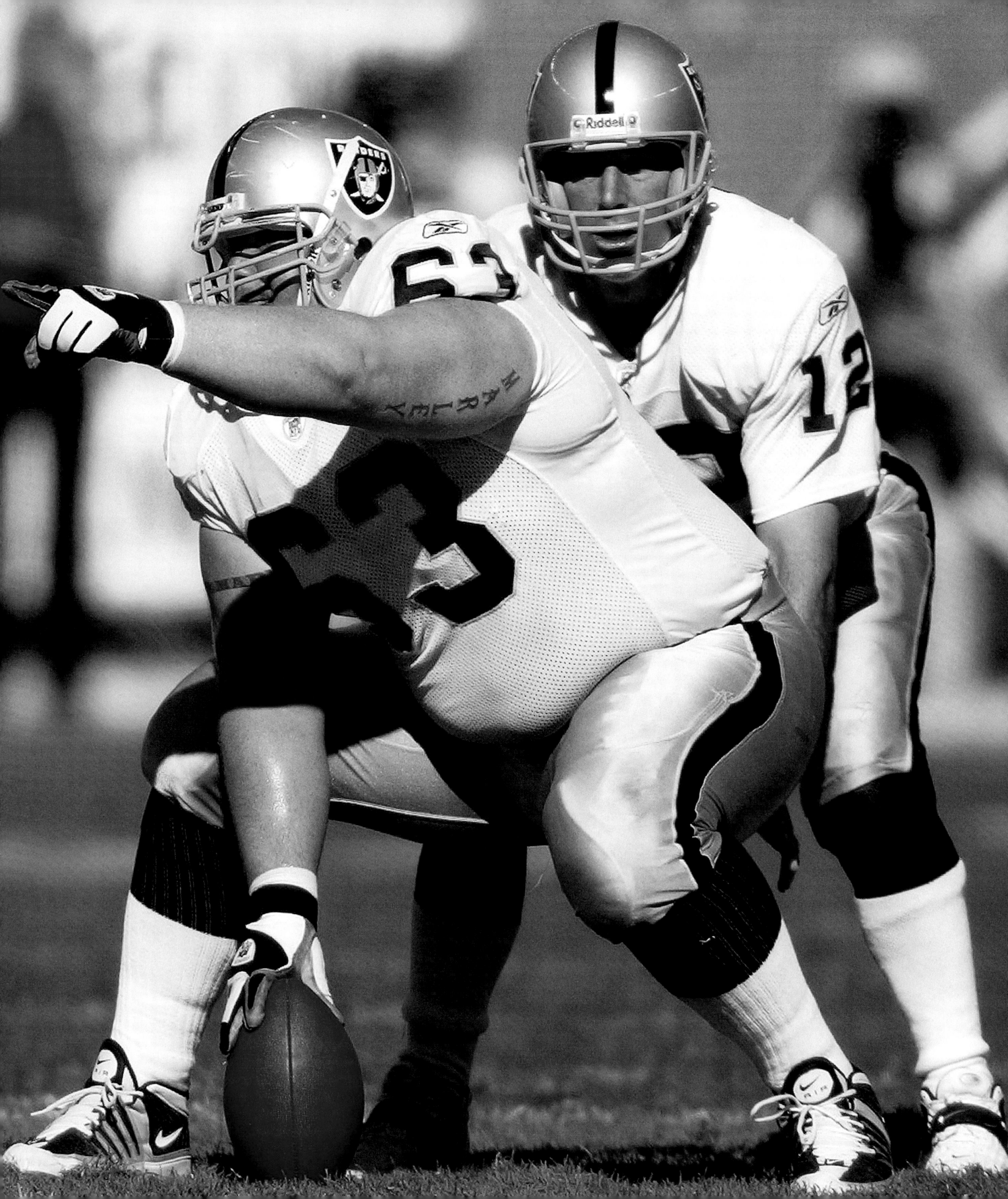
Riddell
63
12
HARLEY

84

2001 | VIKINGS WIDEOUT Randy Moss took matters into his own hand to make this reception against the Steelers | *Photograph by* DAMIAN STROHMEYER

1983 | THE CHARGERS' Mike Williams got up high to cover Dolphins tight end Bruce Hardy, who went even higher for this catch | *Photograph by* WALTER IOOSS JR.

> Artifacts

Tickets to Paradise

The price has gone up over the years, but a ducat still gets you through the turnstile and then makes a perfect souvenir

JETS VS. RAIDERS *August 23, 1963*

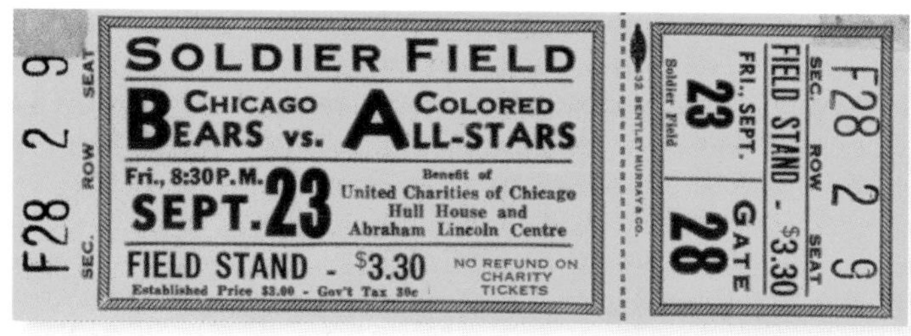

BEARS VS. ALL-STARS *September 23, 1938*

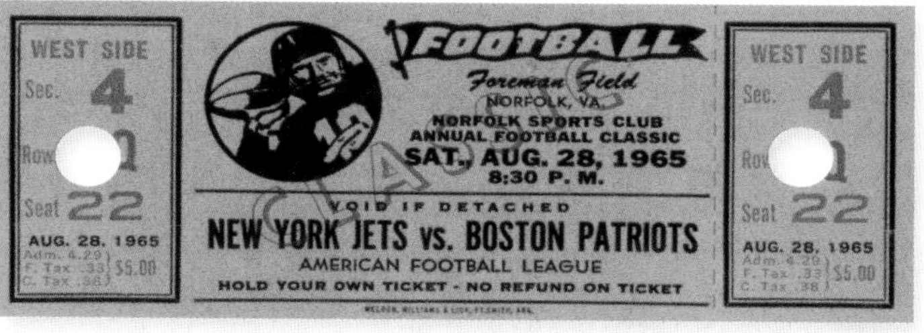

JETS VS. PATRIOTS *August 28, 1965*

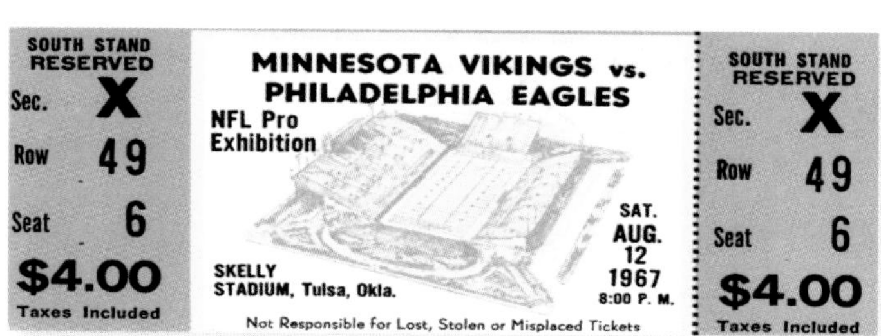

VIKINGS VS. EAGLES *August 12, 1967*

BEARS VS. CARDINALS *December 1, 1946*

COURTESY OF THE PRO FOOTBALL HALL OF FAME

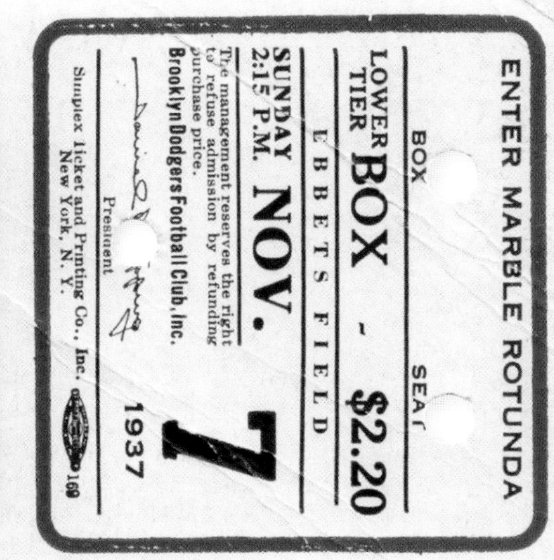

DODGERS vs. EAGLES *November 7, 1937*

BEARS vs. COLLEGE ALL STARS *August 28, 1942*

CARDINALS vs. LIONS *August 15, 1959*

BROWNS vs. COLLEGE ALL-STARS *August 6, 1965*

1962 | THE 49ERS didn't measure up to the Browns in a 13–10 Cleveland victory in San Francisco in December | *Photograph by* NEIL LEIFER

1973 | VIKINGS QB Fran Tarkenton knew exactly what he needed to get past the Cowboys in the NFC title game | *Photograph by* NEIL LEIFER

67
67
10

ZERO OF THE LIONS

BY GEORGE PLIMPTON

For a professional amateur given a chance to play quarterback for Detroit, there were many things to worry about, but none more daunting than the pit. —*from SI, September 7, 1964*

ONE OF THE TROUBLES with wearing a football helmet was that it closed off the outside world, the noise of the crowd, the cheering as the contests wore on—all of this just a murmur—leaving my mind to work away busily inside the amphitheater of the helmet. Voices, my own, spoke quite clearly, offering consolation, encouragement and paternal advice of a particularly galling sort: "The thing to be is calm, son, and remember not to snatch back from the ball until you get it set in your palm."

"I'll hang on to the ball," I murmured back.

"But"—the portentous voice came again like the Ghost's in *Hamlet*—"you must not dally, son. On the handoffs you must get the ball to the halfbacks with dispatch."

These pronouncements were accompanied by short, visual vignettes, subliminal, but which seemed to flash inside my helmet with the clarity of a television screen in a dark room—tumultuous scenes of big tackles and guards in what seemed a landslide, a cliff of them toppling toward me like a slow-moving object in a dream, as I lay in some sort of a depression gaping up in resigned dismay. Raymond Berry, the knowledgeable Baltimore receiver, once told me that I would survive a scrimmage if I played his position and was sure to stay out of what he referred to as the "pit"—a designation that often came to mind just before my participation in scrimmages. It was an area, as he described it, along the line of scrimmage, perhaps 10 yards deep, where at the centering of the ball the Neanderthal struggle began between the opposing linemen. The struggle raged within a relatively restricted area that was possible to avoid. Berry had wandered into the pit only three times—coming back to catch poorly-thrown passes—and he spoke of each instance as one might speak of a serious automobile accident. The particulars were embalmed in his memory in absolute clarity: that year, in that city, at such-and-such a game, during such-and-such a quarter, when so-and-so, the quarterback, threw the ball short, his arm jogged by a red-dogging linebacker, so that Berry had to run back toward the scrimmage line so many yards to catch it, and it was so-and-so, the 290-pounder, who reached an arm out of the ruck of the pit and dragged him down into it.

"One thing to remember when you do get hit," Berry told me in his soft Texas accent, "is to try to fall in the foetus position. Curl up around the ball, and keep your limbs from being extended, because there'll be other people coming up out of the pit to see you don't move any, and one of them landing on an arm that's outstretched, y'know, can snap it."

"Right," I said.

"But the big thing is just stay out of that area."

"Sure," I said.

But when I arrived to train with the Lions I disregarded his advice. What I had to try to play was quarterback, because the essence of the game was involved with that position. The coaches agreed, if reluctantly, and after the front office had made me sign some papers absolving them of any responsibility, I became the "last-string" quarterback, and thus stood in Berry's pit each time I walked up behind the center to call signals. He was right, of course. One of my first plays landed me in the pit. It was a simple handoff. Opposite me the linebackers were all close up, shouting, "Jumbo! Jumbo! Jumbo!" which is one of the Lion code cries to rush the quarterback. When the snap came I fumbled the ball, gaping at it, mouth ajar, as it rocked back and forth gaily at my feet, and I flung myself on it, my subconscious shrilling, "Foetus! Foetus!" as I tried to draw myself in like a frightened pill bug, and I heard the sharp strange whack of gear, the grunts—and then a sudden weight whooshed the air out of me.

It was Dave Lloyd, a 250-pound linebacker, who got to me. A whistle blew and I clambered up, seeing him grin inside his helmet, to discover that the quick sense of surprise that I had survived was replaced by a pulsation of fury that I had not done better. I swore lustily at my clumsiness, hopping mad, near to throwing the ball into the ground, and eager to form a huddle to call another play and try again. The players were all standing up, some with their helmets off, many with big grins, and I heard someone calling, "Hey, man, hey, man!" and someone else called out, "Beautiful, real beautiful." I sensed then that an initiation had been performed, a blooding ceremony. Linebacker Wayne Walker said, "Welcome to pro ball." Something in the tone of it made it not only in reference to the quick horror of what had happened when I fumbled but in appreciation that I had gone through something that made me, if tenuously, one of them, and they stood for a while on the field watching me savor it. . . .

THE PAPER LION was a big zero on the Detroit bench between Nick Pietrosante (left) and Jim Gibbons.

WALTER IOOSS JR.

ALLEN

1995 | CHIEFS BACK Marcus Allen scored the 100th of his 123 career rushing TDs, in Denver | *Photograph by* TIM DEFRISCO

1992 | THE CARDINALS' Chris Chandler unloaded the ball before the 49ers' John Johnson (55) and David Whitmore unloaded on him | *Photograph by* PETER READ MILLER

1961 | LIONS LINEBACKER Joe Schmidt made sure the Packers' Jim Taylor had no place to go but down | *Photograph by* MARVIN E. NEWMAN

17
41

> SI's TOP 25 The Offensive Linemen

DAN DIERDORF
Photograph by NEIL LEIFER

JIM OTTO
Photograph by JAMES FLORES

MEL HEIN
Photograph by AP

JIM RINGO
Photograph by LEFEBVRE-LUEBKE

ANTHONY MUNOZ
Photograph by PETER BROUILLET

GENE UPSHAW
Photograph by HEINZ KLUETMEIER

JIM PARKER
Photograph by DARRYL NORENBERG

CLYDE (BULLDOG) TURNER
Photograph by NFL

MIKE WEBSTER
Photograph by TSN

ROOSEVELT BROWN
Photograph by DAN RUBIN

Bob Brown

Roosevelt Brown

Lou Creekmur

Joe DeLamielleure

Dan Dierdorf

Frank Gatski

Forrest Gregg

Russ Grimm

John Hannah

Mel Hein

Jim Langer

Larry Little

Mike Munchak

Anthony Munoz

Jim Otto

Jim Parker

Jim Ringo

Bob St. Clair

Billy Shaw

Jackie Slater

Dwight Stevenson

Mick Tingelhoff

Clyde (Bulldog) Turner

Gene Upshaw

Mike Webster

1948 | BEARS QBS (from left) Bobby Layne, Johnny Lujack and Sid Luckman took target practice | *Photograph by* HANK WALKER

1979 | GEORGIA ROSENBLOOM put her best foot forward as the Rams' owner | *Photograph by* RICHARD MACKSON

'I'LL DO ANYTHING I CAN GET AWAY WITH'

BY DAPHNE HURFORD

What's a little holding and biting among NFL linemen? For Conrad Dobler, "anything goes" on a football field seemed to mean everything short of a neutron bomb. — *from* SI, JULY 25, 1977

ONE OF THE QUESTIONS on the NFL's personnel survey form is, "Did you take up football for any particular reason?" Conrad Dobler's answer was, "It is still the only sport where there is controlled violence mixed with careful technical planning. Football is still a very physical game."

What Dobler, the All-Pro right guard for the St. Louis Cardinals, means by "controlled violence," "careful technical planning" and "a very physical game" is that "I'll do anything I can get away with to protect my quarterback." And according to his opponents, what Dobler gets away with is holding, eye gouging, face-mask twisting, leg-whipping, tripping, even biting.

Outside St. Louis, Dobler is considered the dirtiest player in the league. In one game Dobler's tactics so infuriated Merlin Olsen, the now-retired defensive tackle of the Los Angeles Rams, that Olsen swore he would never utter Dobler's name again. However, there is one player who has good reason to utter Dobler's name in his prayers—Cardinal quarterback Jim Hart. Thanks to the protection—legal or otherwise—afforded by Dobler and his linemates, Hart has been sacked only 41 times over the last three seasons, an NFL low. Among others who recognize Dobler's prowess are the NFL coaches, who have twice picked him to start in the Pro Bowl.

Dobler was just another obscure lineman until 1974, his third season in the league, when some Minnesota Vikings jokingly requested rabies shots before a game against the Cardinals. Suddenly Dobler had acquired an image. "What you need when you play against Dobler," said one rival, "is a string of garlic buds around your neck and a wooden stake. If they played every game under a full moon, Dobler would make All Pro. He must be the only guy in the league who sleeps in a casket."

Dobler says that he holds no more than any other player, that he would get caught more often if he did, and that reports of his dastardly deeds have been exaggerated. In the next breath he says that rules are made to be broken and adds, with a slightly superior air, "If you're going to break the rules, you've got to have a little style and class." Asked if he really bites opponents, Dobler usually replies that he would never do such a tasteless thing, believing as he does in good oral hygiene. Of course, he adds, "If someone stuck his hand in your face mask and put his fingers in your mouth, what would you do?"

While Dobler insists that he is an aggrieved party as far as holding is concerned, he willingly offers a few hints on the best way to hold a defensive lineman or a blitzing linebacker. "Always keep your hands inside your chest because it's much harder for the referees to see them when they're in there," he says, "and if a guy does get past you, grab his face mask, not his jersey." Dobler also recommends "hooking"—clamping the opponent with your arm and dragging him down—as an effective means of detaining defenders.

"Sometimes I hold by accident," he says. "I get my hand caught in a face mask. But always remember this: At no time do my fingers leave my hand."

Surprisingly, Dobler rarely uses his tongue on rivals. "You have to get just the right comment to make them mad," he says. "Verbal abuse could take all day. A faster and more efficient way to aggravate and intimidate people is to knock the stuffing out of them." Dobler particularly likes to aggravate and intimidate Pro Bowlers, first-round draft choices and players whose salaries are higher than his $50,000 a year. "Of course I'm vindictive," he says. "I was a fifth-round draft choice. . . . "

Drafted by the Cardinals in 1972, Dobler was released before his rookie season. Luckily for him a number of the Cardinals' linemen were injured early on, and they re-signed Dobler in time for their third game. "When I came back I decided that I'd just play my own game," he says. "I'd do what I do best and make the other guys play into my hands, make them have to beat me."

Jim Hanifan, St. Louis' offensive line coach, says of his right guard, "You'd have to kill him to beat him." Dobler smiles. "When you're fighting in the dirt for a position, climbing up from the bottom, you know what it is to compete," he says. "If we both wanted it, I'd want it more. I'd mow 'em right down with no compassion, no mercy." . . .

DURING HIS 10 years in the NFL trenches Dobler, though often called the league's dirtiest player, earned three trips to the Pro Bowl.

WALTER IOOSS JR.

ADAMS
FCNR-23

1950 | LIONS ROOKIE Doak Walker, with New York Yanks in hot pursuit in Tiger Stadium, flashed the form that earned him five trips to the Pro Bowl | *Photograph by* AP

50
325

COURTESY OF THE PRO FOOTBALL HALL OF FAME

c. 1950 | DOAK WALKER played both ways and kicked for the Lions, so he had to be a quick-change artist; hence the zipper on his kicking shoe | *Photograph by* DAVID N. BERKWITZ

2004 | THE FALCONS' Michael Vick became a true rollout quarterback when he was nailed by Broncos cornerback Champ Bailey | *Photograph by* KEVIN KRECK

2004 | SAN DIEGO running back LaDainian Tomlinson charged into the end zone for one of his 17 touchdowns of the season | *Photograph by* TAMI CHAPPELL

TOMLINSON
70

EMMITT'S DOMAIN

BY S.L. PRICE

Stiff-arming his opponents and critics, Emmitt Smith became the leading rusher in NFL history. —*from* SI, NOVEMBER 4, 2002

SUDDENLY, LATE ON SUNDAY afternoon, he had nothing left to explain. It was all coming back: The line kept opening holes, and Emmitt Smith kept hitting them hard and gliding through, getting closer. Thirteen years ago he had vowed that he would get here, to this moment in football history, and now it was as if the intervening seasons had barely left a mark. He spun. He juked. He ground out yard after yard against the Seattle Seahawks, 55 in the first quarter alone, each step taking him closer to Walter Payton's NFL rushing record, each step taking the sellout crowd at Texas Stadium back to his prime. Smith wanted it no other way, of course—for Payton's family, for the Dallas Cowboys, for himself most of all. He had struggled all season to find his game, feeling the city turning on him bit by bit, feeling for the first time the sting of words like *old* and *finished* and *selfish*.

All season Smith had tried to pretend that this didn't hurt. In his calmer moments he would smile and take the long view, because he is a religious man, and it is an article of his faith that each blessing brings a curse. Or he would just shrug, as if to say, *What can I do?*, for the Scriptures preach forbearance, and Lord knows he tries to live a righteous life. Still, there's a limit to his patience, and at times the shrug would turn to rage. Then the magnanimous Emmitt Smith was a 33-year-old bear swiping at the hounds at his heels, off and running about "couch potatoes" who "sit on their asses" and "idiots that've got these so-called sports shows" and "media chumps."

Running behind an injury-riddled line that's still learning a new blocking scheme, playing on a mediocre team for a city and franchise happy only with supremacy, Smith has this season entered that paradoxical zone inhabited by so many great athletes nearing the endgame: Even as he was being celebrated for his march into history, teammates and coaches said he was not the force he used to be, fans insisted that his backup was better, commentators wondered if he was hurting the team. Nice career, Legend. Now isn't it time you stepped aside?

"You can just look at my age and say, 'Yeah, he's 33, he should go,' " Smith says. "Yeah, I'm 33. But have I lost my step? Have I lost my vision? Have I lost my power? Have I lost my ability to make a person miss? If I answer yes to those questions, then you might be right. But don't tell me I should quit just because of my age. That's what makes this frustrating. You have to know who you are. I know who I am."

Indeed, long before Sunday, Smith could always look up from his desk at home and see a wood-carved reminder: EMMITT SMITH #22, WORLD'S ALLTIME GREATEST RUSHER. Finally, against a notoriously porous Seattle defense, he set the notion in stone. Averaging only 63.9 yards entering the game—and needing 93 to break Payton's mark of 16,726 yards—Smith heard Seahawks defensive lineman Chad Eaton say during the coin toss, "You're not going to get it today on us," then saw him flail helplessly as Smith uncorked his best effort of the year. By the fourth quarter, with Dallas down 14–7 and flashbulbs popping, he stood just 13 yards short of the record. Not for a moment did he seem surprised. The Cowboys' next two games were on the road. Smith wanted to grab history at home.

Yes, Smith knows who he is, and he knows *where* he is too. More than speed or power or balance, awareness has been his greatest asset. He's always been able to read the men shifting in front of him, anticipate where and when a hole would open, when to make that famous cutback. So it was: On first-and-10 at Dallas's 27-yard line Smith churned for three yards. On second down he took the ball from rookie quarterback Chad Hutchinson, cut left, found a seam, stumbled over a defender's arm, placed his right hand on the turf, kept his balance and kept on chugging until he had caught Payton and passed him by. Then Smith bounced to his feet, face alight, knowing without being told that the record was his.

On this day, he didn't look like a man about to go away; he won't do that until he's good and ready. Should anyone be surprised? Smith is, after all, pro football's ultimate survivor. Passed over by 16 teams on draft day in 1990, considered too small and too slow, he has outlasted all competition. Over the past five years at least a half-dozen backs have been more highly regarded than him: The list of those who began their careers after Smith, rose to stardom and then vanished is long and distinguished. Those are the vagaries in the life of an NFL running back—for everyone but Smith. He has endured concussions, bone chips, a broken hand. He is still here.

"By all the laws of nature and careers, he shouldn't be sitting in this locker room," says Cowboys owner Jerry Jones. "Every time I look over there, something inside me smiles." . . .

SMITH WAS the biggest star on the field after he broke Walter Payton's career rushing record against the Seahawks in Texas Stadium.

IRWIN THOMPSON/DALLAS MORNING NEWS

96
95

1991 | NEW ORLEANS tackle Stan Brock was sitting pretty during a Saints victory over the Falcons in Atlanta | *Photograph by* JOHN BIEVER

2003 | BILLS DEFENSIVE tackle Sam Adams scored a rare touchdown after intercepting a Tom Brady pass | *Photograph by* DAMIAN STROHMEYER

1969 | CARDINALS BACK Willis Crenshaw had to get up in the grill of Bears linebacker Dick Butkus to slow him down | *Photograph by* NEIL LEIFER

1976 | JACK LAMBERT led the way as the Steel Curtain dropped on Colts running back Lydell Mitchell | *Photograph by* WALTER IOOSS JR.

Coca-Cola

from A BRILLIANT CASE FOR THE DEFENSE

BY PAUL ZIMMERMAN | *SI February 3, 1986*

IT WILL BE MANY YEARS BEFORE we see anything approaching the vision of hell that Chicago inflicted on the poor New England Patriots Sunday in Super Bowl XX. It was near perfect, an exquisite mesh of talent and system, defensive football carried to its highest degree. It was a great roaring wave that swept through the playoffs, gathering force and momentum, until it finally crashed home in pro football's showcase game.

The game wasn't exciting. So what? Go down to Bourbon Street if you want excitement. It wasn't competitive. The verdict on Chicago's 46–10 victory was in after two Patriot series. Don't feel cheated. Louis–Schmeling II wasn't very competitive, either. Nor was the British cavalry charge at Balaklava, but Tennyson wrote a poem about it. This game transcended the ordinary standards we use in judging football. It was historic.

The events of the next few weeks and months will determine if this is the beginning of a mighty defensive dynasty or its culmination. The forces of erosion already were at work. Buddy Ryan, the assistant coach who crafted this defense, was close to the Philadelphia head coaching job when his work was done in New Orleans. With two minutes to go, the defensive players gathered around Mike McCaskey, the Bears' president, and practically begged him to do everything he could to keep Ryan. "Dan Hampton was our spokesman," strong safety Dave Duerson said. "He told Mr. McCaskey that if we lose Buddy Ryan we'll be a good defensive unit, but if we keep him we'll be in the Super Bowl the next five years." Such is the hold that Ryan has on his players; his is a driving spirit that causes hard-eyed veterans like middle linebacker Mike Singletary to say, "Without him we don't have much. I feel honored to have been coached by him."

Money problems could inflict further damage. Right end Richard Dent, the Super Bowl MVP, is in a sticky salary situation. He could be gone, as Todd Bell and Al Harris were from last season's team. Others could follow. Win a title and the price of poker goes up.

O.K., let's not look for trouble. Mike Ditka's Bears have given Chicago its first title in any major professional sport since 1963, when Ditka himself played tight end for those champion Bears. And Ryan's defense, which virtually eliminates traditional positions, put together an astonishing string of conquests, a three-game playoff series that has never been duplicated. . . .

1986 | THE BEARS' Reggie Phillips returned this interception for a TD in Chicago's rout of the Patriots in Super Bowl XX | *Photograph by* WALTER IOOSS JR.

83
46
15

1963 | WILLIE GALIMORE (28) and Mike Ditka (89) were keys to the Bears' offense on a championship team known for its D | *Photograph by* JAMES DRAKE

1954 | PAUL BROWN looked dapper even while squatting in the mud during the title game in which his Browns beat the Lions 56–10 | *Photograph by* HY PESKIN

> Artifacts

Pad to the Bone

They began as flimsy padding sewn into players' shirts and evolved, over the next 100 years, into the body armor that sits upon the shoulders of Giants (and Lions and Bears), making big men look even bigger

c.1920

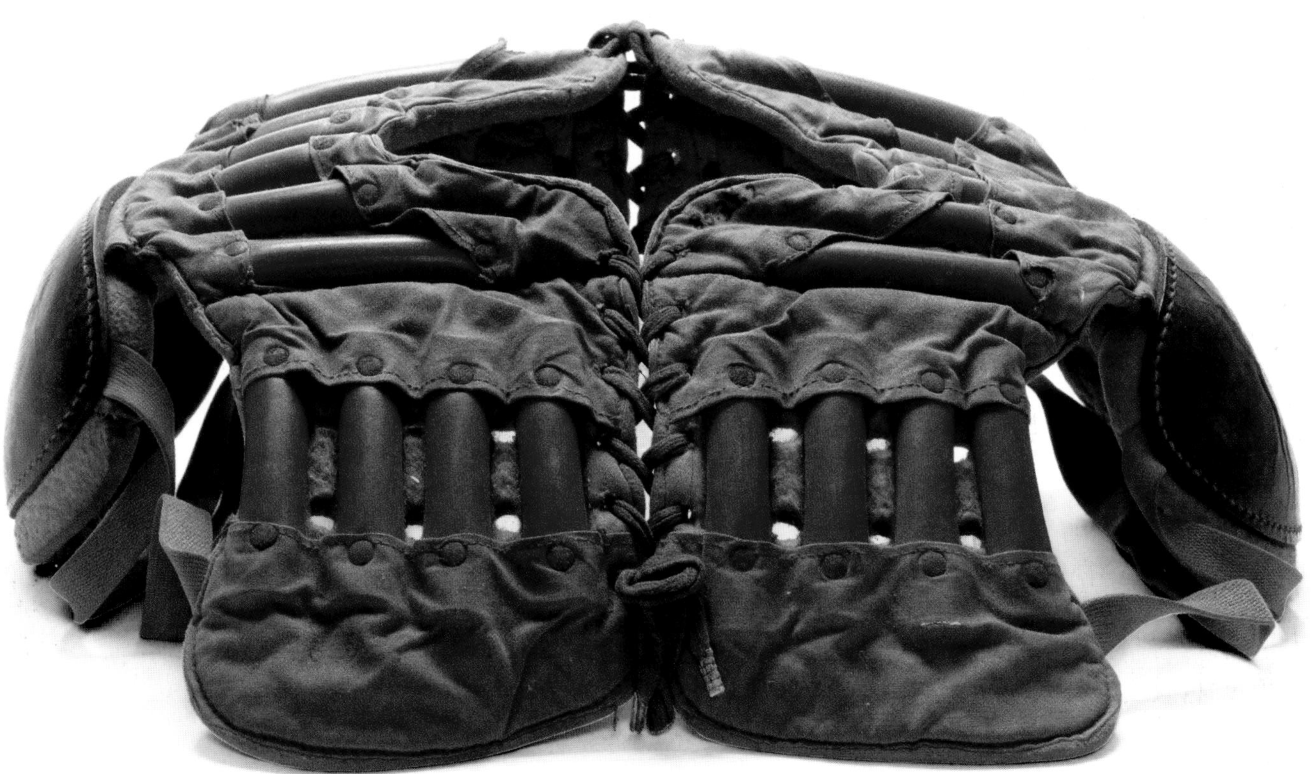

1925

COURTESY OF THE PRO FOOTBALL HALL OF FAME

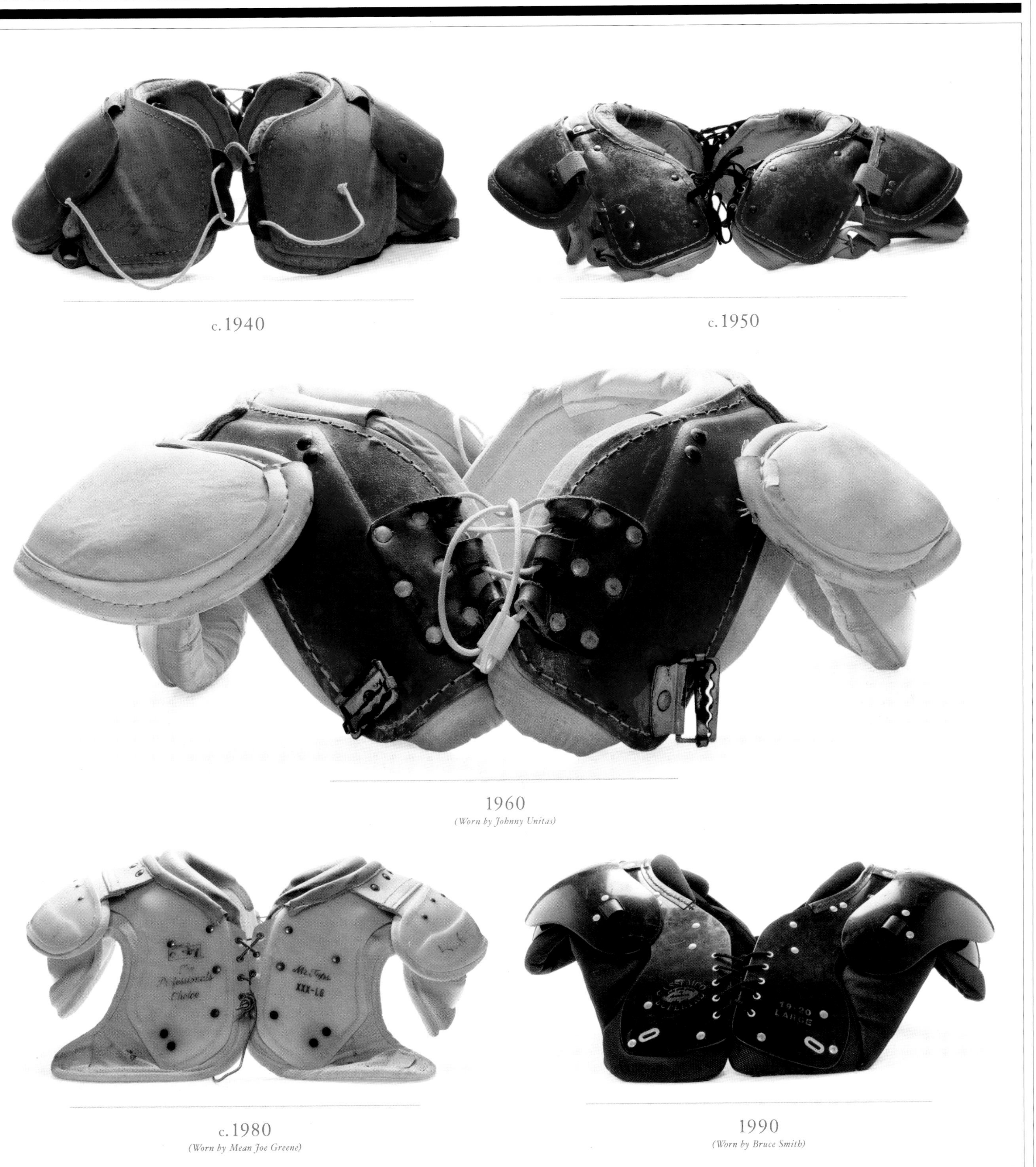

c.1940

c.1950

1960
(Worn by Johnny Unitas)

c.1980
(Worn by Mean Joe Greene)

1990
(Worn by Bruce Smith)

THE GREATEST PLAYER YOU NEVER SAW

BY PETER KING

Packers receiver Don Hutson was too early for prime time, but grainy film from the 1940s helps make the case that he was the best player ever. —*from* SI, *November 29, 1999*

YOU'RE THE GUY WHO named Don Hutson the best player of all time," a West Coast talk show host said to me on the air a few years ago. "Did people take that seriously?" That's the kind of reaction I got when, in a 1993 pro football history book, I called the Green Bay Packers wide receiver the best player ever. Hutson had never played a game on TV. He hadn't suited up in 48 years. But when he left the game in 1945 after 11 seasons, his 99 touchdown receptions were three times as many as any player in NFL history. Naturally, as I told Hutson a few years back (he died in 1997), I wish I could have seen him in action. The ideal day? October 7, 1945, against Detroit in Milwaukee.

The 32-year-old Hutson, in his final NFL season, scored 29 points that day.

In one quarter.

The stadium in Milwaukee's State Fair Park was a cavernous place with ramshackle bleachers. On a bright Indian summer Sunday, 25,500 showed up to see two title contenders knock heads. The Packers were defending NFL champs, and coach Curly Lambeau was breaking in a new halfback (the position from which most passes were thrown in the '30s and '40s), a young fellow named Roy McKay. The Packers' passing game figured to be tested by the Lions, who had one of the league's toughest defenses. Detroit scored first, five seconds into the second quarter, to go up 7–0. Then McKay went to work with the best player who ever lived.

Hutson was football's DiMaggio, a graceful runner who never looked as if he was trying hard. He also had some sprinter in him. At Alabama he had run the 100-yard dash in 9.8 seconds. The grainy, fluttering film I've seen of Hutson shows a 6' 1" man, much taller than most of the defensive backs who covered him. But his leather helmet rode high on his head, making him appear a little nerdy.

You'd never know by listening to Hutson how good he was. He hated talking about himself. But after this game he wouldn't have to. Following the Lions' touchdown, the Packers started at their own 41. On first down Hutson juked Detroit's left cornerback, Art Van Tone, and got two steps on him. McKay's 59-yard scoring pass was perfect—though it didn't have to be—and hit Hutson in effortless stride at the Lions' 40, and he glided to the end zone. Hutson, who at various times in his career was a kicker, defensive end and safety, kicked the extra point. The Packers scored another touchdown on their next drive, and Hutson added the PAT.

Lions coach Gus Dorais then assigned a second defensive back, second-year man Bob Sneddon, to assist Van Tone in shadowing Hutson. A few plays later Hutson blew by Van Tone, who was guarding against a short pass, then turned around Sneddon, who was backpedaling to cover the bomb. Sneddon trailed Hutson by a clear step as the receiver reached the Detroit 15, and McKay's rainbow went over Sneddon's hands and into Hutson's for his second touchdown of the quarter. He then kicked another extra point.

A Packers interception on the next Detroit snap gave Green Bay the ball at the Lions' 17. This time, inexplicably, Dorais put Sneddon man-to-man on Hutson. Sneddon stayed with Hutson to the goal line, but the acrobatic receiver made a leaping catch for a touchdown. Sneddon sank to his knees and began punching the turf.

Finally, in the last minute of the quarter, McKay lofted one more touchdown pass to Hutson, this time from the Detroit six.

Mercifully, halftime came, with Green Bay up 41–7. Hutson had scored 29 points (four touchdowns, five extra points) in 13 minutes, still an NFL record for points in a quarter.

At game's end, a 57–21 final, Dorais looked shell-shocked. "The game can be summed up in three words," he said. "Too much Hutson." . . .

HUTSON, the first star receiver in the NFL, was too big and too fast for the defensive backs of his era.

1970 | LEN DAWSON (16) made enough good calls to lead the Chiefs to a 23–7 win over the Vikings in Super Bowl IV | *Photograph by* NEIL LEIFER

16
73

1988 | JOE MONTANA did the dirty work while burying the Vikings in the NFC playoffs | *Photograph by* ANDY HAYT

1965 | THE BROWNS took the shine off Packers golden boy Paul Hornung (5) in the NFL title game, but Green Bay won | *Photograph by* VERNON BIEVER

MAD DASH

BY IVAN MAISEL

How did the notoriously unreliable 40 become the gold standard of footspeed in the NFL? —*from* SI, AUGUST 10, 1998

FOOTBALL SCOUTS ARE addicted to the 40-yard dash, and like all junkies, they sometimes do very stupid things. Gil Brandt, former personnel director of the Dallas Cowboys, recalls scouting a receiver from Mississippi Valley State in 1985 named Jerry Rice. The Cowboys, who had the 17th pick that year, loved his hands but were concerned about his feet, so they had Rice run the 40 12 times over a three-month period. "We kept thinking this guy played faster and looked faster," Brandt says, sounding wistful, "but he still ran in the 4.6 range. That's why he was drafted 16th. Nobody realized his playing time wasn't his 40 time.

Despite horror stories like that, the 40 remains the gold standard for most NFL scouts. A fast time—4.4 seconds for running backs, receivers and cornerbacks, 4.6 for linebackers and 4.8 for defensive ends—will make a coach more forgiving than wide-leg jeans. A guy who can't run a fast 40 *might* get a chance to prove himself; a guy who runs a fast 40 will *always* get a chance, even if he can't play, because, as Indianapolis Colts president Bill Polian puts it, "Speed is the one thing you can't coach." Which is why every NFL coach is pushing a stopwatch button like a racehorse trainer does.

What's most surprising about all this is that nobody's sure how 40 got to be the magic number. It was not carved into stone tablets by Walter Camp, and there is no proof that a player's time in the 40 is any more indicative of speed than his time for 50 yards—or 39, for that matter. The 40 evolved the way most things do in football—one successful coach used it, so others followed suit. All of which is remarkable because as objective gauges of reality go, 40-yard-dash times fall somewhere between a Chinese election and a World Wrestling Federation decision. "If you have 50 guys timing a player, he will have 50 different times," says Seattle Seahawks coach Dennis Erickson. So it would make sense to entrust the timing to one person, right? Wrong. NFL coaches don't trust any time they get from college coaches, who in turn dismiss every time they get from high school coaches. Even at the annual NFL combine in Indianapolis, where an electronic timer has been in use since 1990, coaches still bring their stopwatches. "Nobody trusts anybody," Erickson says. He cups his hands as if hiding a stopwatch, then casts a furtive glance. "It's like everybody is a damn spy. You'd think we're in the CIA."

The development of the 40 as the definitive measure of speed is attributed to the late coaching legend Paul Brown, who also invented the face bar, the draw play, the 4–3 defense, the two-minute offense, the playbook and the Saturday-night hotel stay for the team. That list is taken from profiles of Brown written late in his life, but none of these stories mentioned the 40, and Brown never brought it up in his 1979 autobiography *PB: The Paul Brown Story*. However, Dante Lavelli, the Hall of Fame end who played for Brown at Ohio State in 1942, remembers being timed in the 40 while with the Buckeyes and later while in Cleveland. "In a training camp with the Browns," Lavelli says, "a guy from North Carolina named Earthquake Smith, a big tackle, never made it in the 40. He fell down a couple of times. Brown sent him home." Brown's son Mike says the distance was not an arbitrary designation. "He did it because he thought that was as far as a player would run on any play," Mike says.

Old-school coaches of the time didn't believe in the 40. A young Marv Levy, then the coach at California, asked Green Bay coach Vince Lombardi in the early '60s how fast Paul Hornung ran. "What the hell difference does it make?" Lombardi boomed. "He gets to the end zone, doesn't he? Fourteen seconds, I don't know."

Well into the '50s, most NFL teams used the 100 or the 50. Veteran scout Bucko Kilroy, now with the New England Patriots, attended the 1957 East-West Shrine Game in San Francisco. "Hornung ran the 50 against Abe Woodson, the Big Ten hurdles champ from Illinois," Kilroy says. "When you think of Hornung, you don't think of him being that fast. Hornung beat him by five yards."

The Cowboys revolutionized scouting in the 1960s and '70s. No detail was too small for Gil Brandt. He sent all of the team's coaches and scouts to Stanford, where track coach Payton Jordan taught them how to properly use a stopwatch. Dallas is believed to have been the first NFL team to go to collegiate spring practices and time entire squads in the 40.

It's not impossible to overcome a poor time in the 40, and the list of players who have done so is impressive: Jerry Rice, Emmitt Smith, Sam Mills, Andre Reed and Zach Thomas, among others. But for every player who makes it in spite of his time, there are dozens and dozens who don't. The NFL has a place for players who run a poor 40. It's called the NFL Europe League.

Says Cowboys director of college and pro scouting Larry Lacewell, "You see a guy who can play, and he doesn't run a 40 well, you kind of wish you hadn't seen his time." . . .

BOB HAYES brought a sprinter's gifts to the Cowboys, the first team to use 40-yard dash as the ultimate test of football speed.

WALTER IOOSS JR

> Artifacts

Going to Extremes

Not all balls were created equal in the NFL's early days, so elaborate efforts were made to subject the equipment—and the elements—to some measure of control

IN THE '50s, long before domed stadiums or heated benches, the league tried using massive ball-warmers to counter the cold—an experiment that was soon abandoned.

VARIATIONS IN the size of balls made during the '30s inspired the creation of a template to be ensure that the ones used in games met the league's standards.

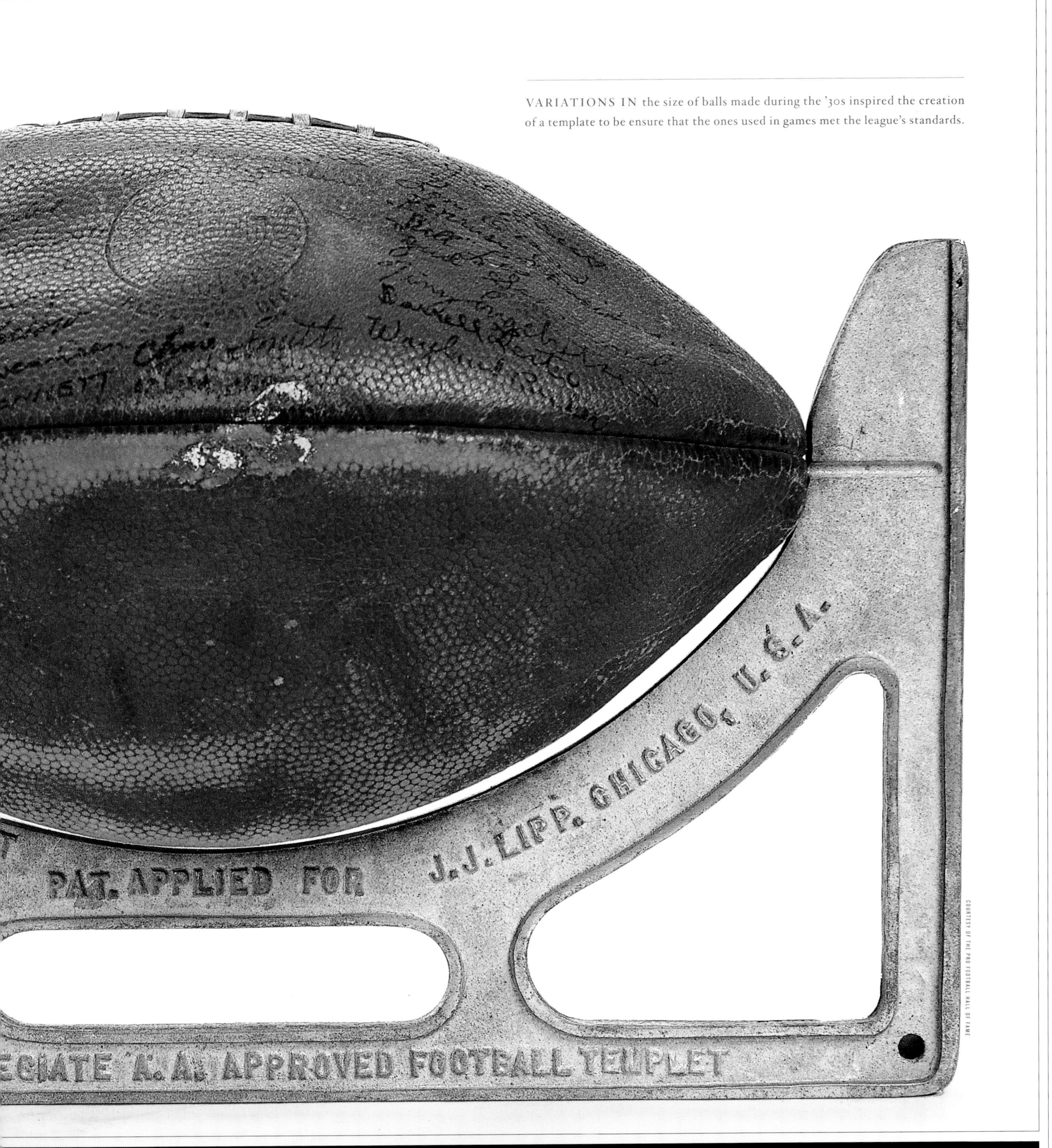

COURTESY OF THE PRO FOOTBALL HALL OF FAME

1954 | THE RAMS' Norm Van Brocklin surveyed the Lions' defense from the comfort of the pocket | *Photograph by* MARK KAUFFMAN

1995 | THE CHARGERS' wedge was in place when Andre Coleman returned a kickoff against the Raiders in Oakland | *Photograph by* BRAD MANGIN

> SI's TOP 25 *The Linebackers*

JACK LAMBERT
Photograph by TONY TOMSIC

JUNIOR SEAU
Photograph by MARC SEROTA

MIKE SINGLETARY
Photograph by JOHN BIEVER

TOMMY NOBIS
Photograph by VERNON BIEVER

DERRICK THOMAS
Photograph by JEFF JACOBSEN

SAM HUFF
Photograph by NEIL LEIFER

LAWRENCE TAYLOR
Photograph by SPORTSCHROME

TED HENDRICKS
Photograph by AL MESSERSCHMIDT

RAY LEWIS
Photograph by TOM DIPACE

BOBBY BELL
Photograph by RICH CLARKSON

CHUCK BEDNARIK
BOBBY BELL
DERRICK BROOKS
NICK BUONICONTI
DICK BUTKUS
HARRY CARSON
GEORGE CONNOR
BILL GEORGE
JACK HAM
TED HENDRICKS
SAM HUFF
JACK LAMBERT
WILLIE LANIER
RAY LEWIS
KARL MECKLENBURG
RAY NITSCHKE
TOMMY NOBIS
DAVE ROBINSON
JOE SCHMIDT
JUNIOR SEAU
MIKE SINGLETARY
LAWRENCE TAYLOR
DERRICK THOMAS
ANDRE TIPPETT
DAVE WILCOX

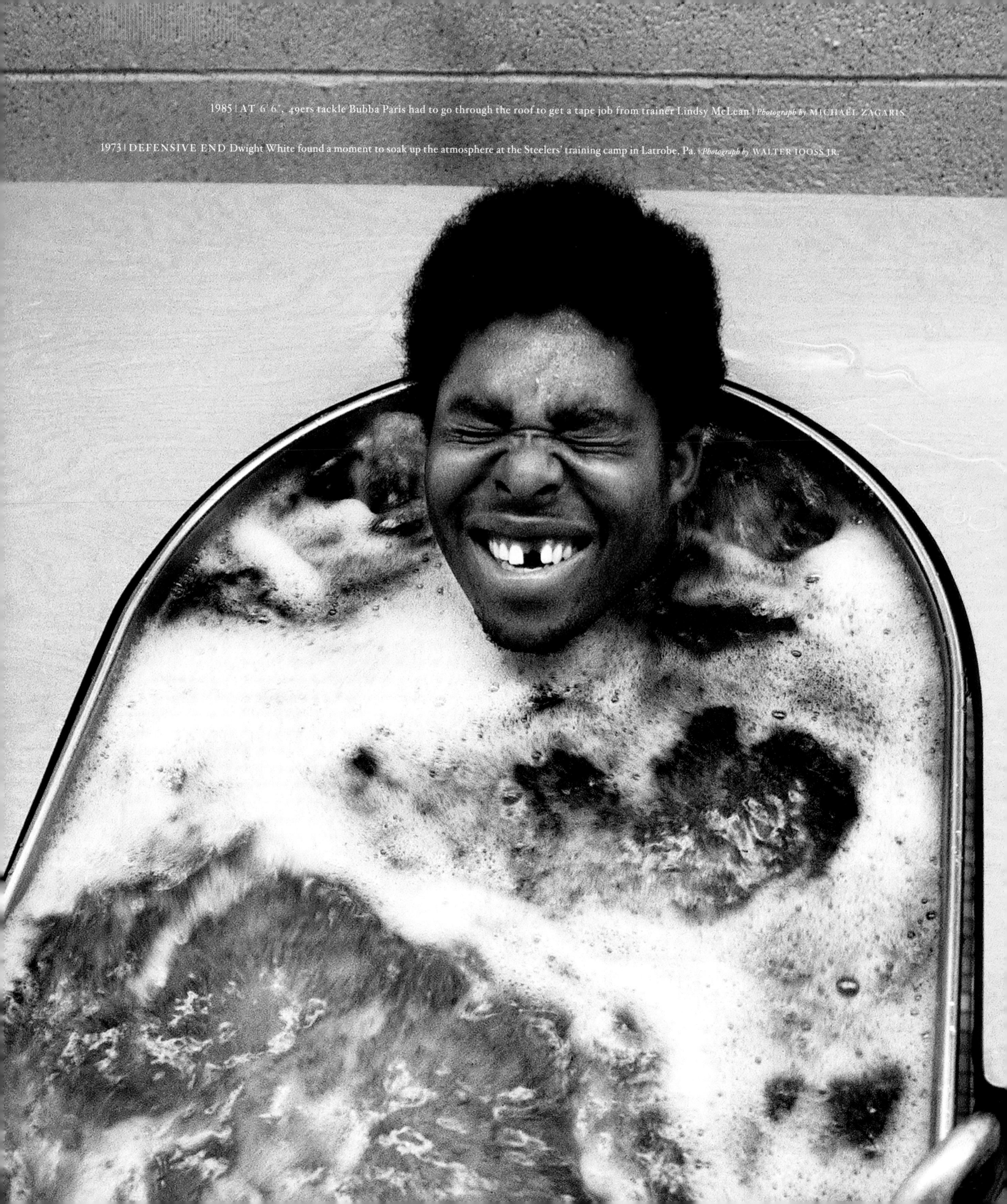

1985 | AT 6' 6", 49ers tackle Bubba Paris had to go through the roof to get a tape job from trainer Lindsy McLean | *Photograph by* MICHAEL ZAGARIS

1973 | DEFENSIVE END Dwight White found a moment to soak up the atmosphere at the Steelers' training camp in Latrobe, Pa. | *Photograph by* WALTER IOOSS JR.

GETTING THERE THE HARD WAY

BY RICK TELANDER

The Broncos were postseason goners until John Elway engineered what will forever be known as the Drive. —*from* SI, JANUARY 19, 1987

HAVE YOU EVER BEEN mean to a nice old dog? Did you sit there with a tail-wagging mongrel at your knee and kindly offer him a meaty bone, hold it in front of the pooch's eager snout and at the last instant, just after his head lunged forward but before his teeth clicked shut, pull the bone away? Have you? Just for fun?

Then you've been John Elway, the Denver Broncos quarterback who yanked the bone from the mouth of the Cleveland Dawgs, er, Browns, 23–20 in overtime, for the AFC Championship before 79,915 stunned fans in Cleveland Stadium on Sunday. No, let's clarify this metaphor. Elway didn't just pull victory from the Browns' mouth. He ripped the thing from halfway down their throat.

The game was over. The Browns had won and the Broncos had lost. It was that simple. But then, with 5:32 remaining and Denver trailing 20–13, Elway led his team 98 yards down the field on as dramatic a game-saving drive as you'll ever see. It was the way Elway must have dreamed it while growing up the son of a football coach, the rifle-armed youngster and his doting father talking over the breakfast table about how to pick defenses apart.

The drive, one of the finest ever engineered in a championship game, was performed directly in the Browns' faces. There was no sneakiness about it; Elway had simply shown what a man with all the tools could do. It was what everybody who had watched him enter the league as perhaps the most heralded quarterback since Joe Namath knew he could do. One was left with the distinct feeling that Elway would have marched his team down a 200-yard- or 300-yard- or five-mile-long field to paydirt.

Playing on unfriendly turf, generating offense where there had been precious little before, Elway ran, passed, coaxed and exhorted his team in magnificent style. Finally, with 39 seconds left and the ball on the Browns' five-yard line, he found Mark Jackson slanting over the middle in the end zone and hit him with a bullet. After that the overtime was a mere formality. Elway took the Broncos 60 yards this time, giving Rich Karlis field goal position at the Cleveland 15-yard line and a sweet piece of advice: "It's like practice." Karlis's 33-yard field goal, his third of the afternoon, cut through the Browns like a knife.

Only a few minutes earlier, back in regulation, when the home team still had that big seven-point lead, nobody in the delirious Cleveland throng could have imagined such a nightmarish turn of events. Browns wide receiver Brian Brennan had just made it 20–13 by twisting safety Dennis Smith into a bow tie on a 48-yard touchdown reception from quarterback Bernie Kosar, a play that seemed destined to go straight into the NFL archives. Super slow motion, voice of doom narrating: "On a frigid afternoon a short, curly-haired young Catholic lad from Boston College snatched glory from the ominous skies over Lake Erie and presented it to this desperate city of rust and steel. . . ." Brennan was Dwight Clark making The Catch against the Dallas Cowboys to send the San Francisco 49ers on to Super Bowl XVI. He was a vivid canvas to be placed in the Cleveland Museum of Art. Hell, he was the glue-fingered kid who caught the Hail Mary bomb against the University of Miami in 1984 to earn Doug Flutie a Heisman Trophy, wasn't he? Well, no, that was Gerard Phelan.

Nonetheless, Brennan sure looked to be the hero of this game. The Broncos misplayed Mark Moseley's ensuing knuckleball kickoff and downed it at their own two-yard line. There was no way they were going to drive 98 yards and score a touchdown. No way. On its two previous fourth-quarter possessions Denver had moved just nine and six yards, respectively.

The Broncos' only touchdown drive had been a mere 37-yarder set up by a fumble recovery. Otherwise Denver had gotten only two short-range field goals from Karlis, a 19-yarder in the second quarter following an interception and a 24-yarder late in the third. To make matters infinitely worse, Elway had a bad left ankle, and the Browns had a ferocious, yapping defense. And straight behind them was the Dawg Pound, the east end-zone section where fans wore doghouses on their heads and bellowed for their Dawgs to treat Denver like a fire hy-

drant. Even from this distance the Broncos were amazed at the insane howling of the Pound.

"I just waited for guys to run into me," said left tackle Dave Studdard. "I could not hear."

It didn't matter. Using hand signals and a silent count, Elway began moving his team.

Now, the image of Elway—blond, 6' 3", 210 pounds, fourth year out of Stanford—conjures up different things to different people. Some see a hot-tempered California beachboy type who runs all over the place throwing heaters without ever winning big games, at least not on the road. (Denver scored only three touchdowns while losing its last three road games of the regular season.) Others see a still-developing athletic prodigy, surrounded by not too much offensive talent, almost ready to take his place at the table of Graham, Unitas and Staubach. His teammates see a leader.

"In the huddle after that kickoff to the two he smiled—I couldn't believe it—and he said, 'If you work hard, good things are going to happen,'" says wide receiver Steve Watson. "And then he smiled again." . . .

WITH THIS fourth-quarter touchdown pass to cap the Drive, John Elway tied the AFC title game—and broke the hearts of all Cleveland fans.

JOHN BIEVER

COURTESY OF THE PRO FOOTBALL HALL OF FAME

1949 | LEATHER HELMETS like this one worn by the postwar Chicago Cardinals sent players into battle with relatively little protection | *Photograph by* DAVID N. BERKWITZ

1925 | THE BEARS knew Red Grange (far right) would be a big draw in Chicago and paid him accordingly (about $12,000) for his first pro game | *Photograph by* UNDERWOOD & UNDERWOOD

18

UNITED APPEAL

> Artifacts

Double Vision

Following in the footsteps of baseball and the movies, the Browns staged twin bills in the '60s that drew legions of fans to preseason games

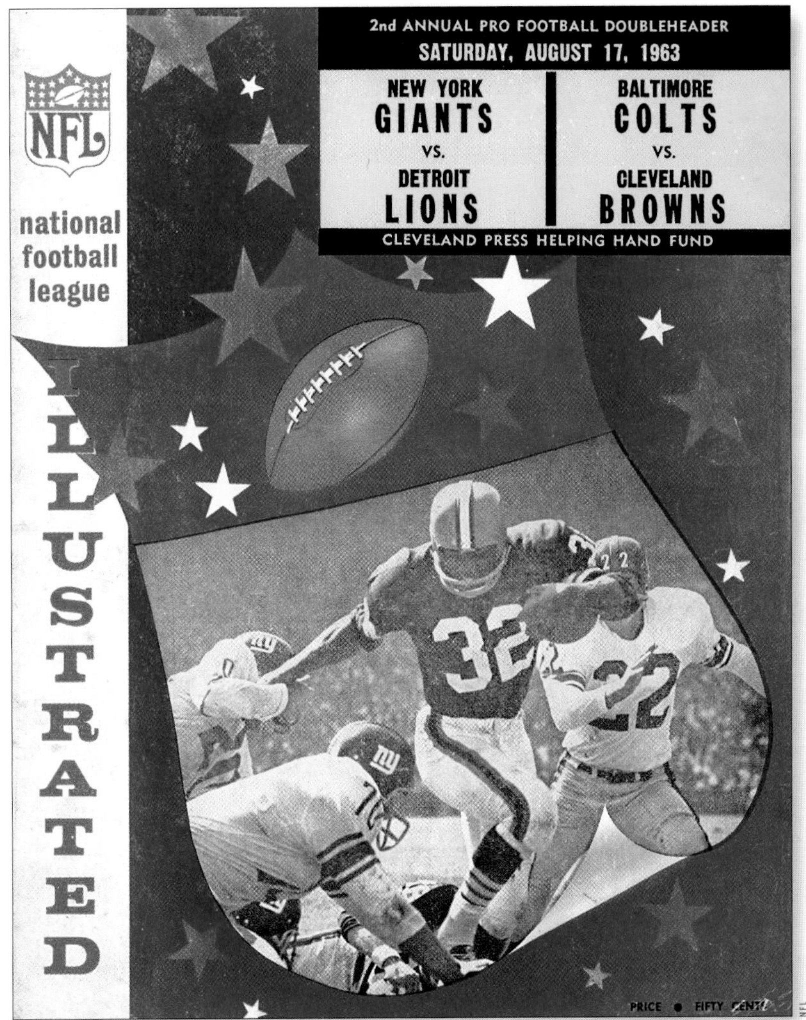

DOUBLE EXPOSURE caught action from both games played in Cleveland Stadium in September '64: Giants versus the Lions (left), and the Packers versus the Browns. Three of those four teams (plus Baltimore) had also played in a doubleheader the year before (above) | *Photograph by* TONY TOMSIC

TITANS
Riddell

1991 | RAIDERS QUARTERBACK Jay Schroeder was an unlucky 13 when Bills defenders put a new twist on the old gang tackle | *Photograph by* JOHN W. MCDONOUGH

2003 | TITANS RECEIVER Justin McCareins had a meeting of the minds with Panthers linebacker Mike Caldwell (59) and safety Jarrod Cooper | *Photograph by* BILL FRAKES

BOSTON
89
21

LORD OF THE REALM

BY JOHN ED BRADLEY

Hard to believe, but Deion Sanders was as good as he often—and loudly—proclaimed himself to be. —*from* SI, OCTOBER 9, 1995

YOU SEE THE MAN IN jewelry, black shades and a do-rag. His mouth is running. Deion Sanders seems anything but a figure to replicate in marble, a statue for the ages. But put him in a football uniform and point out a man for him to cover, and he is the best defensive back in football, among the best of all time.

This is not news to everyone—certainly not to the quarterbacks who dread throwing in his direction, to the receivers who are routinely shut down by him, to the coaches who wish he were on their team. "You play him, it's just intimidating," Rams receiver Isaac Bruce says. Bruce was a rookie last season when he faced Sanders. "I kept thinking he'd come out ragging me or talking a lot of noise. You know the image he has. I didn't have any nightmares beforehand, but during warmups when I saw him come out on the field, it was hard to look at anything else."

This is what a receiver sees when he stands across the line of scrimmage from Deion Sanders: a man somewhat thick of hip, cut square and hard on top and long-limbed. His stance is like nobody else's. He crouches low. On occasion he will hold his hands in front of his face, his fingers tickling invisible piano keys. To some he resembles Bruce Lee set to unload on a pile of bricks. One foot is thrown back, set there until the ball is snapped and he throws it forward to deliver what he calls a quick jam. A quick jam is just that: a fast and artful check on the receiver, designed to slow him and upset his rhythm. Sanders can pin you to the line. He can stop you cold.

Bruce, the greenhorn, looked at Sanders across the line, and what he saw was something altogether different from what he had been expecting. Standing there as mute as a scarecrow in a deep winter field, Sanders was smiling. He was smiling as if he and Bruce were old pals, linked to each other in ways too profound and mysterious to describe. "That's all he did," Bruce says. "Smiled. Then later I'm running my routes, and instead of giving me a hard time, he's kind of coaching me. He's saying, 'Look, you need to stay low when coming out of your cuts, so I won't be able to tell where you're going.' "

Bruce took Sanders's advice, but alas, he finished the game

without any catches while Sanders was covering him. Bruce wasn't the first receiver to get dusted by Sanders. Nor was he the first to come away feeling slightly awed by the experience. The man was even better than his hype: quicker, faster, stronger. And, on top of everything else, Sanders could coach. To offer advice to your own teammates is one thing; to give it to the player you are engaged in trying to stop reveals a self-confidence that is downright spooky. Sanders told Bruce how to beat him; then he went out and beat Bruce anyway. "When we played him last year, we talked about not even bothering to throw his way," says New Orleans Saints receiver Michael Haynes. "It was part of our game plan to keep the ball away from him. There were routes we wouldn't run toward Deion. He can take away that much."

"He takes one third to one half of the field away from the offense," says Flipper Anderson, the former star Rams receiver. "Think about it," Bruce says, in perhaps the most succinct evaluation of Sanders's importance to a defense. "Deion doesn't need any deep help. He doesn't need any help behind him like other defensive backs do. I mean, that alone tells you how good he is. It's like he's this lone man out there. He's on an island, protecting that island all by himself."

And nobody's going to get close. . . .

IN HIS prime Sanders could shut down big receivers, fast receivers and even big, fast receivers such as the Cardinals' David Boston.

OTTO GREULE/GETTY IMAGES (LEFT); LOUIS DELUCA

1978 | STEVE LARGENT, a Seahawk for 14 years, held six major career receiving records when he retired in 1989 | *Photograph by* MANNY MILLAN

1954 | BROWNS RECEIVER Ray Renfro was wide open for this TD catch in Cleveland's 56–10 win over the Lions in the NFL title game | *Photograph by* RONNY PESKIN

MUTUAL OF OMAHA
PAYS UP TO
$475.00 HOSPITALIZATION
$300.00 SURGICAL CARE
463
435

MUDDIED BUT UNBOWED

BY JEFF MACGREGOR

This was the season he was going to ascend to the cosmology of one-name stars. This was the year his team was going to the Big Show. This was the year it all fell apart . . . yet Keyshawn Johnson continued to shine. —*from* SI, NOVEMBER 8, 1999

KEYSHAWN JOHNSON has to stick his head up over the knot of reporters in front of his locker and yell to the clubhouse guy for a jockstrap. This happens almost every day before practice. Then, still talking—seamless, uninterruptible—he goes back to the questions. Can you? Will you? Did you? Minicamp, training camp, preseason, real season; this is New York, so there are always questions.

For the past three years he's had answers, too, answers that are by turns funny and incendiary and smart, audacious or elusive or self-congratulatory, right, wrong, contradictory, contentious, sweet, sour, true and false. He is a 72-point banner headline waiting to happen. His relationship with the press is as vivid a part of his life as the game itself. Sometimes it *is* the game.

He'll crack you up. He'll piss you off. He'll ask better questions than you do. If he doesn't think a question makes any sense, he'll repeat it. Slowly. Like he's doing a lab at Berlitz. He'll stand there holding his practice pants—so small they look as if they came from Baby Gap but threaded with that long, swashbuckler's belt—and repeat the question. Eventually it makes sense to no one, not even the blushing knucklehead who asked it. Sometimes he ignores the question and answers a question nobody thought to ask. Sometimes he asks *and* answers the questions. Man!

He is as brash and self-referential as the young Ali, minus the poetry; as irritating and engaging and confounding to conventional wisdom as Ali before he leveled Liston. Is he really as good as he says he is? "I can hurt you all over the field." Who can be that good? "I can carry this team." Nobody's that good! "Reinvent the position"? Who would even say this kind of stuff!

He stands 6' 3". He weighs 212 pounds. He trains year-round for his day job as a wide receiver for the New York Jets: weights, plyometrics, running. Off-season he runs in the California hills. Or he runs those famous stairs that lead down to the sand at Santa Monica beach. There are hundreds of them. This might take a couple of hours. He runs until he's ready to puke. Matinee-idol jock millionaire, and he's about to puke in front of tourists on their way to the Santa Monica pier. This is when James Strom, his strength coach, tells him to run some more. That way, when reporters call Strom to ask what sort of shape Keyshawn is in, he can answer in simple declarative sentences: "Nobody works any harder. Pound for pound he's up there with the strongest guys in the league."

If Keyshawn Johnson didn't exist, the press would have to create him. The way he created himself.

THIS IS how he works: Under a sky as high and hot as scalded milk, Keyshawn is running patterns on a practice field at Hofstra University, catching long, elegant passes.

He comes off the line of scrimmage like Walter Brennan. For the first three steps he's all crotchet and fuss and pistoning forearms, his big feet flapping. Then on the fourth step his feet are under him again, so he unfolds himself and he's daddy longlegs now, football fast, going, pumping—he plants one of those size-13 shoes, cutting, fakes, fakes again with a shake of the head that seems like an angry denial, pumping, going. Part of him is headed upfield now, and the other part isn't. You can see him from every angle at once, a cubist painting of a man running, and the ball is in the air, drilling an arc into those hands as big and soft as oven mitts.

During the worst of this unseasonal heat wave it feels as if you're wearing clothes made out of steel wool, but Keyshawn is running flat-out up the sideline, going deep, hitch and go, over and over—fast, as if he's chasing something. Or something's chasing him. . . .

THE TOP draft pick in 1996, Johnson averaged 13.6 yards per catch and almost 1,000 receiving yards over the next three seasons.

WALTER IOOSS JR.

adidas

2003 | NINERS WIDEOUT Brandon Lloyd went all out to catch this touchdown pass from Tim Rattay | *Photograph by* PETER READ MILLER

1960 | RAYMOND BERRY, Johnny Unitas's favorite target, led the NFL in receptions three times | *Photograph by* AP

COLTS

> SI's TOP 25 The Defensive Linemen

MEAN JOE GREENE
Photograph by GEORGE GOJKOVICH

ALAN PAGE
Photograph by NFL

HOWIE LONG
Photograph by LOUIS DELUCA

MERLIN OLSEN
Photograph by JOHN G. ZIMMERMAN

BOB LILLY
Photograph by TSN

BRUCE SMITH
Photograph by ELSA HASCH

CHARLES HALEY
Photograph by JAMES D. SMITH

DOUG ATKINS
Photograph by NFL

BUCK BUCHANAN
Photograph by RICH CLARKSON

REGGIE WHITE
Photograph by JEFFREY PHELPS

DOUG ATKINS
ELVIN BETHEA
BUCK BUCHANAN
WILLIE DAVIS
ART DONOVAN
CARL ELLER
LEN FORD
JOE GREENE
L.C. GREENWOOD
CHARLES HALEY
DAN HAMPTON
DEACON JONES
HENRY JORDAN
BOB LILLY
HOWIE LONG
GINO MARCHETTI
LEO NOMELLINI
MERLIN OLSEN
ALAN PAGE
LEE ROY SELMON
BRUCE SMITH
ERNIE STAUTNER
RANDY WHITE
REGGIE WHITE
JACK YOUNGBLOOD

A VIKING CONQUEST

BY STEVE RUSHIN

Alan Page, the first defensive player to be named the NFL's MVP, was a fearsome presence on the field . . . and in the lobby of a Holiday Inn if you were a young fan looking for an autograph.

—*from* SI, JULY 31, 2000

YOU COULDN'T BUY A number 88 Vikings jersey in Minnesota in 1974. You could buy the 10 of Fran Tarkenton or the 44 of Chuck Foreman, but if you wanted the 88 of Alan Page your parents had to find a blank purple football shirt and have the numbers ironed on. As far as I know, my parents were the only ones who ever did. The jersey became my security blanket—what psychologists call a "transition object," the item that sustains a child in moments away from his mother. I wore the shirt until it disintegrated in the wash and blew away one day like dandelion spores.

I grew up in the town in which the Vikings played their home games, in the decade in which they played in four Super Bowls. Yet even in Bloomington, Minn., in the 1970s, I was alone among my schoolmates in worshipping Page, who was fearsome and had a reputation for brooding silence, a reputation that I scarcely knew of as an eight-year-old. I knew only that Page had gone to Notre Dame, that he was genuinely great—the first defensive player to be named MVP of the NFL—and that his Afro sometimes resembled Mickey Mouse ears when he removed his helmet. Lithe and almost feline, Page went wherever the ballcarrier was, often pulling the runner down with one hand. He won his MVP award in his fifth year. I at once loved Alan Page and knew nothing whatsoever about him.

Then one unfathomable day in September '74, the month in which I turned eight, a second-grade classmate named Troy Chaika invited me to a Saturday night sleepover at the Airport Holiday Inn, which his father managed and where the Vikings, as everyone knew, bivouacked on the night before each home game. I could meet the players when they checked in and, if I asked politely and addressed each of them as "Mister," get their autographs, a prospect that thrilled and terrified me in equal measure. So every night for two weeks, toothbrush in hand, I practiced my pitch to the bathroom mirror: "Please, Mr. Page, may I have your autograph?"

Time crawled, clocks ticked backward, but, after an eternity, Saturday came. My mom—God bless her, for it must have pained her beyond words—allowed me to leave the house in my 88 jersey, now literally in tatters, the kind of shirt worn by men in comic strips who have been marooned on a tiny desert island with one palm tree.

So I took my place in the Holiday Inn lobby—Bic pen in one damp hand, spiral notebook in the other—and recited my mantra rapid-fire to myself, like Hail Marys on a rosary: "*Please Mr.PagemayIhaveyour autograph?PleaseMr.PagemayIhaveyourautograph?PleaseMr.Page. . . .*"

Moments before the Vikings' 8 p.m. arrival, my friend's father, the innkeeper, cheerily reminded me to be polite and that the players would in turn oblige me. "Except Page," he added offhandedly, in the oblivious way of adults. "Don't ask him. He doesn't sign autographs."

Which is how I came to be blinking back tears when the Vikings walked into the Holiday Inn, wearing Stetsons and suede pants and sideburns like shag-carpet samples. Their shirt collars flapped like pterodactyl wings. They were truly terrifying men, none more so than Page, whose entrance—alone, an overnight bag slung over his shoulder—cleaved a group of bellhops and veteran teenage autograph hounds, who apparently knew to give the man a wide berth.

Page strode purposefully toward the stairwell. I choked as he breezed past; I was unable to speak, a small and insignificant speck whose cheeks, armpits and tear ducts were suddenly bursting into flames. It was to be an early lesson in life's manifold disappointments: two weeks of excruciating anticipation dashed in as many seconds. Still, I had never seen Page outside a television set and couldn't quite believe he was incarnate, so—my chicken chest heaving, hyperventilation setting in—I continued to watch as he paused at the stairs, turned and looked back at the lobby, evidently having forgotten to pick up his room key.

But he hadn't forgotten any such thing. No, Page walked directly toward me, took the Bic from my trembling hand and signed his name, ALAN PAGE, in one grand flourish. He smiled and put his hand on top of my head, as if palming a grapefruit. Then he disappeared into the stairwell, leaving me to stand there in the lobby, slack-jawed, forming a small puddle of admiration and urine. . . .

QUICK AND STRONG, Page was the first defensive player to be named the league's MVP, in 1971.

NEIL LEIFER

COURTESY OF THE PRO FOOTBALL HALL OF FAME

1950 | MARION MOTLEY (76) helped break pro football's color barrier when he signed with the Browns in 1946; his shoes, which carried him to the rushing title in '50, are in Canton. | *Photograph by* AP *(opposite)*

2001 | THE GIANTS' Tiki Barber and the Chiefs' Greg Wesley showed good hand-eye coordination when they met in September | *Photograph by* DAVID EULITT

GIANTS
21

Riddell
71

from CRASH COURSE | BY PETER KING
SI October 30, 2000

FOUR DECADES AGO THE NFL fullback was a force, in many cases more of an impact player than the halfback and wideouts were. Jim Taylor, with the Green Bay Packers in 1962, was the last pure fullback to win the league rushing title. For most of today's spread offenses, plodding is out and speed is in, making fullbacks as anonymous as linemen. Which is, in effect, what most of them are. "I see the position as being a glorified guard," says Jacksonville Jaguars fullback Daimon Shelton.

"Name me five or six fullbacks," says Bill Parcells, the New York Jets' director of football operations. "See? You can't do it."

On about 80% of the snaps the traditional fullback in today's game either delivers a crushing block on a defender who's usually much bigger, while leading the running back into a hole, or he shields the quarterback from a pass rusher. On maybe 15% of the plays the fullback is an option in the passing game, though often only a safety valve. On 5%—and this is generous when you consider that five of the 31 first-unit fullbacks do not have a rushing attempt through the first eight games of this season—they carry the ball.

"Besides being unselfish," says Denver Broncos running backs coach Bobby Turner, "a fullback has to be mentally tough. On 60 out of 70 plays he has no chance to touch the ball. On a great day he might have five balls thrown at him, and three won't even be catchable. But he's got to come back on every snap and be positive, put his face in there, slam into people, pick up blitzes, pick up linemen. Then after doing all that, he's quietly taking his shower and the halfback's got the microphones and minicams in front of him."

They are anonymous, and they are sore, and they'd better like it that way. "The only thing I could compare us to are the crash-test dummies flying around in those cars, crashing at 30 mph," says Cincinnati Bengals fullback Clif (Totally) Groce.

"You see those big-horned sheep on *National Geographic* get about 10 yards apart, and they charge at each other and *bam!*" says the Atlanta Falcons' Bob Christian. "That's what we do." . . .

2002 | MIKE ALSTOTT'S job was to level whatever stood between him and the yardage that Tampa Bay needed. | *Photograph by* BILL FRAKES

> Artifacts

The Tops of Their Game

NFL helmets got bigger and stronger over the years, much like the players they protected

1919 | KNUTE ROCKNE
Massillon Tigers

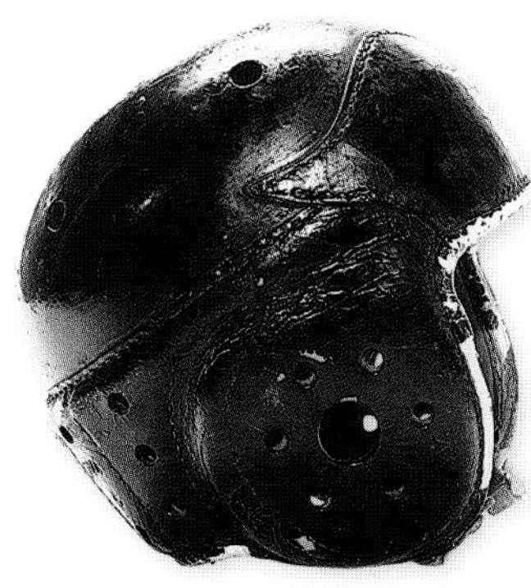

1934 | GEORGE MUSSO
Chicago Bears

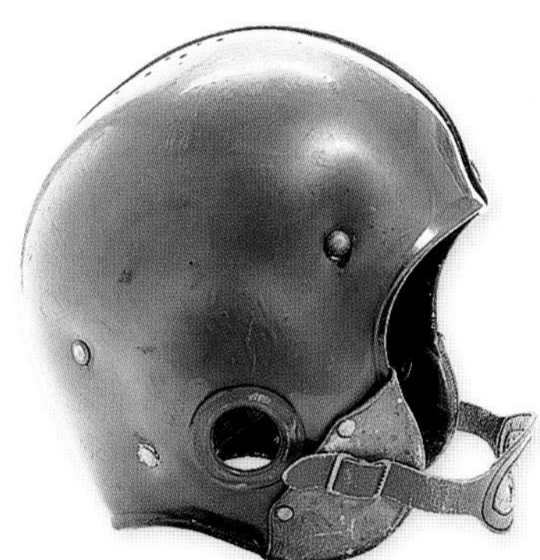

c. 1949 | SAMMY BAUGH
Washington Redskins

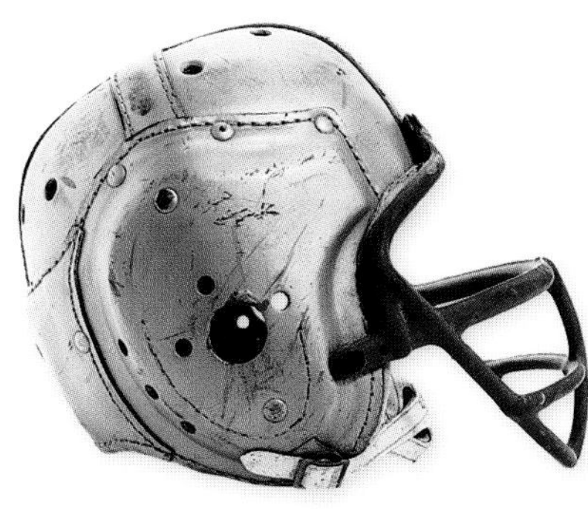

c. 1950 | LOU CREEKMUR
Detroit Lions

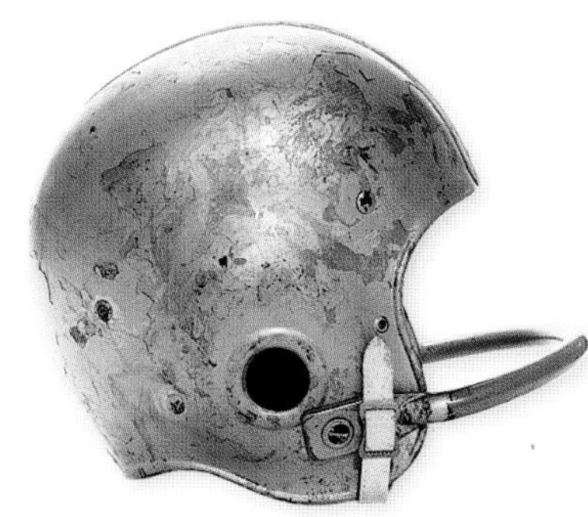

c. 1950 | JACK CHRISTIANSEN
Detroit Lions

c. 1956 | JOE PERRY
San Francisco 49ers

c. 1960 | CHUCK BEDNARIK
Philadelphia Eagles

1961 | BILLY HOWTON
Dallas Cowboys

1990 | BRUCE SMITH
Buffalo Bills

1970 | E.J. HOLUB, a five-time Pro Bowler at linebacker and center, banged heads in 127 games for the Chiefs and the Texans | *Photograph by* TONY TOMSIC

COURTESY OF THE PRO FOOTBALL HALL OF FAME

THE IMMACULATE RECEPTION AND OTHER MIRACLES

BY MYRON COPE

The Steelers dynasty was built on the most famous fluke play in NFL history, but who could deny that their long-suffering fans—and owner—deserved a little divine intervention? —*from* SI, AUGUST 20, 1973

IN THE SPACE OF 40 YEARS, infants have grown to become Watergate plotters and beauty queens have retired to nursing homes. So 40 years is a long time, and unless you were one of us—that is to say, a part or partisan of the Pittsburgh Steelers, who after four desolate decades in the NFL won their first divisional title—you cannot possibly know the sweetness. Sweetness, did I say? More, it was the *ne plus ultra* of fruition when, as if to compensate for the lost years, everything fell into place.

I am 13, walking, sometimes skipping down the hill to the foot of Bouquet Street, heading for the bowels of old Forbes Field. I pass through a narrow entrance into the vendor's hole, a dungeon furnished with two battered picnic tables and a few benches. No problem gaining entrance, for during the baseball season I had appeared regularly for the shape-up. On days when big crowds were expected and a great many vendors needed, boss Myron O'Brisky would force himself to look my way. He would sign, distressed at having run out of strong backs, and say, "O.K., kid, *soo-vaneers.*"

But this was football season and I had no intention of working. An iron gate separated the vendor's hole from a ramp leading into the park to keep the no-goods among us from sneaking off to spend the day as spectators. I had learned that if I arrived early enough one of the bosses going

FRANCO HARRIS had to get past Raiders cornerback Jimmy Warren to score on the miracle catch that put the Steelers into the AFC championship.

HARRY CABLUCK/AP/WIDE WORLD PHOTOS

to and fro would leave the gate unlocked for a few moments. I would dash through, sprint clear to the top of the ballpark in rightfield and hide in a restroom. It would be 2½ hours till the ballpark gates opened, but I passed the cold mornings memorizing the rosters I had torn from the Sunday sports section. At 11 a.m. I would be in position for a front-row space amid the standing-room crowd.

We came knowing we would suffer. Picture, if you will, a chunky man named Fran Rogel who, if given a football and told to run through a wall, would say "On what count?" It is 1955, and the Steelers have a splendid passer named Jim Finks and a limber receiver named Goose McClairen. They also have Fran Rogel at fullback and a head coach named Walt Kiesling, who in training camp a few months before cut a rookie named John Unitas. A big, narrow-eyed German, Kiesling wears the expression of a man suffering from indigestion and has the view that there is only one way to start a football game. On the first Steelers play from scrimmage, Sunday after Sunday, rain or shine, he sends Fran Rogel plowing up the middle.

The word having gotten around, the enemy is stacked in what might be called an 11-0-0 defense. From the farthest reaches of Forbes Field 25,000 voices send down a thunderous chant, hoping ridicule will dissuade Kiesling: "Hi-diddle-diddle, Rogel up the middle!" And up the middle he goes, disappearing in a welter of opponents battling like starved wolves for a piece of his flesh. From his seat in the press box Art Rooney—the Chief—tightens the grip on his cigar till his knuckles whiten. Never has he interfered with a coach. But he has absorbed all he can bear, so for the next game he furnishes an opening play. "Kies," he tells the coach, "we are going to have Jim Finks throw a long pass to Goose McClairen. That's an order."

McClairen breezes into the open field, there being nobody in the 11-0-0 defense remotely concerned about him, takes Finks's pass at a casual lope and trots into the end zone. The touchdown is called back. A Steelers lineman was offside. After the game Rooney confronts the offender, only to learn from the poor fellow that Kiesling ordered him to lurch offside. "If that pass play works," Kies hissed at the lineman, "that club owner will be down here every week giving us plays." A philosophical man, the Chief never again makes the attempt.

So you see, it was not that we always had the worst talent in the league. On the contrary, Jim Brown used to say, "You'll usually find a way to beat the Steelers, but on Monday you'll ache as you haven't ached all season." Heroes we always had. From Johnny Blood to Bullet Bill Dudley (who as a rookie complained of being driven from the huddle by the whiskey on his teammates' breath) to Bobby Layne and John Henry Johnson, we had football players to cheer, but usually not enough of them.

THE BALL richocheted off the shoulder pads of Tatum, who was covering Fuqua, and fell miraculously into the hands of Harris at the 42-yard line.

DONALD J. STETZER/PITTSBURGH POST-GAZETTE/AP/WIDE WORLD PHOTOS

Our ascent to glory began on a gray winter's afternoon in 1969, in an upstairs suite of the Roosevelt, an aging downtown hotel where the Steelers had their headquarters. Dan Rooney, then 36, the Chief's eldest son, was presenting the Steelers' 16th head coach to the press.

Chuck Noll, 36, defensive backfield coach at Baltimore under Don Shula, scarcely cut a figure to trigger excitement. Vaguely handsome with an F.D.R. chin and the sloping shoulders of a linebacker, he wore a tweed jacket and in a light voice evaded pointed questions. He did it with the same tactful smile he would employ four years later when, barring cameramen from practice, he explained, "Fellas, it's icy out here. You might slip and break your expensive equipment."

During his first season in Pittsburgh Noll would look into the stands and say to himself, "My goodness! What strange football crowds." He thought back to his first pro coaching stint with the Chargers in Los Angeles and San Diego, where he had seen brightly frocked women on the arms of their husbands and often, too, the little ones tagging along from Sunday school. Here he saw middle-aged boisterous men wearing their old high school football jackets, their faces grown beefy on Polish sausage or Italian bread or corned beef and cabbage. These men invariably showed up in high humor only to plunge, as often as not, into teeth-gnashing rage. The previous season, under coach Bill Austin, the Steelers had won but two games; now they won but one. If all those ex-high school tackles from the river towns of Aliquippa and Beaver Falls and McKees Rocks had known that the new coach frequently tied on an apron to prepare gourmet dishes, that he religiously attended concerts of the Pittsburgh Symphony or that his fondest wish (granted by his wife last Christmas) was to putter among geraniums in his very own greenhouse, they might have passed up the deer season for an armed assault on Steeler headquarters.

Noll is, beyond anything, resolute. While a low-salaried linebacker and messenger guard for Paul Brown's Cleveland Browns, he completed three years of a four-year night-school law course, with no intention of ever practicing law. When he coached in Baltimore, the newspapermen there dubbed him, not entirely without envy, Knowledge, and when Pittsburgh sportswriters assayed his efforts he privately objected less strenuously to pieces that panned him than to those written without style.

The son of a Cleveland laboring man who died in his 40s of Parkinson's disease, Chuck Noll thinks of himself not so much as a coach as a teacher, and is totally confident of his ability. Steelers crowds booed him when he refused to call plays for Terry Bradshaw who, after having quarterbacked at Louisiana Tech, was finding the transition to the NFL roughly equivalent to trying to fly a lunar rocket after having six lessons in a Piper Cub, but Noll was serene.

"I have never had an extended conversation with the man," said one Steeler the day the team clinched the Central Division title. Noll's premise, no doubt, was that attachment to players destroys objectivity. "On Monday morning he'll smile passing you in the hall and say, 'Good morning' and just from the way he smiles you're damn sure he's telling you, 'You played a terrible game yesterday.' The feeling you get is not that you're only as good as your last game, it's that you're only as good as your *next* game. You never know where you stand with Noll, so you're always working like hell to keep your job. But he is so knowledgeable, so cool under fire, that you have tremendous respect for him."

STEELERS COACH Chuck Noll and quarterback Terry Bradshaw (12) won together, although they didn't see eye to eye on many occasions.

BEGINNING IN the summer of 1970, the Chief would enter the vast, lavishly appointed new dressing room in Three Rivers Stadium each day, pause inside the doorway to get his bearings and then wander from locker to locker. To players dressing for practice he would offer his hand and say, in a dialect surviving Pittsburgh's long-gone Irish First Ward, "How *ahr* ya?" To his favorites he would proffer an expensive cigar.

They had every right, these young studs collected by Chuck Noll, to wonder what is it with this old man whose history of failure lies upon us like a millstone, perpetuating our ridicule. He had, in fact, been a great all-round athlete, one who knew football as well as any owner, but he had run the Steelers as a sportsman torn between two loves, the other being horse racing. More often than not he hired

HEINZ KLUETMEIER

coaches who shared his feelings for the track, and he let them run their teams unencumbered, clear through to making all trades.

At Three Rivers now, his personal attentions to Noll's players, rather than causing him to appear the fumbling fool, dissolved the athletes' worldly veneer to reveal them as boys far from home. Their cynicism crumbled in his presence, for what other owner in the whole of the league knew the names of the lowliest rookies?

The Steelers faced a difficult first month, but they pulled it off by winning two of the four. Victories then accumulated—five in a row. The Steelers tore through the Bengals, Chiefs, Vikings and Browns. Lord, this was more fun than the time fat old Bobby Layne led a jazz band till three in the morning, then went out on a treacherously icy field to establish a Steelers record by passing for 409 yards. Franco Harris was running over cornerbacks, laying them as flat as so many slices of capocollo. Frenchy Fuqua, his natty running mate, was now wearing *two* watches (one on a gold fob across his vest), and one Sunday the congregation of St. Bernard's Roman Catholic Church arose in the middle of mass to give a lusty cheer for linebacker Jack Ham. But it was in the Astrodome at Houston the next to last week of the regular season that our troops, striving to protect a one-game lead over surprising Cleveland, proved what they were made of.

Flu struck five players the morning of the game, but they played. Thirteen Steelers went down with injuries but played on till doctors forbade them. Joe Gilliam, the team's last functioning quarterback, saw his first (and last) action of the season and had his knee torn apart. "Ready to surrender?" said an Oiler, but gimpy Joe, now a black McAuliffe at Bastogne, replied, "Nuts!" The score was tied 3–3 when our stupendous defensive tackle, Mean Joe Greene, told himself, "I have not come this close to a title to see it slip away." Five times he single-handedly sacked the Houston quarterback; on another play he jarred loose the ball from an Oilers running back and recovered the fumble to set up a field goal. Amid the rubble of a 9–3 Steeler victory, passions overwhelmed their normally self-composed coach. "We had guys out there bleeding," Noll said. "Bleeding but simply gutting it out."

How then can anyone insinuate that the Steelers were anything less than deserving of the now-famous Franco Harris miracle, the Terry Bradshaw fourth-down pass that in the first playoff game ricocheted from the shoulder of Oakland defensive back Jack Tatum to be gobbled up on a shoestring catch by Franco? To be sure, as Harris galloped to a touchdown with just five seconds left on the clock, our team stood guilty of receiving 12th-man assistance. But perhaps an even higher power had ordained the astonishing play, had provided a fillip to ensure that Pittsburghers forever more shall celebrate Dec. 23 as the Feast of the Immaculate Reception.

Alas, there was to be no Super Bowl trip, owing to the fact that in the second playoff game, our men lost to the Dolphins. So now we must try again, but our hearts are lifted by the knowledge that ours is a team that is surely meant to taste the best of life. Lest anyone doubt it, let him be told the Battle of the Soft Drink Cooler.

It is last Dec. 3, and the Steelers have just lathered the Browns 30–0—obviously an occasion for great dressing-room jubilation. At the height of it equipment manager Jack Hart, a wiry, brush-cut man, comes upon several small children. To the adult accompanying them he says, "No kids in the dressing room."

"They're O.K.," says Art Rooney Jr., the club's 37-year-old vice president. "They're friends."

"No kids," reiterates Hart.

One word leads to another, whereupon Rooney seizes Hart and deposits him in a soft-drink cooler. From his seat among the Cokes and Dr Peppers, Hart reaches out and pops the vice president two stiff shots to the eye. A while later, after Hart has climbed out of the cooler to ponder prospects for unemployed equipment manager and after the vice president goes to the equipment manager and says, "You did right, Jack," the other vice president, Dan Rooney, seeks him out and says, "It's all right, Jack."

So there you have it, the enduring flavor of the Pittsburgh Steelers. And maybe that is why so many good things came to them in the 40th year and why there's surely more in store. . . .

PITTSBURGH LINEBACKER Jack Ham (59) was both the heart and the brains of the fearsome Steel Curtain defense.

RICH CLARKSON

1954 | BOBBY LAYNE led the Detroit Lions to NFL titles in 1952 and '53, but had to settle for a conference crown in '54 | *Photograph by* HY PESKIN

> SI's TOP 25 The Defensive Backs

LARRY WILSON
Photograph by TONY TOMSIC

MIKE HAYNES
Photograph by RICH CLARKSON

CLIFF HARRIS
Photograph by RUSS RUSSELL

DARRELL GREEN
Photograph by LAWRENCE JACKSON

PAUL KRAUSE
Photograph by AP

RONNIE LOTT
Photograph by AL MESSERSCHMIDT

RODNEY HARRISON
Photograph by TOM DIPACE

ROD WOODSON
Photograph by JOHN BIEVER

MEL RENFRO
Photograph by TONY TOMSIC

HERB ADDERLEY
Photograph by TONY TOMSIC

HERB ADDERLEY

DICK ANDERSON

STEVE ATWATER

LEM BARNEY

MEL BLOUNT

BOB BOYD

WILLIE BROWN

JACK CHRISTIANSEN

KENNY EASLEY

DARRELL GREEN

CLIFF HARRIS

RODNEY HARRISON

MIKE HAYNES

KEN HOUSTON

JIMMY JOHNSON

PAUL KRAUSE

DICK (NIGHT TRAIN) LANE

RONNIE LOTT

MEL RENFRO

DEION SANDERS

EMLEN TUNNELL

ROGER WEHRLI

LARRY WILSON

WILLIE WOOD

ROD WOODSON

from NIGHT MOVES | BY PAUL ZIMMERMAN
SI February 11, 2002

DICK (NIGHT TRAIN) LANE came up in an era when cornerbacks were still called defensive halfbacks. He played a style of football that was born of poverty and desperation. Years later his technique would acquire the catchy name "bump and run," but when he came into the NFL, in 1952, his approach was as elemental as the game itself. Lock on a receiver, rough him up as he makes his way down the field, try to knock him off his pattern, and if he still caught the ball, take his head off.

Lane, who died last week of a heart attack at age 73, was the most feared corner in the game. A big guy at 6' 2" and more than 200 pounds, he was known for the Night Train Necktie, a neck-high tackle that the league eventually banned. "I've never seen a defensive back hit like him," Packers Hall of Famer Herb Adderley once said. "I mean, take them *down*, whether it be Jim Brown or Jim Taylor."

If Lane had been only a roughneck, he wouldn't have put together a 14-year career, which he spent with the Rams, the Chicago Cardinals and the Lions, nor would he have ended up in the Hall of Fame. He had speed, phenomenal leaping ability and great hands. Ironically, when he broke in with the Rams, they switched him from receiver to defense because they thought he had trouble holding on to the ball. He made 14 interceptions in his rookie year (in only 12 games), still the NFL single-season record.

I used to see him from time to time at Hall of Fame gatherings, always smiling, always friendly. "Until he got sick [with diabetes] a few years ago, he'd always be back here for the Hall of Fame weekend," says John Bankert, the Hall's executive director. "He'd always ask me the same thing, 'Is there anything I can do to help?'

"One of the last times I saw him, he said, 'You know, sometimes I feel that I'm not worthy of being here.' "

No one was worthier than Night Train Lane. . . .

1961 | LANE'S TRADEMARK necktie tackle, part of his bruising repertoire, was later banned by the NFL. | *Photograph by* BETTMANN

1957 | THE LIONS' Yale Lary, kicking against the Browns in Briggs Stadium, was the NFL's leading punter three times | *Photograph by* MARVIN E. NEWMAN

1973 | DOLPHINS' KICKER Garo Yepremian tried to pass after a bungled field goal attempt against the Redskins in Super Bowl VII | *Photograph by* NEIL LEIFER

1
BRUNDIGE
77

1967 | A REF'S WHISTLE from the title game known as the Ice Bowl (temperature in Green Bay: -13°, with a windchill of -46°) ended up in Canton. Bart Starr (15) ended up in the end zone on a quarterback sneak that gave the Packers the win over the Cowboys | *Photograph by* AP *(right)*

COURTESY OF THE PRO FOOTBALL HALL OF FAME

34
57
81

80

LET'S HAND IT TO HIM

BY RICK TELANDER

Jerry Rice's dedication to his craft made him the most prolific receiver in the game's history. —*from* SI, DECEMBER 26, 1994

THE BEST? ❧ HE'S HERE, in blue tights and red windbreaker, bitchy as a diva with a headache. ❧ The best ever? ❧ He's right here, sitting at his locker, taking off his rain gear after practice, edgy as a cat in a sawmill. ❧ Around him swirls the clamor of big men winding down, messing around, acting like fools. Two bare-chested linemen lock up and start to grapple, rasslin' and snorting like trash-talking sumos. Other players laugh, but not the best ever. "Guys," he says irritably. "Hey, guys!" Someone could get hurt.

The two wrestlers slowly come apart, his voice bringing them to their senses. They've heard the voice before; it's their fourth-grade teacher scolding them for rolling spitballs. It's the voice of San Francisco 49er Jerry Rice, the best wide receiver ever to play football. The 6' 2", tightly braided coil of nerves, fast-twitch fibers, delicate grasping skills and unadulterated desire is setting such high standards for the position that they will probably never be approached again, and he can't stand distractions while he works.

Rice does not fool around. Ever. He works so hard at his conditioning that during the off-season he virtually exits his body and studies his physical package the way a potter studies clay. "I mess with it," he says. "I like to do different things to motivate myself. I set goals and go after them."

As a rookie in 1985 he came to the 49ers at a muscular 208 pounds, but now he weighs 196. He is so lean that you wonder if he's sick. He likes to mess with his body fat, wants it to know that he is its master. For Rice, fat is a cornerback in man coverage with no safety in sight, a minor and ultimately irrelevant nuisance. Eschewing dietary fat, he got down to 189 a year or so ago, but the weight loss was too much. His starved body was literally eating up his muscles. His trainer ordered him to start eating things like ice cream.

"Under four percent body fat and I don't feel good," Rice states. "I'm a health-food fanatic, but getting that low really hurt my performance. I'm at 4.8 percent now, and I feel good." Well, not really *good*. Not the way you or I might feel good if we knew that not only were we certifiably the best receiver in the history of football but, perhaps, the greatest offensive player ever. That argument can be made. Rice already has more receiving touchdowns and more total touchdowns than anyone in NFL history. He has more 1,000-yard seasons than any other receiver, more touchdown catches in a Super Bowl and more consecutive games with a touchdown reception than anyone.

Was he this good in college? Imagine, for a moment, that it's September, 1984, and you are in sweltering Itta Bena, Miss., watching Mississippi Valley State coach Archie (Gunslinger) Cooley direct his Satellite Express offense, with quarterback Willie Totten flinging passes to a senior wideout named Rice, who races out of a stacked receiver formation that looks something like a Motown chorus line. In the first four games of that season Rice caught 64 passes for 917 yards and 12 touchdowns. As a junior he caught 24 passes in one game, an all-division record. He left school with 18 NCAA I-AA records. Yes, he was good.

Rice never missed a game in college, nor has he missed one as a pro. Since he joined the 49ers the team has gone 126-45-1 (best in the NFL during that period) and won two Super Bowls. And at the seemingly advanced age of 32, he is still in his prime.

Early this season he talked about his compulsion to prove himself, to never let up even for an instant out of fear that everything might come apart. He had started at the bottom, and he could be back there in a heartbeat; people would forget him, and if that happened . . . would he even exist?

Afield, as in life, Rice is evasive. He almost never takes a direct, crushing blow after catching a pass. He controls his body like a master puppeteer working a marionette. A one-handed grab here, a tiptoe up the sideline there, an unscathed sprint through two closing safeties when it seems decapitation is imminent.

"I don't think I've ever seen him all stretched out," says 49ers quarterback Steve Young of Rice's ability to avoid big hits. Rice jumps only when he has to, and unlike almost all other receivers, he catches passes in mid-stride and effortlessly continues running, the ball like a sprinter's baton in his hand. It's almost certain that no one has run for more yardage after catching the ball than Rice. Though he's not particularly fast, Rice has a fluid stride and a sudden burst that, as Young says, "is a speed you can't clock."

And the hands. Clad in gloves, the hands are so supple and sure that last year they snared a touchdown pass by latching onto the *tail end* of a fading ball. "That was not giving up on the ball," explains Rice. Sounds simple. In reality it's like grabbing the back end of a greased pig. . . .

RICE MADE 11 catches—including this one-hander—against the Bengals in Super Bowl XXIII.

WALTER IOOSS JR.

86

1997 | PACKERS GUARD Adam Timmerman got a wet kiss after Green Bay beat the 49ers to reach the Super Bowl | *Photograph by* TONY TOMSIC

1964 | BROWNS RECEIVER Gary Collins was swarmed by Cleveland fans after scoring one of his three touchdowns in the title game | *Photograph by* TONY TOMSIC

1959 | GIANTS QUARTERBACK Charlie Conerly needed two men to protect him from Colts end Gino Marchetti in the title game | *Photograph by* NEIL LEIFER

CODE OF HONOR

BY GARY SMITH

Responding to the 9/11 attacks the only way that made sense to him, Pat Tillman did the unthinkable: He walked away from his NFL career and joined the Army Rangers. —*from* SI, MAY 3, 2004

EVEN BEFORE THE WORLD Trade Center incinerated, even as a linebacker at Arizona State in 1996 and '97, Pat Tillman would lie in bed on the eve of games and picture things that no teammate pictured. He'd envision the American flag and the blood that had been spilled for it and utter words that football players didn't, *shouldn't*, just hours before entering battle. "There's more to life than football," he'd say. "I want to contribute to society and help people."

Then came the phone call one September morning from his brother Kevin, an infielder in the Cleveland Indians organization—*Turn on your TV, right NOW, Pat!*—and the image on the screen of the second airliner hurtling into the second glass tower full of human beings. The next day came Pat's interview with NFL Films, when he said, "I play football, and it just seems so goddam—it *is*—unimportant compared to everything that's taken place.... My grandfather was at Pearl Harbor and a lot of my family has gone and fought in wars, and I really haven't done a damn thing...."

"We're worthless.... We're actors," Pat had muttered as he watched events on a locker room TV the day after the attacks. What did people expect him to say a half year later when, like his brother, he decided, at age 25, that he couldn't do what every other pro athlete did—keep playing ball and leave it to others to do what had to be done? What did they expect him to do—*talk* about it?

Relatives tried to persuade the Tillman boys to change their minds. Their father—Pat Sr., a lawyer and former college wrestler at San Jose State who had told his sons long ago that he regretted not having followed the family footpath into service—knew that dissuasion would be futile. One day Pat pulled a chair around the desk of then Cardinals coach Dave McGinnis and said, "Mac, we've gotta talk," walking away later that day and leaving Mac to do all the talking to the media.

The Tillman brothers made the Rangers. Pat's reward was a pay cut from the $1.2 million a year the Cardinals would have paid him to $17,316. "I can't stop smiling," his old college coach, Bruce Snyder, told *The Miami Herald* at the time, "and I'm not really sure why."

The news [that Pat Tillman was killed in action in Afghanistan] whistled through America's soul and raised the hair on the back of its neck. It tapped into people's admiration, their awe, their guilt. In a country where no civilians have been asked to sacrifice anything and where even the cost of the war is being forwarded to their children and their children's children, a man had sacrificed the biggest dream of all: the NFL. During World War II, 638 NFL players served and 19 died in action, but no well-known U.S. professional athlete in a quarter century had volunteered for service, and none had perished since Buffalo Bills lineman Bob Kalsu in Vietnam in 1970.

Memorials sprang up overnight, balloons and flowers and teddy bears and notes left, and a man stood before a photo of Pat outside Sun Devil Stadium—home to ASU and the Cardinals—and blew *Amazing Grace* through his bagpipes. Scholarships were founded, and the Cardinals announced that a plaza outside their unfinished new stadium will carry his name. Before its story had even been written, SI had received 103 letters about Pat's sacrifice. Pat had no need for the fuss. But the people did. At last they had a face to grieve.

"There is in Pat Tillman's example," said Senator John McCain of Arizona, "in his unexpected choice of duty to his country over the riches and other comforts of celebrity, and in his humility, such an inspiration to all of us to reclaim the essential public-spiritedness of Americans that many of us, in low moments, had worried was no longer our common distinguishing trait."

The mist of human motive is as dense as the fog of war. Pat Tillman may have died in the Middle East last week because it was the only place on earth where he could get a good night's sleep. But anytime a man listens to his inner voice, refuses to wall it off with all the mortar and bricks that his culture can possibly offer, it's a moment to stand in wonder as well as to weep.

Elizabeth McKenrick, the wife of 4th Ranger Training Battalion Commander Terry McKenrick, couldn't help herself last Friday. As a rule she shields her three children from newscasts about the war because otherwise she knows that the next time their dad is shipped from Fort Benning, Ga., to the Middle East, she won't stand a chance of convincing them he'll return home. But when she saw the TV report about Pat Tillman, she called her nine-year-old to her side. "Listen," she said. "Listen to the story of what this man did."...

GENE LOWER/SLINGSHOT

40
CARDINALS
40
40

1973 | **THE PACKERS** defense was very much in its element against Vikings running back Chuck Foreman in Green Bay | *Photograph by* JOHN BIEVER

1964 | **JIM BROWN** led the NFL in rushing in eight of the nine years he played for the Browns, and retired in his prime, at 30 | *Photograph by* NEIL LEIFER

SUPER BOWL - NEW YORK GIANTS - DEFENSIVE CALL SHEET - JANUARY 28, 2001

VS. REGULAR

SERIES 50/50 - Reduce Stir 22K
Tilt FZ I = LT
• (St) Ov Snk Swill 1Lk •
• (St) Under Shunk 63

1ST DN SL Run (20 In)
(St) Ov Snk 63
Eagle Storm
Reduce Op Smoke Sp. 1
(St) Ov Ed 3

INC SL Run
Reduce Tilt 63 Zone X
(St) Ov Snk Stud 1Lk
(St) Ov Ed 3

2ND 7+ SL Pass (Scrn)
Und Stir 22K
Reduce Knife 43 / 63
Tilt FZ
(St) Ov Ed 3 (Tom)

2ND MD 50/50
Reduce Knife 63
Under Shunk Zone X

2ND SHT Run
Ov Ed (Knife) 3
Reduce Tilt Zone X

VS. TIGER

Series Hvy Run
Cyclone Dog 1
Under 63
Open Storm
Ov Snk 63

1st 50/50
(St) Ov Ed 4
Over Whip You 1Y
Ov Ed 3
Ov Snk 63

2nd 7+ Pass
Ov Ed Stir 2B
Reduce Op Smoke Sp. 1
(RS) Strong FZ
(St) Ov Ed Combo 4

VS. 1ST / 2ND PASS

3W 50/50
Und 1/2 7
Ov Combo 4, 3

E
Under Me 63
Und 1/2 7
Und Sam 1
Ov Ed (Combo) 3, 6

BASE VS. 3W

• Flex 78
• Flex Change
BA
Dime Viper
Bear Peel 1
Dime Dog 1

1ST & 2ND DOWN E

Under Me 78
Flex Change
Nickel Dog 1
Dime Viper

Tiger - Flex Change/78
Nickel Dog 1

U / GREY

Vandy -
(St) Ov Snk Stud 1Lk
• Ov Snk 63 •
Ov Ed 3
• Under 1/2 7, 63 -

Hvy -
Over 6 Match
Backer Storm
Over Hammer O

BACKED UP

Eagle Storm / Open Storm
Over Sink 63
Tilt FZ
(St) Ov Ed 3
Reduce Knife (Combo) 22K, 63

4 MINUTE

(St) Ov Snk Stud 1Lk
Eagle Storm
- Hvy-Over 6 Match -
Reduce Tilt 7, 63
Cyclone Dog 1

3RD DOWN SUB

	3W	4W	Reg	E
3RD LNG	30 Blast 1 (RS) Bear Nickel Go 1 30 Rush Str 58 Str Rush 52W 3-2 Rush Auto 30 Ray 55 Rush 55 (30 Peel)	30 Peel 1 30 Hound 1 Rush Change 3-2 Rush 52W 30 Gut O	Rush 58 Str Strong FZ Rush 52W Bear Peel 1	Rush 58 Str BA Bear Peel 1 30 Blast 1
3RD REG	Double Dog 1 Rush 52W BA Bear Hk 78 Rush Change	Strong FZ 30 Blast 1 3-2 Rush Change 30 Trap 52W	Rush 52W 30 Near FZ 3-2 Rush 78	Bear Hk 78 30 Peel 55 Rush 52W
3RD MED	Bear Peel 1 Flex Change 30 NR FZ Tiger	Rush 52W Rush 78	Rush 52W Flex 78 - MA - MA	Max Blitz O Dime Viper Under Me 52W **3rd 3-4**: Rush 52W / 30 Hound 1 / Rush Change

2 MINUTE

Patient - Begin w/ a Run. Screen on 2nd Long. 3WR 2x2-Alert ZSeam - H ✓ Down. Trips=HiLoWk. Ch-78, HiLoStr or H. Regular-Bunch/ Levels concepts.

Rush 58 Str, 78
3-2 Rush 52W
Rush Change / 54
BA
Double Dog 1
Drop Kathy

GOAL LINE

1st Goal Line Banjo
2nd Goal Line Banjo
3rd Goal Line Banjo

REG. RED ZONE

HIGH RED
Reduce Knife/Stir 22K, 63
Ov Ed (Tilt) 3, 4

+ 15
Ov Ed (Tilt/Knife) Red 2
Flex (Tom) Red 2
(Vandy) Ov Ed Red 2

PRESSURE
Eagle Storm
Tilt FZ / Cyclone Dog 1

MUST STOP
Reduce Hammer O
Ov Snk Stud Up OLk
U - (Ok) Sink Stud Up OLk

SUB RED ZONE

HIGH RED
(Sub) Flex/Rush Change 52W

+ 15
Flex/Rush R52
3-2 Rush R52

PRESSURE
30 Blast 1
BA
Strong FZ

2 PT PLAY
30 Gut O
(Sub) Flex R52

MUST STOP
Max Blitz O
30 Gut O

SHORT YARDAGE

REG- Ov Snk Stud 1Lk
Cyclone Dog 1

3W- (BS) Flex Change, 71Y
Under 1/2 7 (Combo)

U- Hvy-Backer Storm
Over Hammer O
(Ok) Sink Stud 1Lk

TIGER- Und Sam 1
Und 1/2 7

JUMBO- SY Under Zone the Set

2001 | RAVENS QUARTERBACK Trent Dilfer (8) could have used a peek at the Giants' play sheet (left) before facing their defense in the Super Bowl | *Photograph by* CHUCK SOLOMON

36

BIG BANG THEORY

BY AUSTIN MURPHY

Increasingly, NFL teams turned to beefy, big-butted backs who could both bowl over and blow past the opposition.

—from SI, NOVEMBER 24, 1997

EVERY SO OFTEN, JUST TO remind the Cincinnati Bengals that he's more than a Sherman tank, Pittsburgh Steelers running back Jerome Bettis would throw in a hip fake or stutter step, but these feints were like a brooch on a hippo. For the most part, the man with the blue-collar nickname, the Bus, flat ran over people.

As the weather turns foul north of the Sunbelt and the playoffs draw nigh, we take this opportunity to celebrate the NFL's bulkier backs, the moundlike men who move the pile on third-and-one, who are at home running between the tackles, who, for the most part, lack abdominal definition. "It used to be I was considered a big linebacker," says the Arizona Cardinals' Eric Hill, a ninth-year player who goes 6' 2", 253 pounds. "Now there are backs about as big as I am. It's a scary profession."

Big backs have been around since the league's Pleistocene epoch. What is unprecedented about the current crop is the array of skills its members boast. The ability to pound the ball inside is but a single line on their résumés. When there is no daylight, they have the vision to find a seam, the agility to step over bodies and the speed to get outside. What's more, they can make people miss, break long runs and catch the ball out of the backfield. Says Steelers coach Bill Cowher, "They're unique people. They're hard to find." And hard to feed.

Along with the Bus (5' 11", 243 pounds), the Tennessee Oilers' Eddie George (6' 3", 232), the Jacksonville Jaguars' Natrone Means (5' 10", 240) and the Baltimore Ravens' Bam Morris (6 feet, 245)—come to think of it, the AFC Central is also Big Back Central—this fraternity of dancing bears includes ball-carriers with whom you may be less familiar. Buffalo Bills rookie first-round pick Antowain Smith (6' 2", 224 pounds, 4.48 in the 40) was identified last week by Denver Broncos coach Mike Shanahan as the "toughest, strongest" back his team would face this season. Jamal Anderson, a 5' 11", 234-pound wrecking ball of a runner, is the Falcon who made 250-pound Craig (Ironhead) Heyward expendable in Atlanta.

"They're broadening their horizons," says Tampa Bay Buccaneers coach Tony Dungy of today's abnormally large, swift runners, one of whom, 248-pound Mike Alstott, plays for him. "They're like basketball guards. Guys who are six-six, six-seven are doing things little men used to do."

Consider Atlanta's Anderson, who has been known to line up as a wide receiver and run a "go" route on one play and then run an off-tackle blast on the next.

As he worked his way through a basket of tortilla chips at a Mexican restaurant near his apartment recently, the Bus related some of the sights and sounds experienced by a big back on game day: "First series, they're coming at you like gangbusters. They're swarming to the ball, talking a lot of mess. 'Bus grounded today, baby.' Stuff like that. By the last series guys aren't coming to the ball nearly as fast. I'm coming at them, and they're looking around, like, O.K., who's with me?"

It is Bettis's appetite for collisions, as much as the fact that he has surpassed 100 yards rushing in 18 of his 27 games as a Steeler, that has caused Pittsburgh fans to embrace him. (We mean this figuratively. One reason the ample-bellied, massively derriered, thunderously thighed Bettis is so hard to bring down, says Steelers running backs coach Dick Hoak, is that "it's hard to get your arms around him.")

Investors take note: We are approaching that time of year when the stock of the big back rises. The nastier the weather, the tougher it becomes to throw. Games with playoff implications are followed by playoff games; coaches become more conservative. Asked last week if big backs are more valuable late in the year, Shanahan replied, "We'll find out shortly." He already knows. One of last season's most shocking sights was that of Means gashing Shanahan's defense—the NFL's best against the run in 1996—for 140 rushing yards in the Jaguars' 30–27 second-round playoff upset of the Broncos. A week earlier Means had run for 175 yards in Jacksonville's wild-card playoff win in Buffalo.

Means still doesn't see why everyone was so surprised by his big games. "Those were cold, loud places, where you're going to have trouble calling audibles, where you can't line up and throw it on every down," he says. "The best thing to do is to snap the ball on the quick count and pound it up in there."

Like Bettis, Means is blessed with sweet feet. Like Bettis, he wears down defenders. How does he know? They tell him. "What I like is in the second half, when guys start making arm tackles," says Means. "They start groaning when they get up and saying things like, 'I'm tired of tackling your big ass.' " . . .

LONGTIME STEELERS back Jerome Bettis could sometimes run away from defenders, but he much preferred running over them.

JOHN BIEVER

1966 | RUNNING BACK Lenny Moore and guard Jim Parker were a Pro Bowl duo for the Colts for six years | *Photograph by* WALTER IOOSS JR.

1967 | RAMS QB Roman Gabriel beat Willie Davis and the Packers on his way to earning the NFL's MVP in '69 | *Photograph by* WALTER IOOSS JR.

Reebok

1994 | HATS OFF to Raiders linebacker Mike Jones for not flagging the ref for holding on this play | *Photograph by* RICHARD MACKSON

1995 | THE PANTHERS' Lamar Lathon found himself in a cat fight when he tried to drag down Jaguars QB Steve Beuerlein (7) | *Photograph by* GEORGE TIEDEMANN

> SI's TOP 25 The Coaches

TOM LANDRY
Photograph by NEIL LEIFER

DICK VERMEIL
Photograph by GEORGE TIEDEMANN

JOHN MADDEN
Photograph by RICH CLARKSON

DON SHULA
Photograph by WALTER IOOSS JR.

PAUL BROWN
Photograph by RICHARD MEEK

BILL PARCELLS
Photograph by PETER READ MILLER

BILL WALSH
Photograph by JOHN BIEVER

JOE GIBBS
Photograph by JOE ROBBINS

BILL BELICHICK
Photograph by JOHN BIEVER

GEORGE HALAS
Photograph by CURT GUNTHER

GEORGE ALLEN
BILL BELICHICK
PAUL BROWN
WEEB EWBANK
RAY FLAHERTY
JOE GIBBS
SID GILLMAN
BUD GRANT
GEORGE HALAS
CHUCK KNOX
CURLY LAMBEAU
TOM LANDRY
MARV LEVY
VINCE LOMBARDI
JOHN MADDEN
EARLE (GREASY) NEALE
CHUCK NOLL
STEVE OWEN
BILL PARCELLS
DAN REEVES
MIKE SHANAHAN
DON SHULA
HANK STRAM
DICK VERMEIL
BILL WALSH

THE DAY OF THE GAME

BY VINCE LOMBARDI WITH W.C. HEINZ

In this SI excerpt from his book, Run to Daylight!, *the great Packers coach chronicled the hours leading to kickoff on a football Sunday.* —*from* SI, SEPTEMBER 9, 1963

AFTER BREAKFAST ON the Sunday of the game, I look out the window and the sky is low and the air is loaded with moisture that has condensed into droplets on the shrubs and the lawn. Later, as I drive across the bridge, the first drops of rain hit the windshield. This is not going to help us a bit, but it is not going to help the other guys either. If we are going to take it right to them, I think, let's do it on the first play. Go to their strength, and if that's where we're going, our Brown Right-73 might be the one to open with. I like it because their middle linebacker is a great one and the sooner we go to work on him the better. It will give us at least two people on him. While I don't think we will discourage him, we should, if Jim Ringo and Ron Kramer both get good shots at him, force him to be a little concerned. That could help.

Except for half a dozen cars parked up by the entrance to the dressing rooms, the area is empty, and when I walk inside it is 10:25 and Hank Jordan is there, getting out of his jacket in front of his dressing stall. I look around the room at the stalls, each with the name card and jersey number on it, each with the gold helmet and shoulder pads above it, the gold pants hanging inside on the right, the green jerseys and blue warm-up sweaters on hangers on the left, the floor of each stall covered with six or eight or 10 pairs of football shoes at $23.50 a pair.

Earl Gros and Gary Barnes are undressing and in the trainer's room Ed Blaine and Ron Gassert, our two other first-year men, are having their left knees taped.

The veterans are coming in now—Forrest Gregg and Dave Hanner and Jim Ringo—and Hank Gremminger is getting out of his street clothes in front of his stall. "You give the doctor another workout?" Ringo is saying to Hanner.

"That's right," Hanner answers.

"What's the matter with you?" I ask Hanner.

"I felt hot and cold yesterday," he says.

"Did you go to the doctor?"

"Yes, sir. Then last night I went to bed at 8. I woke up at 10 sweatin' like anything, but I feel better today."

I hope you do, I say to myself, and I hope Jimmy Taylor walks in saying he feels better, too.

"How's Jim?" Ringo says. "Anybody know?"

"He says he had 101," Hanner says, "but he says he's gonna play."

I walk in the coaches' room. Red Cochran is holding his Packer blazer in his left hand and, with his right hand wrapped in white tape, brushing lint off it. Phil Bengtson is talking to Norb Hecker about UCLA's upset of Ohio State yesterday, and Bill Austin is on the phone checking with the airport about the weather. "It could be off and on," he says when he hangs up. "Light rains all afternoon. The wind is east-northeast, 10 to 12 knots."

"That's not the way the flags are blowing," Phil says.

"They're liable to be any way out there," Bill says.

I am at my desk now, thinking about Brown Right-73, our opening play. What I like about it is that it really goes to work on that middle linebacker. Ringo sets him up with a drive block for Ron Kramer, who releases from his tight-end spot and comes across and bull-blocks him. Taylor fakes up the middle and then takes that big 76. It's a tough block for Jerry Kramer on that 71, but if they give Paul Hornung any daylight and his thigh is all right he should go. Another nice thing about it, too, is that it is a good influence play on their left end. Forrest Gregg pulls across his face, making him think the play is going outside, and when it goes inside you've got that trap on him.

I look at our ready list, in its plastic envelope, the right formations on a 8 × 11 card, the left formations on the other side. I jot down half a dozen plays, any of which could be logical calls in our first sequence, depending on the result of our 73. "How's Taylor?" I say to Gene Brusky as I see him walk in.

"He had 101 last night," Gene says. "It's normal this morning."

I walk out then and find Jim Taylor. "Jim?" I say "How do you feel? The doctor says you're going to be all right."

"I hope so," he says, and I hope so, too. He is one of those performers who has to be emotionally up and I'm hoping not only that the fever hasn't drained him physically but also that it hasn't defeated him psychologically.

"Jim? Bubba?" I say, and I get Ringo and Bubba Forester, our two captains, together. "If you win the toss, receive. If we have to kick off, take the north goal."

In the coaches' room I change into slacks and pull on a pair of white woolen socks and the ripple-soled coaching shoes.

"All right," I say, "I want the quarterbacks in here."

"Bart! Johnny Roach!" Cochran calls as the others leave.

THE PACKERS won only one game in 1958, the year before Lombardi arrived; three years later, they were the NFL champs.

NEIL LEIFER

When Starr and Roach come in, I sit down across from them. "Generally," I say, "your sweeps should be to your left. As far as your pitchout is concerned, I'd use 48 to the left side. When you're going for short yardage, you can expect the 6–1, so use those short-yardage plays we've been working on." They are intent and nodding. "Now for our first play let's try the 73. That's whether they're in the 6–1 or 4–3 or whatever they do. O.K.?"

"Yes, sir," Starr says.

They get up and leave. I put on my topcoat and transparent raincoat over it. I walk to the door of the dressing room and look at the players. They are now in uniform and wearing olive-green rain jackets and dark blue knitted skull caps. All of them are waiting.

"Let's go!" they shout, and they clap in unison and start filing out. Their cleats make the sound of hailstones hitting the concrete and, as I follow them out and look up, the rain, still light and hesitant, hits my face.

The stands are about two-thirds full. I pick a couple of tufts of grass and throw one up and then the other. The wind is not too strong and out of the northeast. If we lose the toss and have to kick off we will stay with the north goal.

In the far end zone Ringo and Forester are leading the calisthenics. Behind me I hear the roar from the stands and I turn and see the other team, in silver and white uniforms, coming out, down the ramp and out onto the field. I search the other side of the field until I find my counterpart, and I walk over.

"How are you," I say, and we shake hands.

"Fine," he says. "You?"

"All right," I say. "We drew a rotten day."

"We can't do anything about that."

"I'm sorry about the condition of the field, though," I say. "We've had rain most of the week, and they had a high school game here Friday night."

"I understand," he says.

"Well," I say, "good luck, and I'll see you."

"Thanks," he says. "The same to you."

As I turn I see that the referee is bringing over No. 56, that great middle linebacker of theirs. All week, day and night, he has been invading my thoughts, and now we shake hands. Ringo and Forester have joined us. Then I leave, and I'm aware that the light rain seems to have stopped.

"We won the toss," Ringo says when he and Forester come back. "We receive and they have the north goal."

"Good," I say.

I walk down to where Austin and Bengtson have the offensive and defensive lines facing one another. They are reviewing assignments. It is now 12:45. We have been out on the field for half an hour, so I send them in.

When they are all seated in front of their stalls, the other coaches and I go into our room and shut the door. It is 10 minutes to game time, and these three minutes that will follow, with just the squad members alone in the dressing rooms, is something I started when I first came here in 1959. I was reaching for anything then that would give them a feeling of oneness, of dependence upon one another and of strength to be derived from their unity, so I told the captains that before each game this period would belong solely to the players. I do not know what is said in that room. I know that Ringo or Forester, or perhaps both, speak, and that if someone else wants to say something, he does. I know that at the end—and this is completely their thought and desire—they all join in the Lord's Prayer.

Someone knocks on our door and the other coaches and I walk back into the room. Now I have seven minutes, and I walk among them. I start out by going over the automatic we're going to use, the plays our quarterback will call on the line when he sees that the defensive alignment will negate what he called in the huddle. "We're going to receive," I say then, "and we've got the south goal. Remember that this club puts their speediest men as third men out from each side and they must be blocked. So let's take them out of there. Let's impress them, all of them, right on that kickoff. I don't have to tell you about the importance of this ball game. You know as well as I do that you're meeting today the top contender, and that no one can win it now but you. For two years these people have been on our necks, but if you beat them today you'll be making your job easier for the rest of this year. For you to do it, though, is going to require a top effort. You know that they think they can beat you, that they've said they will. That's why I say it's going to take a top effort.

"And now," I say, "I want all of you to know this. Regardless of the outcome today I'll still be proud of you."

"Let's go!" they shout, standing now, and they bring their hands together in unison again. "Let's go! Go!"

There is the roar of the crowd again, the faces and bodies bordering the walkway. There is the jam-up going down the ramp, and we stand, waiting amid the shouts, for the P.A. announcer to introduce our offensive team.

"At center," he says, the sound of his voice filling the air, and Jim Ringo runs out onto the field through the V formed by the cheerleaders and the Green Bay Lumberjacks' band, "Number 51—Jim Ringo! At right guard, Number 64—Jerry Kramer! At left guard, Number 63—Fuzzy Thurston! At right tackle. . . . "

We coaches then follow the rest of the squad out. The roar from the stands is beating down in waves around us and I am in the middle, crouching, with the squad pressing in around me. "Go out there and hustle," I tell them.

OUR KICKOFF-receiving team runs out. From the other sideline the other team is peeling out of its huddle. And now that nervousness which I have forestalled, which I have learned to control up to a point, starts to come. I watch the referee's arm come down and then I hear the whistle, and to my left that line of white shirts and silver pants and helmets moves forward and I see that ball rise. . . .

BART STARR, drafted in the 17th round in 1956, blossomed under Lombardi, leading the Packers to five NFL championships and two Super Bowls.

NEIL LEIFER

31
Riddell

1998 | TERRELL OWENS seemed to smell six points as he turned a catch into a TD against the Vikings in San Francisco | *Photograph by* V.J. LOVERO

2003 | THE PYLON left no doubt that Bengals running back Jeremi Johnson had scored against the Chiefs in Cincinnati | *Photograph by* JOHN BIEVER

2003 | STEELERS WIDEOUT Antwaan Randle El provided a turning point of sorts when he was face-masked by the Browns' Chris Akins | *Photograph by* BOB ROSATO

1999 | THE MAJORITY of the Browns defenders turned out to greet Vikings back Leroy McFadden in a 24–17 Minnesota win | *Photograph by* DAVID LIAM KYLE

PASSING TIME

BY LEIGH MONTVILLE

At 35 and with nothing left to prove in Canada, little Doug Flutie took one last shot at making it big in the NFL. —*from* SI, JUNE 22, 1998

THE BASKETBALL IS finished at 2 o'clock on a Monday afternoon at the Longfellow Sports Club in Natick, Mass. The businessmen are showering, dressing, talking about the stock market and personal relationships and missed layups, getting ready to go back to the job. Doug Flutie is getting ready to go to lunch. He is still wearing his shorts and sneakers.

"You're not taking a shower?" he is asked.

"No," he replies.

"Really?"

"I don't need it," he explains. "I kind of, you know, just stay sweaty all day."

His schedule for this day is pretty typical. Let's see, he has run four or five miles, lifted weights for an hour, played basketball with the same lunchtime group that gathers every noon. After lunch he will meet his brother, Darren, and they will run sprints and go through drills, throwing a football back and forth. Then he will return to the gym and play a higher grade of basketball with college kids.

On other days there might be variations—a game with his rec-league soccer team, perhaps, or a session on the drums with his band—but this is his usual off-season routine. He is 35, still flying around like a teenager. He could be Peter Pan in a damp sweatshirt.

"Take away the part where you go to classes, and he's like a college kid," says Jack Mula, Flutie's agent. "Remember when you'd get up in the morning, throw on any clothes that were around the room, clean or not, and just go? Not worry about shaving? Nothing? That's Doug."

His life—his athletic life, at least—seems frozen in time and place and circumstance. His hair is still long and black, rock-and-roll hair. His weight is still 175. His height is still 5' 10" in any program, 5' 9" in stocking feet, about 2' 11" in the estimation of most NFL scouts. He looks no different from the way he did in 1984, when he was a Boston College quarterback, when he made a miracle pass in Miami, when he stood behind the Heisman Trophy at the Downtown Athletic Club. He feels no different. He's free from chronic injury, and even after 12 seasons of professional football on six teams in three leagues in two countries, his knees are intact.

The place is still the same: his hometown, Natick. His parents have moved to Florida, and he has moved into a big house (with a full-sized basketball court) designed by his wife, Laurie, but he still goes to the same bank, eats in the same restaurants, shops in the same stores. He still has the same friends.

The eeriest aspect of a life that appears frozen in time is his career. He is back at the beginning. The misconceptions and preconceptions, the computer-printout prejudices that he has battled all these years, that he quieted with eight seasons of excellence in the Canadian Football League, have returned. *Too small. Too short. Too . . . too something. Can't play. Can't survive. Can't.* He is back in the NFL, back behind some other quarterback on the depth chart. He is the underdog again, this time with the Buffalo Bills.

"Do you think you'll get a chance in Buffalo?" he is asked.

"We'll see," the 35-year-old teenager replies, as he moves to the next event in his teenager's day. "All I can worry about is me. The rest will be decided by other people."

He knows the rules. He has been here before.

"I could retire tomorrow and be perfectly happy," Flutie says. "Well, 90 percent happy."

The NFL is his one bit of unfinished business. He was the best college player in the country his senior year. He was the best player in CFL history, winner of six Most Outstanding Player awards in eight years, quarterback of three Grey Cup champions, holder of most of the league's passing records. Even in the old USFL, as quarterback of the New Jersey Generals in 1985, he was a diamond in Donald Trump's little showcase.

Only the NFL has resisted his scrambling, free-form charm, the sight of a little man weaving through fat-boy peril to complete passes on the run. By signing with the Bills in January, by taking a pay cut from the $1 million he made last year in Canada to the NFL minimum $275,000 plus a $50,000 signing bonus and incentives, by surrendering all-out control of the show in Toronto with the defending-champion Argonauts to stand behind recently acquired Buffalo quarterback Rob Johnson, Flutie has given himself one more chance. . . .

DAMIAN STROHMEYER

Riddell
Wilson
7

78

1955 | BROWNS QUARTERBACK Otto Graham scored the last touchdown of his 10-year career in Cleveland's 38–14 title game win over the Rams | *Photograph by* AP

66
80

A GAME NO ONE SHOULD HAVE LOST

BY JOHN UNDERWOOD

In the muggy heat of Miami's Orange Bowl, two heavyweight offenses exchanged body blows for five quarters . . . and then staggered to the sidelines to watch as a kicker decided their fates in the greatest game ever played. —*from* SI, JANUARY 11, 1982

IT IS THE ONE GREAT IRONY of professional football that magnificent games such as San Diego's wonderful, woeful 41–38 overtime AFC playoff victory over Miami are almost always decided by the wrong guys. Decided not by heroic, bloodied men who play themselves to exhaustion and perform breathtaking feats, but by men in clean jerseys. Men with names you cannot spell, and the remnants of European accents, and slender bodies and mystical ways. Men who cannot be coached, only traded. Men whose main objective in life, more often than not, is to avoid the crushing embarrassment of a shanked field goal in the last 30 seconds.

There, at the end, in a moist, numbed Orange Bowl, still jammed with disbelievers after 74 minutes and 1,030 yards and 79 points of what San Diego coach Don Coryell called "probably the most exciting game in the history of pro football," was Dan Fouts. Heroic, bloodied Fouts, the nonpareil Charger quarterback. His black beard and white jersey crusted with dirt. His skinny legs so tired they could barely carry him off the field after he had thrown, how many? A playoff-record 53 passes? And completed, how many? A playoff-record 33? For a playoff-record 433 yards? And three touchdowns?

Ah, Fouts. The guy Otto Graham says activates "the greatest offense" in pro football history. (Outrageous comparisons are a dime a dozen around the Chargers these days.) Fouts sets records with every other breath. If he'd only pay his union dues, what a terrific fellow he would be. Fouts should have decided this game.

Or Kellen Winslow. There, at the end, his magnificent body battered and blued by a relentless—if not altogether cohesive—Miami defense, Winslow *had* to be carried off. Time after time during the game he was helped to the sidelines, and then, finally, all the way to the dressing room, the last man to make the postgame celebration. Staggering, sore-shouldered, one-more-play-and-let-me-lie-down Winslow, looking as if he might die any minute (the only sure way he could have been stopped), catching, how many? A playoff-record 16 passes? For a playoff-record 166 yards?

Winslow is listed as a tight end. The Dolphins know better. Like the 800-pound gorilla, Winslow plays just about wherever he wants to play: tight end, wide receiver, fullback, wingback, slotback. Even on defense, as Miami discovered when he blocked what would have been the winning field goal and thereby spoiled what Dolphin guard Ed Newman called—another drum roll, please—"the greatest comeback in the history of professional football." Winslow should have decided this game.

Or there, on the other side, Don Strock, the gutty, heroic Miami relief pitcher. Strock coming in with the Dolphins submerged at 0–24 and not only matching Smilin' Dan pass for pass, but doing him better than that for so long a stretch that it looked for sure the Dolphins would pull it out. Throwing for 397 yards and *four* touchdowns, and getting Miami ahead and into a position to win at 38–31, and then at the threshold of victory twice again at 38–38. In the end, breakdowns not of his doing cost Strock exactly what Newman said it would have been—the greatest playoff comeback in the NFL's history. "Strock," said Fouts, "was awesome." Strock should have decided this game.

Fittingly, all of the above helped make it what Fouts himself called "the greatest game I ever played in." (See? It's catching.) But, typically, none of them had even a bit part in the final scene. Overtime games almost always come to that because in overtime the objective shifts to a totally conservative aim: The first team close enough tries a field goal. Be cool, play it straight, pop it in. Thus, after a day-into-night parade of exquisite offensive plots and ploys, the final blow was a comparative feather duster, struck by a former 123-pound weakling in a dry, spotless uniform. After the haymakers that kept the old bowl rocking for almost four hours, it was a finishing jab that buckled the Dolphins. A tidy little 29-yard love tap that Rolf Benirschke put slightly right of center, 13 minutes and 52 seconds into overtime. . . .

WINSLOW (80) WAS helped to the sidelines repeatedly, then finally carried from the field before the Chargers beat the Dolphins in overtime.

AL MESSERSCHMIDT/WIREIMAGE

1943 | SID LUCKMAN threw for seven touchdowns in this game against the Giants, a record that still stands | *Photograph by* CHICAGO TRIBUNE

1995 | STEVE YOUNG quarterbacked the 49ers to a 38–28 win over the Cowboys to advance to the Super Bowl—where they drubbed the Chargers | *Photograph by* V.J. LOVERO

8
HENNINGS
95
JEFFCOAT
COWBOYS
U
103

1999 | TITANS QB Steve McNair paid a high price to reach paydirt against the Steelers. | *Photograph by* AL TIELEMANS

Titans
Radio 1045

from BLITZES | BY PAUL ZIMMERMAN
SI September 17, 1984

THERE ARE BLITZES AND THERE are blitzes. There are safety blitzes and delayed blitzes; there are blitzes that look like blintzes because they're so ineffective. Then there are Lawrence Taylor blitzes. ❧ They are like nothing else in the NFL, or any other FL. They are like messages from Thor, or as Taylor's former New York Giant teammate Beasley Reece once said, "When Lawrence is coming, you can hear sirens going off."

Random House's unabridged dictionary defines a blitz this way: "War waged by surprise, swiftly and violently, as by the use of aircraft, tanks, etc." Etcetera stands for Lawrence Taylor.

Swiftly? Yes. The Giants' right outside linebacker runs a 4.5 40, a time no man who stands 6' 3" and weighs 243 pounds should be allowed to run. Gary Hogeboom, the young Dallas quarterback who went down three times in a game last Sunday under Taylor blitzes, said, "I never saw him coming." And Doug Cosbie, the tight end who tried to block Taylor, said, "When you're four yards away from him, what can you do? He's too quick."

In 1981, when Taylor burst into the league from the University of North Carolina, a running back was assigned to pick up his blitzes—the conventional blocker-blockee relationship. Taylor was too fast, too strong and too nasty for that matchup. Better use the big people on him. The 49ers solved the problem in a playoff game. They had a 265-pound guard, John Ayers, peeling off to pick up Taylor, and they got a standoff out of it.

Back to the drawing board went Bill Parcells, then the defensive coordinator, now the Giants' head coach: You want to pull a guard and leave a hole in the middle? Fine. We'll send other people through it. Or maybe we'll send Taylor on a wide, looping rush and make a footrace out of it.

The 49ers' guard idea was soon mothballed, and various combinations of two or more blockers were assigned to Taylor. Sure, we're tying up a lot of people, the offensive coaches said, but it's better than having to face the quarterback's parents the next day. . . .

1985 | TAYLOR LOWERED the boom on Dallas' Gary Hogeboom—and just about every other QB in the league | *Photograph by* JOHN BIEVER

56
56
56

COWBOYS
SAINTS
QTR
DOWN
TO GO
BALL ON
American Airlines
DEJA BLUE

1994 | THE BROWNS' Eric Metcalf hit his celebratory stride to end a 92-yard punt return for a TD against the Bengals | *Photograph by* PATRICK MURPHY-RACEY

2004 | END ZONE seats at Texas Stadium took a turn for the better when the Dallas Cowboys cheerleaders got behind their team | *Photograph by* BILL FRAKES

COURTESY OF THE PRO FOOTBALL HALL OF FAME

1895 | THERE WERE no shoulder pads in the game's early days; the only shock absorbers were a heavy canvas vest and jacket | *Photograph by* DAVID N. BERKWITZ

1930 | THE BEARS' backfield of Red Grange (left) and Bronko Nagurski was one of the league's great attractions | *Photograph by* AP

28

2002 | **JETS WIDEOUT** Laveranues Coles was third in line, but he was still able to make a touchdown catch in Foxboro | *Photograph by* EZRA SHAW

2004 | **STEELERS CORNERBACK** Ike Taylor picked off a Tom Brady pass intended for the Patriots' Bethel Johnson in Pittsburgh | *Photograph by* JOHN BIEVER

GETTING NOWHERE FAST

BY ROBERT F. JONES

They call it hard living, but it looked awfully easy when Kenny Stabler did it. —*from* SI, SEPTEMBER 19, 1977

THE BIG KNUCKLES bulge around a beaded can of beer, second of the morning though it is scarcely 9 a.m. "This is home," says Kenny Stabler. "I'll die here." The flat tone of the statement, issuing as it does from a face masked by a grizzled brown beard and mirrored sunglasses, raises questions. Does the premier quarterback of the NFL, the 1976 MVP, the star of Super Bowl XI, whose deft passes and clever calls eviscerated the Minnesota Vikings, mean that he's outgrown his hometown? That the rustic pleasures of Foley, Ala. (pop. 4,000) are beginning to pall? That he would die of boredom if he had to live here year-round?

Not a bit.

"I love this place," says Stabler, gunning the motor as he hits the edge of town. "It's got everything I'll ever need. Come on, let's get some beer and go for a boat ride."

A week with Stabler shot by like a long wet blur. Through it ran the sounds of Stablerian pleasure: the steady gurgle of upturned beer bottles, the clack and thunk of pool balls, the snarl of outboard motors, the whiny cadences of country music. At the end of it, anyone following in Stabler's wake would be ready for a body transplant: liver and lights, heart and kidneys, eardrums—maybe even a few new teeth.

It began in Memphis, where Stabler was expected to perform in the pro-am of the Danny Thomas-Memphis Classic. Stabler was waiting at the airport. He was, of course, in the bar. He had been there since noon. It was now close to 5 p.m. Surrounded by reeling pals, beautiful girls and an array of empty or partially drained glassware—beer bottles, Bloody Marys, Salty Dogs, Seven and Sevens—he grinned at a newcomer. "You're late," he exulted. "Thank God. Here"—he unwrapped his thick left arm from a petite blonde, who emerged like a bauble from the shadow of his armpit—"meet Wanda." She smiled demurely, then stuck out her tongue.

The next morning a caravan of Continental Mark Vs wound erratically through southeastern Memphis. "Where the hayull is the golf course?" snarled a Southern voice. "Danged if *Ah* know," answered another. "Turn on the goldurned *ayer* conditioner," gasped a third. "It's runnin' full blast, you knucklehead," was the response.

"Wayull, shore," continued Bear Bryant, as if he hadn't been interrupted. "Ah remember that boy. He looked like a good 'un but he always left his football game in some parked car the night before we played. Ah remember that Auburn game in. . . ." Bryant, Stabler's coach during his college All-America days at Alabama, was paired with Stabler for the pro-am. His deep, hoarse, mellifluous voice, eroded by hard living and the football wars of a quarter of a century, filled the car with meaningless magic, reminiscence. Stabler giggled like a schoolboy at the great man's mots.

Later, under a scorching sun, Stabler, his shots snaking into the rough, pleaded "migraine" and quit short of nine holes. "Hayull," grumped Bear in mock chagrin as Kenny was departing for the clubhouse. "Ah was gonna pull that one myself but you beat me to it."

STABLER IS now dining at a Gulf Shores squat-'n-gobble. Wanda at his side, before him his third Scotch of the meal and a heaping plate of scampi in garlic sauce. "Scotch and scampi," he crows between chomps. "I love 'em. Johnnie Walker Red. Namath drinks it. Sonny Jurgensen is a Scotch drinker too. Maybe all the great quarterbacks drink Scotch. And I love seafood, particularly these babies." (Munch, crunch, gulp.) "I told Pete Banaszak last season, just after we beat Pittsburgh in the opening game, that I'd eat scampi for 14 weeks in a row if it would guarantee us winning all our games." Like Proust's madeleine, the jumbo shrimp provoke a remembrance of the season past.

"We really didn't know what to expect from the Vikings in the Super Bowl. We knew they were an experienced team, disciplined, and well-coached at all levels, a no-nonsense bunch of guys, straight up, older than us but not necessarily wiser. We didn't think they'd add any new wrinkles for the Super Bowl, and we didn't plan to either. We'd stick with what had worked, what got us there. Some of our guys got up so high that they vomited before the game. I remember Freddie Biletnikoff was tying his shoes over and over again. He'll do it maybe 50 times before a regular-season game, but that day Freddie must have hit 1,000.

"After the game was over, for the first time I felt real happy for myself. I remember thinking that there are only about six quarterbacks who have ever won the Super Bowl, and now I'm one of them. A great feeling, a great release, an ego balloon. Freddie was crying and Coach Madden was all red and grinning and guys were hugging each other like a bunch of fruits and pouring champagne over each other and then I suddenly had this tremendous urge for a great big plate of scampi and a bottle of Johnnie Red." . . .

THE SNAKE led the Raiders to a win over the Steelers in the 1976 AFC Championship game, and then went on to thump the Vikings in Super Bowl XI.

MICHAEL ZAGARIS

Wilson

26

1970 | EIGHT MONTHS after Super Bowl IV, Dave Osborn and the Vikings avenged their loss to Willie Lanier (63) and the Chiefs | *Photograph by* HEINZ KLUETMEIER

1968 | TIGHT COVERAGE by Packers DB Herb Adderley couldn't prevent this catch by the Colts' Willie Richardson in Green Bay | *Photograph by* NEIL LEIFER

1969 | THE BEARS' Dick Butkus made eight straight Pro Bowls and led the Monsters of the Midway in intimidation for nine years | *Photograph by* NEIL LEIFER

1948 | A BLIZZARD in Philadelphia couldn't ground the Eagles, who beat the Chicago Cardinals 7–0 in the title game | *Photograph:* PRO FOOTBALL HALL OF FAME

51

THREE-RING CIRCUS

BY MICHAEL SILVER

The Patriots staked their claim as the century's first dynasty and the Greatest Show on Turf by beating the Eagles for their third NFL title in four seasons. —*from* SI, FEBRUARY 14, 2005

BECAUSE THEY DO NOT beat you over the head with their excellence or beat their chests in triumph, the New England Patriots are forever being cast as commonplace champions. They are great in the way that a chocolate milkshake is great, as poised and proficient as the Beach Boys' doing background harmonies onstage. What we are slowly but surely learning from the Pats as they forge the first football dynasty of the 21st century is that dominance comes in many forms, and that sometimes doing the little things well can provide the biggest satisfaction of all.

As these Patriots keep escaping with three-point victories and kicking dirt on the Super Bowl's heritage of wretched excess, skipping individual pregame introductions and engaging in comparatively low-key locker room celebrations, isn't it time we stop being perplexed by their success? Yes, New England's 24–21 victory over the Philadelphia Eagles in Super Bowl XXXIX on Sunday night in Jacksonville was another testament to teamwork, tenacity and the strategic acumen of coach Bill Belichick and his staff. But in vanquishing a brasher opponent to claim the NFL's ultimate prize for the second consecutive year—and the third time in four seasons, matching the record run of the Dallas Cowboys from 1992 to '95—the Pats' players proved they are even more potent than typically perceived.

"Someday I'm going to have kids and tell them I played on one of the greatest teams of all time, a team with a whole lot of great players," said 11th-year outside linebacker Willie McGinest, whose deployment at defensive end was the key to New England's surprise scheme change for the title game. "You might not call them stars, but they just went out and embarrassed people in the biggest game of their lives, so why wouldn't they be stars? It doesn't matter if we won by three or 103—we don't give a damn if people downplay our accomplishments, because all we want to do is win."

So before the coronation of the plucky Patriots as the team of the decade, let's get this much straight: As they proved again in front of 78,125 fans at Alltel Stadium and an estimated 80 million television viewers worldwide, the Pats are more than Belichick's brain and quarterback Tom Brady's golden right arm. Defenders like McGinest, fellow linebackers Tedy Bruschi and Mike Vrabel and strong safety Rodney Harrison, whose second interception of Donovan McNabb iced the game with nine seconds remaining, showed that they're elite players, while unheralded wideout Deion Branch seized footballs out of the cool night sky and the MVP award from Brady's grasp.

"It's awesome to see a guy like Deion win it," said Brady (23 of 33, 236 yards, two touchdowns), a two-time Super Bowl MVP. "The guy has done everything he can for this team, and this is a team full of guys who cheer for one another. The MVP is nice, but that's not why you play. I'm playing for that diamond ring that's as big as a belt buckle." . . .

TOM BRADY (12) got the most attention, but the Patriots had many stars in Super Bowl XXXIX, including MVP Deion Branch and Tedy Bruschi (above).

PETER READ MILLER; DAMIAN STROHMEYER (BRUSCHI)

Riddell
12
Riddell
67

Team	1920	1921	1922	1923	1924	1925	1926	1927	1928	1929	1930	1931
ARIZONA *Cardinals**	6-2-2	3-3-2	8-3-0	8-4-0	5-4-1	11-2-1	5-6-1	3-7-1	1-5-0	6-6-1	5-6-2	5-4-0
CHICAGO *Bears**	10-1-2	9-1-1	9-3-0	9-2-1	6-1-4	9-5-3	12-1-3	9-3-2	7-5-1	4-9-2	9-4-1	8-5-0
GREEN BAY *Packers*		3-2-1	4-3-3	7-2-1	7-4-0	8-5-0	7-3-3	7-2-1	6-4-3	12-0-1	10-3-1	12-2-0
NEW YORK *Giants*						8-4-0	8-4-1	11-1-1	4-7-2	13-1-1	13-4-0	7-6-1
DETROIT *Lions**											5-6-3	11-3-0
WASHINGTON *Redskins**												
PHILADELPHIA *Eagles*												
PITTSBURGH *Steelers**												
ST. LOUIS *Rams**												
CLEVELAND *Browns*												
SAN FRANCISCO 49*ers*												
INDIANAPOLIS *Colts**												
DALLAS *Cowboys*												
BUFFALO *Bills*												
DENVER *Broncos*												
TENNESSEE *Titans**												
KANSAS CITY *Chiefs**												
OAKLAND *Raiders**												
NEW ENGLAND *Patriots*												
NEW YORK *Jets**												
SAN DIEGO *Chargers**												
MINNESOTA *Vikings*												
ATLANTA *Falcons*												
MIAMI *Dolphins*												
NEW ORLEANS *Saints*												
CINCINNATI *Bengals*												
SEATTLE *Seahawks*												
TAMPA BAY *Buccaneers*												
CAROLINA *Panthers*												
JACKSONVILLE *Jaguars*												
BALTIMORE *Ravens*												
HOUSTON *Texans*												

Team	1932	1933	1934	1935	1936	1937	1938	1939	1940	1941	1942	194
ARIZONA *Cardinals**	2-6-2	1-9-1	5-6-0	6-4-2	3-8-1	5-5-1	2-9-0	1-10-0	2-7-2	3-7-1	3-8-0	0-10
CHICAGO *Bears**	7-1-6	10-2-1	13-0-0	6-4-2	9-3-0	9-1-1	6-5-0	8-3-0	8-3-0	10-1-0	11-0-0	8-1
GREEN BAY *Packers*	10-3-1	5-7-1	7-6-0	8-4-0	10-1-1	7-4-0	8-3-0	9-2-0	6-4-1	10-1-0	8-2-1	7-2
NEW YORK *Giants*	4-6-2	11-3-0	8-5-0	9-3-0	5-6-1	6-3-2	8-2-1	9-1-1	6-4-1	8-3-0	5-5-1	6-3
DETROIT *Lions**	6-2-4	6-5-0	10-3-0	7-3-2	8-4-0	7-4-0	7-4-0	6-5-0	5-5-1	4-6-1	0-11-0	3-6
WASHINGTON *Redskins**	4-4-2	5-5-2	6-6-0	2-8-1	7-5-0	8-3-0	6-3-2	8-2-1	9-2-0	6-5-0	10-1-0	6-3
PHILADELPHIA *Eagles*		3-5-1	4-7-0	2-9-0	1-11-0	2-8-1	5-6-0	1-9-1	1-10-0	2-8-1	2-9-0	5-4
PITTSBURGH *Steelers**		3-6-2	2-10-0	4-8-0	6-6-0	4-7-0	2-9-0	1-9-1	2-7-2	1-9-1	7-4-0	5-4
ST. LOUIS *Rams**						1-10-0	4-7-0	5-5-1	4-6-1	2-9-0	5-6-0	X
CLEVELAND *Browns*												
SAN FRANCISCO 49*ers*												
INDIANAPOLIS *Colts**												
DALLAS *Cowboys*												
BUFFALO *Bills*												
DENVER *Broncos*												
TENNESSEE *Titans**												
KANSAS CITY *Chiefs**												
OAKLAND *Raiders**												
NEW ENGLAND *Patriots*												
NEW YORK *Jets**												
SAN DIEGO *Chargers**												
MINNESOTA *Vikings*												
ATLANTA *Falcons*												
MIAMI *Dolphins*												
NEW ORLEANS *Saints*												
CINCINNATI *Bengals*												
SEATTLE *Seahawks*												
TAMPA BAY *Buccaneers*												
CAROLINA *Panthers*												
JACKSONVILLE *Jaguars*												
BALTIMORE *Ravens*												
HOUSTON *Texans*												

Key

10-5-1	Super Bowl Champions
10-5-1	NFL-NFC Champions
10-5-1	AFL-AFC Champions
10-5-1	AAFC Champions
10-5-1	Members of AAFC
10-5-1	Members of AFL
X	Did not operate
*	Team moved and/or changed name

CHART CONCEPT COURTESY OF THE PRO FOOTBALL HALL OF FAME

Past Teams of the NFL

Team	*Years*	*Record*	*Team*	*Years*	*Record*
CHICAGO *Tigers*	1920	2-5-1	WASHINGTON *Senators*	1921	2-2-0
DETROIT *Heralds*	1920	2-3-3	EVANSVILLE *Crimson Giants*	1921-22	3-5-0
CLEVELAND *Tigers*	1920-21	5-9-2	LOUISVILLE *Brecks***	1921-26	1-12-0
MUNCIE *Flyers*	1920-21	0-3-0	MINNEAPOLIS *Marines***	1921-30	6-33-4
ROCHESTER *Jeffersons*	1920-25	8-27-4	OORANG *Indians*	1922-23	3-16-0
ROCK ISLAND *Independents*	1920-25	27-14-12	TOLEDO *Maroons*	1922-23	8-5-4
AKRON *Pros*	1920-26	27-26-11	MILWAUKEE *Badgers*	1922-26	15-27-6
CANTON *Bulldogs***	1920-26	38-19-11	RACINE *Legion***	1922-26	15-15-6
COLUMBUS *Panhandles*	1920-26	13-45-3	ST. LOUIS *All-Stars*	1923	1-4-2
HAMMOND *Pros*	1920-26	7-28-4	CLEVELAND *Indians***	1923-27	23-14-6
BUFFALO *All-Americans***	1920-29	40-37-12	DULUTH *Kelleys*	1923-27	16-20-3
DAYTON *Triangles*	1920-29	18-51-8	KENOSHA *Maroons*	1924	0-4-1
CINCINNATI *Celts*	1921	1-3-0	KANSAS CITY *Blues*	1924-26	12-15-1
DETROIT *Tigers*	1921	1-5-1	FRANKFORD *Yellow Jackets*	1924-31	69-45-1
NEW YORK *Giants*	1921	0-2-0	DETROIT *Panthers*	1925-26	12-8-4
TONAWANDA *Kardex*	1921	0-1-0	POTTSVILLE *Maroons*	1925-29	31-24-1

Teams of the Decade

by Peter King

1920s

Canton Bulldogs

UNBEATEN IN 1922 AND '23, THE 'DOGS WERE led by two-way tackles Fats Henry and Link Lyman, who controlled both lines. Against the Toledo Maroons in '22, Henry drop-kicked a 50-yard field goal, the longest such kick ever. In 1924, under financial pressure, Canton merged with Cleveland and moved to that city, where the Bulldogs won their third straight championship.

1930s

Green Bay Packers

THEY FOLLOWED A 12-0-1 TITLE SEASON IN 1929 with four championships in the '30s. Wide receiver Don Hutson was the biggest star. Most years the league stacked the deck against the Packers, having them play at home early in the season and on the road in the second half, when the bitter Green Bay weather would have given them another edge. It didn't matter.

1940s

Chicago Bears

THE WINNINGEST FRANCHISE IN NFL HISTORY? THE BEST TIGHT END FROM THE 50S? THE FIRST HELMET LOGO? IT'S ALL HERE, ALONG WITH AMAZING STATS, DR. Z'S ALL-DECADE TEAMS AND THE SEASON-BY-SEASON RECORDS OF EVERY TEAM SINCE THE LEAGUE OPENED FOR BUSINESS IN 1920

The Final Score

1966 | THE MERGER that would join the NFL and the AFL in '70 was more than just a glimmer in commisioner Pete Rozelle's eye when this picture was snapped.

1977	1978	1979	1980	1981	1982	1983	1984	1985	1986	1987	1988	1989	1990	1991	1992	1993	1994	1995	1996	1997	1998	1999	2000	2001	2002	2003	2004
-7-0	6-10-0	5-11-0	5-11-0	7-9-0	5-4-0	8-7-1	9-7-0	5-11-0	4-11-1	7-8-0	7-9-0	5-11-0	5-11-0	4-12-0	4-12-0	7-9-0	8-8-0	4-12-0	7-9-0	4-12-0	9-7-0	6-10-0	3-13-0	7-9-0	5-11-0	4-12-0	6-10-0
-5-0	7-9-0	10-6-0	7-9-0	6-10-0	3-6-0	8-8-0	10-6-0	15-1-0	14-2-0	11-4-0	12-4-0	6-10-0	11-5-0	11-5-0	5-11-0	7-9-0	9-7-0	9-7-0	7-9-0	4-12-0	4-12-0	6-10-0	5-11-0	13-3-0	4-12-0	7-9-0	5-11-0
-10-0	8-7-1	5-11-0	5-10-1	8-8-0	5-3-1	8-8-0	8-8-0	8-8-0	4-12-0	5-9-1	4-12-0	10-6-0	6-10-0	4-12-0	9-7-0	9-7-0	9-7-0	11-5-0	13-3-0	13-3-0	11-5-0	8-8-0	9-7-0	12-4-0	12-4-0	10-6-0	10-6-0
-9-0	6-10-0	6-10-0	4-12-0	9-7-0	4-5-0	3-12-1	9-7-0	10-6-0	14-2-0	6-9-0	10-6-0	12-4-0	13-3-0	8-8-0	6-10-0	11-5-0	9-7-0	5-11-0	6-10-0	10-5-1	8-8-0	7-9-0	12-4-0	7-9-0	10-6-0	4-12-0	6-10-0
-8-0	7-9-0	2-14-0	9-7-0	8-8-0	4-5-0	9-7-0	4-11-1	7-9-0	5-11-0	4-11-0	4-12-0	7-9-0	6-10-0	12-4-0	5-11-0	10-6-0	9-7-0	10-6-0	5-11-0	9-7-0	5-11-0	8-8-0	9-7-0	2-14-0	3-13-0	5-11-0	6-10-0
-5-0	8-8-0	10-6-0	6-10-0	8-8-0	8-1-0	14-2-0	11-5-0	10-6-0	12-4-0	11-4-0	7-9-0	10-6-0	10-6-0	14-2-0	9-7-0	4-12-0	3-13-0	6-10-0	9-7-0	8-7-1	6-10-0	10-6-0	8-8-0	8-8-0	7-9-0	5-11-0	6-10-0
-9-0	9-7-0	11-5-0	12-4-0	10-6-0	3-6-0	5-11-0	6-9-1	7-9-0	5-10-1	7-8-0	10-6-0	11-5-0	10-6-0	10-6-0	11-5-0	8-8-0	7-9-0	10-6-0	10-6-0	6-9-1	3-13-0	5-11-0	11-5-0	11-5-0	12-4-0	12-4-0	13-3-0
-5-0	14-2-0	12-4-0	9-7-0	8-8-0	6-3-0	10-6-0	9-7-0	7-9-0	6-10-0	8-7-0	5-11-0	9-7-0	9-7-0	7-9-0	11-5-0	9-7-0	12-4-0	11-5-0	10-6-0	11-5-0	7-9-0	6-10-0	9-7-0	13-3-0	10-5-1	6-10-0	15-1-0
)-4-0	12-4-0	9-7-0	11-5-0	6-10-0	2-7-0	9-7-0	10-6-0	11-5-0	10-6-0	6-9-0	10-6-0	11-5-0	5-11-0	3-13-0	6-10-0	5-11-0	4-12-0	7-9-0	6-10-0	5-11-0	4-12-0	13-3-0	10-6-0	14-2-0	7-9-0	12-4-0	8-8-0
-8-0	8-8-0	9-7-0	11-5-0	5-11-0	4-5-0	9-7-0	5-11-0	8-8-0	12-4-0	10-5-0	10-6-0	9-6-1	3-13-0	6-10-0	7-9-0	7-9-0	11-5-0	5-11-0	X	X	X	2-14-0	3-13-0	7-9-0	9-7-0	5-11-0	4-12-0
-9-0	2-14-0	2-14-0	6-10-0	13-3-0	3-6-0	10-6-0	15-1-0	10-6-0	10-5-1	13-2-0	10-6-0	14-2-0	14-2-0	10-6-0	14-2-0	10-6-0	13-3-0	11-5-0	12-4-0	13-3-0	12-4-0	4-12-0	6-10-0	12-4-0	10-6-0	7-9-0	2-14-0
)-4-0	5-11-0	5-11-0	7-9-0	2-14-0	0-8-1	7-9-0	4-12-0	5-11-0	3-13-0	9-6-0	9-7-0	8-8-0	7-9-0	1-15-0	9-7-0	4-12-0	8-8-0	9-7-0	9-7-0	3-13-0	3-13-0	13-3-0	10-6-0	6-10-0	10-6-0	12-4-0	12-4-0
2-2-0	12-4-0	11-5-0	12-4-0	12-4-0	6-3-0	12-4-0	9-7-0	10-6-0	7-9-0	7-8-0	3-13-0	1-15-0	7-9-0	11-5-0	13-3-0	12-4-0	12-4-0	12-4-0	10-6-0	6-10-0	10-6-0	8-8-0	5-11-0	5-11-0	5-11-0	10-6-0	6-10-0
-11-0	5-11-0	7-9-0	11-5-0	10-6-0	4-5-0	8-8-0	2-14-0	2-14-0	4-12-0	7-8-0	12-4-0	9-7-0	13-3-0	13-3-0	11-5-0	12-4-0	7-9-0	10-6-0	10-6-0	6-10-0	10-6-0	11-5-0	8-8-0	3-13-0	8-8-0	6-10-0	9-7-0
2-2-0	10-6-0	10-6-0	8-8-0	10-6-0	2-7-0	9-7-0	13-3-0	11-5-0	11-5-0	10-4-1	8-8-0	11-5-0	5-11-0	12-4-0	8-8-0	9-7-0	7-9-0	8-8-0	13-3-0	12-4-0	14-2-0	6-10-0	11-5-0	8-8-0	9-7-0	10-6-0	10-6-0
-6-0	10-6-0	11-5-0	11-5-0	7-9-0	1-8-0	2-14-0	3-13-0	5-11-0	5-11-0	9-6-0	10-6-0	9-7-0	9-7-0	11-5-0	10-6-0	12-4-0	2-14-0	7-9-0	8-8-0	8-8-0	8-8-0	13-3-0	13-3-0	7-9-0	11-5-0	12-4-0	5-11-0
-12-0	4-12-0	7-9-0	8-8-0	9-7-0	3-6-0	6-10-0	8-8-0	6-10-0	10-6-0	4-11-0	4-11-1	8-7-1	11-5-0	10-6-0	10-6-0	11-5-0	9-7-0	13-3-0	9-7-0	13-3-0	7-9-0	9-7-0	7-9-0	6-10-0	8-8-0	13-3-0	7-9-0
-3-0	9-7-0	9-7-0	11-5-0	7-9-0	8-1-0	12-4-0	11-5-0	12-4-0	8-8-0	5-10-0	7-9-0	8-8-0	12-4-0	9-7-0	7-9-0	10-6-0	9-7-0	8-8-0	7-9-0	4-12-0	8-8-0	8-8-0	12-4-0	10-6-0	11-5-0	4-12-0	5-11-0
-5-0	11-5-0	9-7-0	10-6-0	2-14-0	5-4-0	8-8-0	9-7-0	11-5-0	11-5-0	8-7-0	9-7-0	5-11-0	1-15-0	6-10-0	2-14-0	5-11-0	10-6-0	6-10-0	11-5-0	10-6-0	9-7-0	8-8-0	5-11-0	11-5-0	9-7-0	14-2-0	14-2-0
-11-0	8-8-0	8-8-0	4-12-0	10-5-1	6-3-0	7-9-0	7-9-0	11-5-0	10-6-0	6-9-0	8-7-1	4-12-0	6-10-0	8-8-0	4-12-0	8-8-0	6-10-0	3-13-0	1-15-0	9-7-0	12-4-0	8-8-0	9-7-0	10-6-0	9-7-0	6-10-0	10-6-0
7-7-0	9-7-0	12-4-0	11-5-0	10-6-0	6-3-0	6-10-0	7-9-0	8-8-0	4-12-0	8-7-0	6-10-0	6-10-0	6-10-0	4-12-0	11-5-0	8-8-0	11-5-0	9-7-0	8-8-0	4-12-0	5-11-0	8-8-0	1-15-0	5-11-0	8-8-0	4-12-0	12-4-0
)-5-0	8-7-1	7-9-0	9-7-0	7-9-0	5-4-0	8-8-0	3-13-0	7-9-0	9-7-0	8-7-0	11-5-0	10-6-0	6-10-0	8-8-0	11-5-0	9-7-0	10-6-0	8-8-0	9-7-0	9-7-0	15-1-0	10-6-0	11-5-0	5-11-0	6-10-0	9-7-0	8-8-0
7-7-0	9-7-0	6-10-0	12-4-0	7-9-0	5-4-0	7-9-0	4-12-0	4-12-0	7-8-1	3-12-0	5-11-0	3-13-0	5-11-0	10-6-0	6-10-0	6-10-0	7-9-0	9-7-0	3-13-0	7-9-0	14-2-0	5-11-0	4-12-0	7-9-0	9-6-1	5-11-0	11-5-0
)-4-0	11-5-0	10-6-0	8-8-0	11-4-1	7-2-0	12-4-0	14-2-0	12-4-0	8-8-0	8-7-0	6-10-0	8-8-0	12-4-0	8-8-0	11-5-0	9-7-0	10-6-0	9-7-0	8-8-0	9-7-0	10-6-0	9-7-0	11-5-0	11-5-0	9-7-0	10-6-0	4-12-0
-11-0	7-9-0	8-8-0	1-15-0	4-12-0	4-5-0	8-8-0	7-9-0	5-11-0	7-9-0	12-3-0	10-6-0	9-7-0	8-8-0	11-5-0	12-4-0	8-8-0	7-9-0	7-9-0	3-13-0	6-10-0	6-10-0	3-13-0	10-6-0	7-9-0	9-7-0	8-8-0	8-8-0
3-6-0	4-12-0	4-12-0	6-10-0	12-4-0	7-2-0	7-9-0	8-8-0	7-9-0	10-6-0	4-11-0	12-4-0	8-8-0	9-7-0	3-13-0	5-11-0	3-13-0	3-13-0	7-9-0	8-8-0	7-9-0	3-13-0	4-12-0	4-12-0	6-10-0	2-14-0	8-8-0	8-8-0
-9-0	9-7-0	9-7-0	4-12-0	6-10-0	4-5-0	9-7-0	12-4-0	8-8-0	10-6-0	9-6-0	9-7-0	7-9-0	9-7-0	7-9-0	2-14-0	6-10-0	6-10-0	8-8-0	7-9-0	8-8-0	8-8-0	9-7-0	6-10-0	9-7-0	7-9-0	10-6-0	9-7-0
-12-0	5-11-0	10-6-0	5-10-1	9-7-0	5-4-0	2-14-0	6-10-0	2-14-0	2-14-0	4-11-0	5-11-0	5-11-0	6-10-0	3-13-0	5-11-0	5-11-0	6-10-0	7-9-0	6-10-0	10-6-0	8-8-0	11-5-0	10-6-0	9-7-0	12-4-0	7-9-0	5-11-0
																		7-9-0	12-4-0	7-9-0	4-12-0	8-8-0	7-9-0	1-15-0	7-9-0	11-5-0	7-9-0
																		4-12-0	9-7-0	11-5-0	11-5-0	14-2-0	7-9-0	6-10-0	6-10-0	5-11-0	9-7-0
																			4-12-0	6-9-1	6-10-0	8-8-0	12-4-0	10-6-0	7-9-0	10-6-0	9-7-0
																									4-12-0	5-11-0	7-9-0

MS IN THE AFC,
e of the alltime
owls in a six-year
win?" linebacker
an all-star team."
to that Steelers
the Hall of Fame,
ny other dynasty.

1980s
San Francisco 49ers

JUST LIKE THE STEELERS OF THE 1970S, they made four trips to the Super Bowl in a decade, winning every time. One of their strengths was the ability to rebuild on the fly, drafting Jerry Rice in 1985 and trading for the rights to Steve Young in '87. Moves like those allowed the 49ers to sustain greatness as few teams have.

1990s
Dallas Cowboys

WITH FREE AGENCY AND THE NEWFANGLED salary cap taking hold, the Cowboys collected draft picks and stars better than any other franchise. Coach and team architect Jimmy Johnson, who was around for the first two titles, rubbed half the league the wrong way with his brashness, but Dallas won three Super Bowls in a four-year period by a combined 62 points.

2000s
New England

MOST SAID IT COULD not be done in the era of parity and the salary cap. But the resourceful Patriots won three Super Bowls titles in a four-year span, in dominating and diverse fashion.

SHOSTAK STUDIOS

1944	1945	1946	1947	1948	1949	1950	1951	1952	1953	1954	1955	1956	1957	1958	1959	1960	1961	1962	1963	1964	1965	1966	1967	1968	1969	1970	1971	1972	1973	1974	1975	1976
-10-0	1-9-0	6-5-0	9-3-0	11-1-0	6-5-1	5-7-0	3-9-0	4-8-0	1-10-1	2-10-0	4-7-1	7-5-0	3-9-0	2-9-1	2-10-0	6-5-1	7-7-0	4-9-1	9-5-0	9-3-2	5-9-0	8-5-1	6-7-1	9-4-1	4-9-1	8-5-1	4-9-1	4-9-1	4-9-1	10-4-0	11-3-0	10-4-0
6-3-1	3-7-0	8-2-1	8-4-0	10-2-0	9-3-0	9-3-0	7-5-0	5-7-0	3-8-1	8-4-0	8-4-0	9-2-1	5-7-0	8-4-0	8-4-0	5-6-1	8-6-0	9-5-0	11-1-2	5-9-0	9-5-0	5-7-2	7-6-1	7-7-0	1-13-0	6-8-0	6-8-0	4-9-1	3-11-0	4-10-0	4-10-0	7-7-0
-2-0	6-4-0	6-5-0	6-5-1	3-9-0	2-10-0	3-9-0	3-9-0	6-6-0	2-9-1	4-8-0	6-6-0	4-8-0	3-9-0	1-10-1	7-5-0	8-4-0	11-3-0	13-1-0	11-2-1	8-5-1	10-3-1	12-2-0	9-4-1	6-7-1	8-6-0	6-8-0	4-8-2	10-4-0	5-7-2	6-8-0	4-10-0	5-9-0
8-1-1	3-6-1	7-3-1	2-8-2	4-8-0	6-6-0	10-2-0	9-2-1	7-5-0	3-9-0	7-5-0	6-5-1	8-3-1	7-5-0	9-3-0	10-2-0	6-4-2	10-3-1	12-2-0	11-3-0	2-10-2	7-7-0	1-12-1	7-7-0	7-7-0	6-8-0	9-5-0	4-10-0	8-6-0	2-11-1	2-12-0	5-9-0	3-11-0
6-3-1	7-3-0	1-10-0	3-9-0	2-10-0	4-8-0	6-6-0	7-4-1	9-3-0	10-2-0	9-2-1	3-9-0	9-3-0	8-4-0	4-7-1	3-8-1	7-5-0	8-5-1	11-3-0	5-8-1	7-5-2	6-7-1	4-9-1	5-7-2	4-8-2	9-4-1	10-4-0	7-6-1	8-5-1	6-7-1	7-7-0	7-7-0	6-8-0
6-3-1	8-2-0	5-5-1	4-8-0	7-5-0	4-7-1	3-9-0	5-7-0	4-8-0	6-5-1	3-9-0	8-4-0	6-6-0	5-6-1	4-7-1	3-9-0	1-9-2	1-12-1	5-7-2	3-11-0	6-8-0	6-8-0	7-7-0	5-6-3	5-9-0	7-5-2	6-8-0	9-4-1	11-3-0	10-4-0	10-4-0	8-6-0	10-4-0
7-1-2	7-3-0	6-5-0	8-4-0	9-2-1	11-1-0	6-6-0	4-8-0	7-5-0	7-4-1	7-4-1	4-7-1	3-8-1	4-8-0	2-9-1	7-5-0	10-2-0	10-4-0	3-10-1	2-10-2	6-8-0	5-9-0	9-5-0	6-7-1	2-12-0	4-9-1	3-10-1	6-7-1	2-11-1	5-8-1	7-7-0	4-10-0	4-10-0
-10-0	2-8-0	5-5-1	8-4-0	4-8-0	6-5-1	6-6-0	4-7-1	5-7-0	6-6-0	5-7-0	4-8-0	5-7-0	6-6-0	7-4-1	6-5-1	5-6-1	6-8-0	9-5-0	7-4-3	5-9-0	2-12-0	5-8-1	4-9-1	2-11-1	1-13-0	5-9-0	6-8-0	11-3-0	10-4-0	10-3-1	12-2-0	10-4-0
-6-0	9-1-0	6-4-1	6-6-0	6-5-1	8-2-2	9-3-0	8-4-0	9-3-0	8-3-1	6-5-1	8-3-1	4-8-0	6-6-0	8-4-0	2-10-0	4-7-1	4-10-0	1-12-1	5-9-0	5-7-2	4-10-0	8-6-0	11-1-2	10-3-1	11-3-0	9-4-1	8-5-1	6-7-1	12-2-0	10-4-0	12-2-0	10-3-1
		12-2-0	12-1-1	14-0-0	9-1-2	10-2-0	11-1-0	8-4-0	11-1-0	9-3-0	9-2-1	5-7-0	9-2-1	9-3-0	7-5-0	8-3-1	8-5-1	7-6-1	10-4-0	10-3-1	11-3-0	9-5-0	9-5-0	10-4-0	10-3-1	7-7-0	9-5-0	10-4-0	7-5-2	4-10-0	3-11-0	9-5-0
		9-5-0	8-4-2	12-2-0	9-3-0	3-9-0	7-4-1	7-5-0	9-3-0	7-4-1	4-8-0	5-6-1	8-4-0	6-6-0	7-5-0	7-5-0	7-6-1	6-8-0	2-12-0	4-10-0	7-6-1	6-6-2	7-7-0	7-6-1	4-8-2	10-3-1	9-5-0	8-5-1	5-9-0	6-8-0	5-9-0	8-6-0
									3-9-0	3-9-0	5-6-1	5-7-0	7-5-0	9-3-0	9-3-0	6-6-0	8-6-0	7-7-0	8-6-0	12-2-0	10-3-1	9-5-0	11-1-2	13-1-0	8-5-1	11-2-1	10-4-0	5-9-0	4-10-0	2-12-0	10-4-0	11-3-0
																0-11-0	4-9-1	5-8-1	4-10-0	5-8-1	7-7-0	10-3-1	9-5-0	12-2-0	11-2-1	10-4-0	11-3-0	10-4-0	10-4-0	8-6-0	10-4-0	11-3-0
																5-8-1	6-8-0	7-6-1	7-6-1	12-2-0	10-3-1	9-4-1	4-10-0	1-12-1	4-10-0	3-10-1	1-13-0	4-9-1	9-5-0	9-5-0	8-6-0	2-12-0
																4-9-1	3-11-0	7-7-0	2-11-1	2-11-1	4-10-0	4-10-0	3-11-0	5-9-0	5-8-1	5-8-1	4-9-1	5-9-0	7-5-2	7-6-1	6-8-0	9-5-0
																10-4-0	10-3-1	11-3-0	6-8-0	4-10-0	4-10-0	3-11-0	9-4-1	7-7-0	6-6-2	3-10-1	4-9-1	1-13-0	1-13-0	7-7-0	10-4-0	5-9-0
																8-6-0	6-8-0	11-3-0	5-7-2	7-7-0	7-5-2	11-2-1	9-5-0	12-2-0	11-3-0	7-5-2	10-3-1	8-6-0	7-5-2	5-9-0	5-9-0	5-9-0
																6-8-0	2-12-0	1-13-0	10-4-0	5-7-2	8-5-1	8-5-1	13-1-0	12-2-0	12-1-1	8-4-2	8-4-2	10-3-1	9-4-1	12-2-0	11-3-0	13-1-0
																5-9-0	9-4-1	9-4-1	7-6-1	10-3-1	4-8-2	8-4-2	3-10-1	4-10-0	4-10-0	2-12-0	6-8-0	3-11-0	5-9-0	7-7-0	3-11-0	11-3-0
																7-7-0	7-7-0	5-9-0	5-8-1	5-8-1	5-8-1	6-6-2	8-5-1	11-3-0	10-4-0	4-10-0	6-8-0	7-7-0	4-10-0	7-7-0	3-11-0	3-11-0
																10-4-0	12-2-0	4-10-0	11-3-0	8-5-1	9-2-3	7-6-1	8-5-1	9-5-0	8-6-0	5-6-3	6-8-0	4-9-1	2-11-1	5-9-0	2-12-0	6-8-0
																	3-11-0	2-11-1	5-8-1	8-5-1	7-7-0	4-9-1	3-8-3	8-6-0	12-2-0	12-2-0	11-3-0	7-7-0	12-2-0	10-4-0	12-2-0	11-2-1
																						3-11-0	1-12-1	2-12-0	6-8-0	4-8-2	7-6-1	7-7-0	9-5-0	3-11-0	4-10-0	4-10-0
																						3-11-0	4-10-0	5-8-1	3-10-1	10-4-0	10-3-1	14-0-0	12-2-0	11-3-0	10-4-0	6-8-0
																							3-11-0	4-9-1	5-9-0	2-11-1	4-8-2	2-11-1	5-9-0	5-9-0	2-12-0	4-10-0
																								3-11-0	4-9-1	8-6-0	4-10-0	8-6-0	10-4-0	7-7-0	11-3-0	10-4-0
																																2-12-0
																																0-14-0

Team	*Years*	*Record*
Providence *Steam Roller*	1925-31	41-32-11
Brooklyn *Lions*	1926	3-8-0
Hartford *Blues*	1926	3-7-0
Los Angeles *Buccaneers*	1926	6-3-1
New York *Yankees*	1927-28	11-16-2
Detroit *Wolverines*	1928	7-2-1
Orange *Tornadoes*	1929-30	4-14-5
Staten Island *Stapletons*	1929-32	14-22-9
Brooklyn *Dodgers*	1930-44	60-100-9
Cleveland *Indians*	1931	2-8-0
Cincinnati *Reds*	1933-34	3-14-1
St. Louis *Gunners*	1934	1-2-0
New York *Bulldogs*	1949-51	9-24-3
Boston *Yanks*	1944-48	14-38-3
Baltimore *Colts*	1950	1-11-0
Dallas *Texans*	1952	1-11-0

** *Did not play every season*

HE FIRST OF THEIR FOUR TITLES IN THE ecade was the most amazing. Three weeks fter losing to the Redskins 7–3, the Bears turned to D.C. and waxed them 73–0 for the hampionship. In 1942 Chicago was 5–0 hen coach George Halas left for military uty. The Bears lost to Washington, then beat e Redskins for the '43 title. What a rivalry.

1950s

Cleveland Browns

AFTER WINNING ALL FOUR ALL-AMERICA Football Conference titles to close the '40s, the Browns were one of three AAFC franchises to merge with the NFL in '50. With Otto Graham at QB, they continued their dominance, earning a trip to the title game the first six years and winning it all in '50, '54 and '55. Paul Brown's Browns were arguably the best team of all time.

1960s

Green Bay Packers

"YOU WILL MAKE MISTAKES," VINCE Lombardi told his players upon taking over a poor team in 1959, "but not very many if you want to play for the Green Bay Packers." Lombardi kept 14 starters from a team that went 1-10-1 in '58 and won the first of his five titles in '61. The Packers are the only team in the last 70 years to win three titles in a row.

1970s

Pittsburgh Steelers

WITH SO MANY GOOD TE the Steelers had to be o greats to win four Super B period. "How could you no Andy Russell said. "We had In all, 12 men connected club have been elected to a number unsurpassed by a

> Time Capsule THE 40s

1948 | STEVE VAN BUREN (15), led the league in rushing yardage and touchdowns in four of his eight seasons with the Eagles.

AP/WIDE WORLD PHOTOS; COURTESY OF LIZ CLARE (WEDEMAYER)

> DR. Z's ALL DECADE TEAMS

1940s

END	HALFBACK	FULLBACK	QUARTERBACK	HALFBACK	END
DON HUTSON	**STEVE VAN BUREN**	**MARION MOTLEY**	**SID LUCKMAN**	**SPEC SANDERS**	**MAC SPEEDIE**
Mal Kutner	Bill Dudley	Norm Standlee	Otto Graham	Tony Canadeo	Jim Benton
Pete Pihos	George McAfee	Buddy Young	Sammy Baugh	Chet Mutryn	Ken Kavanaugh
TACKLE	**GUARD**	**CENTER**	**GUARD**	**TACKLE**	**KICKER**
AL WISTERT	**DANNY FORTMANN**	**BULLDOG TURNER**	**BILL WILLIS**	**BRUISER KINARD**	**HARVEY JOHNSON**
Lou Rymkus	Riley Matheson	Mel Hein	Buster Ramsey	Vic Sears	Ben Agajanian
Al Blozis	Dick Barwegen	Alex Wojciechowicz	Len Younce	Nate Johnson	Bob Waterfield

1920s–30s

END	BLOCKING BACK	TAILBACK	FULLBACK	WINGBACK	END
DON HUTSON	**FATHER LUMPKIN**	**DUTCH CLARK**	**BRONKO NAGURSKI**	**JOHNNY (BLOOD) MCNALLY**	**BILL HEWITT**
Ray Flaherty	Bo Molenda	Benny Friedman	Clarke Hinkle	Ernie Caddel	Lavie Dilweg
Red Badgro	Riley Smith	Cliff Battles	Ernie Nevers	Tony Latone	Dick Plasman
TACKLE	**GUARD**	**CENTER**	**GUARD**	**TACKLE**	**PUNTER-KICKER**
CAL HUBBARD	**DANNY FORTMANN**	**MEL HEIN**	**MIKE MICHALSKE**	**TURK EDWARDS**	**PADDY DRISCOLL**
Turk Edwards	George Musso	George Trafton	Walt Kiesling	Duke Slater	Ken Strong
Wilbur (Fats) Henry	Ed Healey	Joe Alexander	Gus Sonnenberg	Link Lyman	Verne Lewellen

> NFL NEWS

THE 1940 CHAMPIONSHIP GAME, in which the Bears defeat the Redskins 73–0, is the first NFL game broadcast nationally on the radio (Red Barber at the mike). The Mutual Broadcasting System paid $2,500 for the rights.

ELMER LAYDEN, Notre Dame's head coach and athletic director, is elected as the NFL's first commissioner, in 1941.

IN 1943 the NFL mandates that every player on the field must wear a helmet.

THE LIONS AND GIANTS play to a 0–0 tie on Nov. 7, 1943 in Detroit, the last scoreless game in NFL history.

BILL DUDLEY of the Steelers wins the 1945 MVP by leading the NFL in rushing, interceptions and punt returns.

THE DEFENDING CHAMPION RAMS move from Cleveland to Los Angeles for the 1946 season.

THE ALL-AMERICA FOOTBALL CONFERENCE begins play in 1946. In a merger four years later, the San Francisco 49ers, Cleveland Browns and Baltimore Colts join the NFL.

IN 1946 Woody Strode and Kenny Washington sign with the Rams to become the first African-Americans to play in the NFL since '33. Marion Motley and Bill Willis break the color barrier in the AAFC that same season, signing with the Browns.

IN 1948 officials other than referees are issued whistles to replace the horns that had been part of their standard equipment.

IN 1948 Rams halfback Fred Gehrke paints horns on his helmet, the first headgear logo in NFL history.

>NICKNAMES<

[Slingin'] Sammy Baugh
Edward [Ty] Coon
Bob [Twenty Grand] Davis
Gil [Cactus Face] Duggan
Nello [Flash] Falaschi
Kenneth [Kayo] Lunday
Earle [Greasy] Neale
Bob [Stoneface] Waterfield
^ [Squirmin] Herman Wedemeyer
Bill [Bubbles] Young

RECORD OF THE DECADE

The Chicago Bears scored 258 points in 1944, placing second in the league—a pedestrian statistic until you consider that those Bears are still the only team since 1938 to play an entire season without attempting a field goal.

> GO FIGURE

50,000 Fee, in dollars, for a franchise to join the National Football League in 1940.

1,000 Rushing total, in yards, surpassed by Steve Van Buren of the Eagles and Tony Canadeo of the Packers in 1949, the first time two runners gained 1,000 yards in the same season.

7 Touchdown passes thrown by Bears quarterback Sid Luckman in a 1943 game against the New York Giants—a record equaled four times.

638 Number of NFL players, coaches and front office personnel who served in the U.S. military during World War II, including 22 who were killed in action.

0 First downs picked up by the Giants in a 1942 game against the Redskins, which New York won, 14–7, Washington's only loss of the season.

47 Number of catches separating Don Hutson (74) and the second leading receiver, Pop Ivy, during the 1942 season.

51.4 Average, in yards, of Sammy Baugh's punts in 1940, still the NFL record.

5 Weeks in 1941 that Buff Donelli coached both the Duquesne University football team and the Pittsburgh Steelers before he was forced to choose by the NFL. He picked Duquesne.

64 Percentage of players in 1949 who worked in the off-season.

7 Field goals made, in 15 tries, in 1949 by Bears rookie kicker George Blanda, who went on to play a record 26 years in the NFL.

DECADE HIGHS

RUSHING
YARDS: 4,904 / STEVE VAN BUREN
TDs: 59 / STEVE VAN BUREN

PASSING
YARDS: 17,002 / SAMMY BAUGH
TDs: 149 / SAMMY BAUGH

RECEIVING
CATCHES: 329 / DON HUTSON
YARDS: 5,089 / DON HUTSON
TDs: 63 / DON HUTSON

SCORING
589 POINTS / DON HUTSON

SEASON HIGHS

RUSHING
YARDS: 1,146 / STEVE VAN BUREN 1949
TDs: 15 / STEVE VAN BUREN 1945

PASSING
YARDS: 2,938 / SAMMY BAUGH 1947
TDs: 28 / SID LUCKMAN 1943

RECEIVING
CATCHES: 77 / TOM FEARS 1949
YARDS: 1,211 / DON HUTSON 1942
TDs: 17 / DON HUTSON 1942

SCORING
138 POINTS / DON HUTSON 1942

GAME HIGHS

RUSHING
205 YARDS / STEVE VAN BUREN 11/27/49

PASSING
468 YARDS / JOHNNY LUJACK 12/11/49

RECEIVING
303 YARDS / JIM BENTON 11/22/45

SCORING
31 POINTS / DON HUTSON, 4 TDs,
7 EXTRA POINTS 10/7/45

> Time Capsule THE 50s

1959 | FRANK GIFFORD earned his ticket to Canton as a multithreat back, piling up more yards receiving than rushing and even throwing for 14 TDs during his Giants career.

NEIL LEIFER; VIC STEIN (HIRSCH)

> DR. Z's ALL DECADE TEAM

OFFENSE

END	HALFBACK	QUARTERBACK	FULLBACK	HALFBACK	END
ELROY HIRSCH	**HUGH McELHENNY**	**JOHNNY UNITAS**	**JIM BROWN**	**FRANK GIFFORD**	**RAYMOND BERRY**
Harlon Hill	Ollie Matson	Otto Graham	Joe Perry	Dan Towler	Billy Wilson
Billy Howton	Lenny Moore	Norm Van Brocklin	Tank Younger	Doak Walker	Tom Fears
GUARD	**TACKLE**	**CENTER**	**TACKLE**	**GUARD**	**KICKER**
DUANE PUTNAM	**MIKE McCORMACK**	**FRANK GATSKI**	**ROOSEVELT BROWN**	**DICK STANFEL**	**LOU GROZA**
Abe Gibron	Jim Parker	Jim Ringo	Lou Creekmur	Dick Barwegen	Fred Cone
Stan Jones	Lou Groza	Bill Johnson	Bob St. Clair	Bruno Banducci	Sam Baker

DEFENSE

HALFBACK	END	TACKLE	TACKLE	END	HALFBACK
DICK (NIGHT TRAIN) LANE	**GINO MARCHETTI**	**ART DONOVAN**	**ERNIE STAUTNER**	**LEN FORD**	**JACK BUTLER**
Tom Landry	Doug Atkins	Gene (Big Daddy) Lipscomb	Leo Nomellini	Andy Robustelli	Jim David
Don Paul	Gene Brito	Arnie Weinmeister	Bob Gain	Norm Willey	Warren Lahr
SAFETY	**LINEBACKER**	**MIDDLE GUARD**	**LINEBACKER**	**SAFETY**	**PUNTER**
EMLEN TUNNELL	**JOE SCHMIDT**	**BILL WILLIS**	**BILL GEORGE**	**BOBBY DILLON**	**HORACE GILLOM**
Jack Christiansen	Chuck Bednarik	Dale Dodrill	George Connor	Yale Lary	Pat Brady
Jimmy Patton	Sam Huff	Les Bingaman	Les Richter	Jerry Norton	Sam Baker

> NFL NEWS

THE FREE SUBSTITUTION RULE is permanently adopted at the start of the 1950 season, making possible the evolution of separate offensive and defensive units.

THE LOS ANGELES RAMS televise all of their games in the 1950 season, the first team to do so. Their attendance drops by 46% from the previous year.

BURT LANCASTER plays the title role in *Jim Thorpe—All American*, the story of the great multisport athlete who was also the first league president of the American Professional Football Association, which would become the National Football League.

THE 1951 CHAMPIONSHIP GAME between the Browns and the Rams is the first nationally televised game. The DuMont Network paid $75,000 for the rights to air the 24–17 Rams win.

THE 1–11 DALLAS TEXANS, operated by the league out of Hershey, Pa., but without a stadium during the second half of the 1952 season, disband at the end of the year. No NFL franchise has gone out of business since.

IN 1953 the United States District Court for the Eastern District of Pennsylvania upholds NFL restrictions on broadcasts of home games into the territory of a team during those games. Commissioner Bert Bell rules in '56 that all home games would be blacked out.

ALAN AMECHE scores the overtime touchdown that ends the Baltimore Colts' 1958 NFL Championship Game against the New York Giants and then appears later that night on *Toast of the Town*, a nationally broadcast variety television show hosted by Ed Sullivan.

>NICKNAMES<

Chuck [Concrete Charlie] Bednarik
Howard [Hopalong] Cassady
L.G. [Long Gone] Dupre
Frank [Gunner] Gatski
Lou [the Toe] Groza
^ Elroy [Crazy Legs] Hirsch
Dick [Night Train] Lane
Eugene [Big Daddy] Lipscomb
Joe [the Jet] Perry
Zollie [Tug Boat] Toth
Tom [the Bomb] Tracy

RECORD OF THE DECADE

Rams rookie defensive back Dick (Night Train) Lane intercepted a record 14 passes during the 12 games of the 1952 season. More than half a century later, with teams now playing 16 games, Lane's record still stands.

> GO FIGURE

5 | NFL players featured on the cover of SPORTS ILLUSTRATED in the 1950s after San Francisco 49ers quarterback Y.A. Tittle became the first, on the Nov. 22, 1954.

6 | Touchdowns by Cleveland halfback Dub Jones in a 42–21 win over the Bears in 1951, including scores on each of his last five touches.

53,676 | Attendance for the first Pro Bowl, in 1951. The American Conference beat the National Conference 28–27.

4 | AAFC teams that did not join the NFL in 1950. The Brooklyn–New York Yankees, Buffalo Bills, Chicago Hornets and Los Angeles Dons were disbanded and their players were dispersed among the NFL's clubs.

8 | Number of clubs in the American Football League, formed in 1959 and scheduled to begin play in 1960. The original AFL cities were Boston, Buffalo, Dallas, Denver, Houston, Los Angeles, Minneapolis and New York.

375 | Combined NFL head coaching victories (including four Super Bowls) for Tom Landry and Vince Lombardi, who in 1954 worked together under coach Jim Lee Howell as the Giants' defensive and offensive coordinators, respectively.

8 | Interceptions thrown by Chicago Cardinals quarterback Jim Hardy in an opening day loss to the Philadelphia Eagles in 1950. At the time Hardy held the NFL record for most consecutive passes without an interception (114).

5,000 | Minimum wage, in dollars, negotiated in 1957 by the newly established Players' Association.

DECADE HIGHS

RUSHING
YARDS: 7,151 / JOE PERRY
TDs: 49 / JOE PERRY

PASSING
YARDS: 20,539 / NORM VAN BROCKLIN
TDs: 151 / BOBBY LAYNE

RECEIVING
CATCHES: 404 / BILLY WILSON
YARDS: 6,091 / BILLY HOWTON
TDs: 49 / ELROY HIRSCH

SCORING
742 POINTS / LOU GROZA

SEASON HIGHS

RUSHING
YARDS: 1,527 / JIM BROWN 1958
TDs: 17 / JIM BROWN 1958

PASSING
YARDS: 2,899 / JOHNNY UNITAS 1959
TDs: 32 / JOHNNY UNITAS 1959

RECEIVING
CATCHES: 84 / TOM FEARS 1950
YARDS: 1,495 / ELROY HIRSCH 1951
TDs: 17 / ELROY HIRSCH 1951

SCORING
128 POINTS / DOAK WALKER 1950

GAME HIGHS

RUSHING
237 YARDS / JIM BROWN 11/24/57

PASSING
554 YARDS / NORM VAN BROCKLIN 9/28/51

RECEIVING
302 YARDS / CLOYCE BOX 12/3/50

SCORING
36 POINTS / DUB JONES, 6 TDs 11/25/51

>Time Capsule THE 60S

1969 | DEACON JONES (75), an obscure 14th-round draft pick in '61, emerged as a perennial all-pro defensive end for the Rams.

JAMES FLORES/WIREIMAGE; WAYNE REYNOLDS (SMITH)

> DR. Z's ALL DECADE TEAM

OFFENSE

WIDE RECEIVER	HALFBACK	QUARTERBACK	FULLBACK	WIDE RECEIVER	KICKER
LANCE ALWORTH	**GALE SAYERS**	**JOHNNY UNITAS**	**JIM BROWN**	**DON MAYNARD**	**JAN STENERUD**
Tommy McDonald	Lenny Moore	Len Dawson	Jim Taylor	Bobby Mitchell	Jim Bakken
Paul Warfield	Clemon Daniels	Joe Namath	Matt Snell	Bob Hayes	Bruce Gossett

GUARD	TACKLE	CENTER	TACKLE	GUARD	TIGHT END
JIM PARKER	**FORREST GREGG**	**JIM OTTO**	**RON MIX**	**BILLY SHAW**	**MIKE DITKA**
Walt Sweeney	Bob Brown	Jim Ringo	Roosevelt Brown	Gene Hickerson	John Mackey
Fuzzy Thurston	Winston Hill	Mick Tingelhoff	Jim Tyrer	Ed Budde	Pete Retzlaff

DEFENSE

CORNERBACK	END	TACKLE	TACKLE	END	CORNERBACK
JIMMY JOHNSON	**DEACON JONES**	**MERLIN OLSEN**	**BOB LILLY**	**RICH JACKSON**	**WILLIE BROWN**
Dick (Night Train) Lane	Gino Marchetti	Alex Karras	Houston Antwine	Willie Davis	Herb Adderley
Dick LeBeau	Doug Atkins	Tom Sestak	Henry Jordan	Earl Faison	Lem Barney

STRONG SAFETY	LINEBACKER	LINEBACKER	LINEBACKER	FREE SAFETY	PUNTER
RICHIE PETITBON	**DAVE WILCOX**	**DICK BUTKUS**	**CHUCK HOWLEY**	**LARRY WILSON**	**TOMMY DAVIS**
Johnny Robinson	Dave Robinson	Ray Nitschke	Bobby Bell	Willie Wood	Yale Lary
Kenny Graham	Wayne Walker	Lee Roy Jordan	Larry Grantham	Eddie Meador	Jerrel Wilson

> NFL NEWS

BYRON (WHIZZER) WHITE, the NFL's rushing leader in 1940, is appointed to the United States Supreme Court in '62.

THE PRO FOOTBALL Hall of Fame opens in Canton, Ohio, in 1963.

PETE GOGOLAK of Cornell becomes the first professional soccer-style kicker when he signs with the Bills in 1964.

ON OCT. 25, 1964, defensive end Jim Marshall picks up a 49ers fumble and rambles 66 yards into the end zone for what he thinks is a touchdown. Marshall ran the wrong way, however, and scored two points for San Francisco.

OAKLAND'S COACH AND G.M. Al Davis becomes commissioner of the AFL in 1966.

IN THE SPRING OF 1966 Tex Schramm of the Cowboys and Lamar Hunt of the Chiefs hold secret meetings to work out the details of a merger between the AFL and NFL for the 1970 season.

WHILE FILMING *The Dirty Dozen*, Jim Brown, 30, the NFL's alltime leading rusher, announces that he's retiring from football to pursue acting full time.

FORMER GIANTS DEFENSIVE BACK Emlen Tunnell becomes the first African-American elected to the Pro Football Hall of Fame.

ON NOV. 17, 1968, NBC switches from its national broadcast of the Jets-Raiders game with 50 seconds remaining to air the children's movie *Heidi*. The Jets are leading 32–29 at the time, but Oakland scores two TDs to win 43–32 while calls from legions of irate viewers overwhelm the NBC switchboard in Manhattan.

> NICKNAMES <

Lance [Bambi] Alworth
Junious [Buck] Buchanan
Elbert [Golden Wheels] Dubenion
Carlton [Cookie] Gilchrist
David [Deacon] Jones
Daryle [the Mad Bomber] Lamonica
Jim [Wrong Way] Marshall
[Broadway] Joe Namath
^ Charles [Bubba] Smith
Fred [Fuzzy] Thurston
Fred [Hammer] Williamson

RECORD OF THE DECADE

Bears rookie Gale Sayers set an NFL record for touchdowns in a season by getting into the end zone 22 times in 1965. Sayers reached pay dirt 14 times on the ground, six times through the air and twice on returns (one punt, one kickoff).

> GO FIGURE

17 Points by which the NFL's Baltimore Colts were favored over the AFL's New York Jets in Super Bowl III. The Jets won, 16–7.

23 Number of ballots it took NFL owners to elect Pete Rozelle commissioner in 1960.

15,000 Winning player's share, in dollars, for the Green Bay Packers from the AFL–NFL World Championship Game (a.k.a. Super Bowl I), played in Los Angeles on Jan. 15, 1967.

14 Regular-season NFL games after two were added to each team's 1961 schedule.

2,000 Dollars paid in fines by Detroit's Alex Karras and Green Bay's Paul Hornung in 1963 for placing bets on NFL games. They were also were suspended indefinitely and sat out one year.

2 Days after the assassination of President Kennedy that the NFL allowed games to be played. Three of the seven games played that day were sellouts.

22 Consecutive games, from 1963 to '65, in which Colts back Lenny Moore scored a touchdown.

18 Consecutive games during the 1962 and '63 seasons in which Raiders defensive back Tom Morrow had an interception.

17 Charter members of the Pro Football Hall of Fame when it opened in 1963: Sammy Baugh, Bert Bell, Joe Carr, Earl (Dutch) Clark, Red Grange, George Halas, Mel Hein, Wilbur (Fats) Henry, Cal Hubbard, Don Hutson, Earl (Curly) Lambeau, Tim Mara, George Preston Marshall, Johnny (Blood) McNally, Bronko Nagurski, Ernie Nevers and Jim Thorpe.

DECADE HIGHS

RUSHING
YARDS: 8,514 / JIM BROWN
TDS: 76 / JIM TAYLOR

PASSING
YARDS: 26,548 / JOHNNY UNITAS
TDS: 207 / SONNY JURGENSEN

RECEIVING
CATCHES: 470 / BOBBY MITCHELL
YARDS: 7,472 / BOBBY MITCHELL
TDS: 64 / SONNY RANDLE

SCORING
870 POINTS / LOU MICHAELS

SEASON HIGHS

RUSHING
YARDS: 1,863 / JIM BROWN 1963
TDS: 19 / JIM TAYLOR 1962

PASSING
YARDS: 3,747 / SONNY JURGENSEN 1967
TDS: 36 / Y.A. TITTLE 1963

RECEIVING
CATCHES: 93 / JOHNNY MORRIS 1964
YARDS: 1,436 / BOBBY MITCHELL 1963
TDS: 15 / SONNY RANDLE 1960

SCORING
176 POINTS / PAUL HORNUNG 1960

GAME HIGHS

RUSHING
237 YARDS / JIM BROWN 11/19/61

PASSING
505 YARDS / Y.A. TITTLE 10/28/62

RECEIVING
269 YARDS / DEL SHOFNER 10/28/62

SCORING
36 POINTS / GALE SAYERS, 6 TDs 12/12/65

> Time Capsule THE 70^S^

1974 | MEAN JOE GREENE (75), the first pick in the '69 draft, became the cornerstone of a Steelers team that dominated with defense and won four Super Bowls in the decade.

WALTER IOOSS JR.; HEINZ KLUETMEIER (JOHNSON)

> DR. Z's ALL DECADE TEAM

OFFENSE	WIDE RECEIVER **HAROLD CARMICHAEL** Cliff Branch Charlie Joiner	RUNNING BACK **WALTER PAYTON** O.J. Simpson Franco Harris	QUARTERBACK **ROGER STAUBACH** Ken Anderson Terry Bradshaw	FULLBACK **LARRY CSONKA** Sam Cunningham Rocky Bleier	WIDE RECEIVER **HAROLD JACKSON** Fred Biletnikoff Lynn Swann	KICKER **GARO YEPREMIAN** Don Cockroft Mark Moseley
	GUARD **JOHN HANNAH** Gene Upshaw Doug Wilkerson	TACKLE **ART SHELL** Jon Kolb Dan Dierdorf	CENTER **MIKE WEBSTER** Jim Langer Dave Dalby	TACKLE **RAYFIELD WRIGHT** Winston Hill George Kunz	GUARD **BOB KUECHENBERG** Bob Young Tom Mack	TIGHT END **DAVE CASPER** Charlie Sanders Ray Chester
DEFENSE	CORNERBACK **JAMES JOHNSON** Mike Haynes Mel Renfro	END **CEDRICK HARDMAN** L.C. Greenwood Claude Humphrey	TACKLE **JOE GREENE** Curley Culp Randy White	TACKLE **BOB LILLY** Alan Page Ernie Holmes	END **ELVIN BETHEA** Jack Youngblood Carl Eller	CORNERBACK **WILLIE BROWN** Mel Blount Roger Wehrli
	STRONG SAFETY **KEN HOUSTON** Charlie Waters Dick Anderson	LINEBACKER **TED HENDRICKS** Matt Blair Robert Brazile	LINEBACKER **WILLIE LANIER** Jack Lambert Lee Roy Jordan	LINEBACKER **JACK HAM** Dave Wilcox Tom Jackson	FREE SAFETY **CLIFF HARRIS** Jake Scott Paul Krause	PUNTER **RAY GUY** Jerrel Wilson Dave Jennings

> NFL NEWS

ABC'S *MONDAY NIGHT FOOTBALL* makes its debut on Sept. 21, 1970, with a game between the Browns and the Jets.

PRESIDENT RICHARD NIXON makes national news by suggesting plays for the 1971 postseason to Redskins coach George Allen and Dolphins coach Don Shula.

ON JULY 13, 1972, Carroll Rosenbloom, who owned the Colts, and Robert Irsay, who had recently taken over the Los Angeles Rams, swap franchises.

CONGRESS ADOPTS LEGISLATION requiring that any NFL game sold out 72 hours before kickoff must be made available on local TV.

PASSER RATING becomes an official NFL statistic in 1973.

THE WORLD FOOTBALL LEAGUE begins play in 1974. A year later Miami's "Butch Cassidy and The Sundance Kid" backfield of Larry Csonka and Jim Kiick, along with receiver Paul Warfield, sign with the Memphis Southmen after contract disputes with the Dolphins.

DOLPHINS QUARTERBACK BOB GRIESE, in 1977, becomes the first NFL player to wear glasses during a game.

RAIDERS TIGHT END Dave Casper bats a loose ball into the end zone and pounces on it to score a game-winning touchdown against the Chargers in 1978. The play, dubbed the Holy Roller, is outlawed the following season.

OILERS ROOKIE Earl Campbell gains 1,450 yards on the ground in 1978 and becomes the first rookie since Jim Brown ('57) to top the NFL in rushing yards.

>NICKNAMES<

Sam [Bam] Cunningham
John [Frenchy] Fuqua
[Mean Joe] Greene
Thomas [Hollywood] Henderson
Ted [the Mad Stork] Hendricks
^ Billy [White Shoes] Johnson
Ed [Too Tall] Jones
Carl [Spider] Lockhart
Eugene [Mercury] Morris
Jack [Hacksaw] Reynolds
Ken [Snake] Stabler

RECORD OF THE DECADE

Vikings defensive end Jim Marshall established an alltime record by playing in 282 consecutive games. Marshall's streak began in 1960, during the Eisenhower Administration, and ended in 1979, with Jimmy Carter in office.

> GO FIGURE

6 Professional heavyweight fights for Cowboys defensive end Ed (Too Tall) Jones during his one-year hiatus from football in 1979. He won all his bouts, five by KO.

63 Length, in yards, of field goal by New Orleans kicker Tom Dempsey against the Lions on Nov. 8, 1970, the longest in NFL history.

26 Consecutive losses by Tampa Bay Buccaneers, a streak that began with the team's inaugural game in 1976.

5 Consecutive losses by the Seattle Seahawks in 1976, a streak that began with the team's inaugural game. Seattle's first win came against Tampa Bay.

2,003 Yards gained in 1973 in 14 games by Bills running back O.J. Simpson, the first man to rush for more than 2,000 yards in a season.

17 Consecutive wins for the 1972 Miami Dolphins, the only team to win every game through the regular season, the playoffs and the Super Bowl.

82:40 Official game time needed to complete Christmas Day playoff in 1971 between the Dolphins and the Chiefs. Garo Yepremian's field goal gave Miami the win in the longest game in NFL history.

98 Yards gained on the longest nonscoring play in NFL history when Cardinals wide receiver Bobby Moore (later known as Ahmad Rashad) caught a Jim Hart pass in a 1972 game against the Rams but was pulled down one yard short of the end zone.

DECADE HIGHS

RUSHING
YARDS: 10,539 / O.J. SIMPSON
TDs: 72 / FRANCO HARRIS

PASSING
YARDS: 23,863 / FRAN TARKENTON
TDs: 156 / FRAN TARKENTON

RECEIVING
CATCHES: 432 / HAROLD JACKSON
YARDS: 7,724 / HAROLD JACKSON
TDs: 61 / HAROLD JACKSON

SCORING
905 POINTS / GARO YEPREMIAN

SEASON HIGHS

RUSHING
YARDS: 2,003 / O.J. SIMPSON 1973
TDs: 19 / EARL CAMPBELL 1979

PASSING
YARDS: 4,082 / DAN FOUTS 1979
TDs: 28 / TERRY BRADSHAW 1978, STEVE GROGAN and BRIAN SIPE 1979

RECEIVING
CATCHES: 88 / RICKEY YOUNG 1978
YARDS: 1,237 / STEVE LARGENT 1979
TDs: 13 / DICK GORDON 1970, HAROLD JACKSON 1973, CLIFF BRANCH 1974, JOHN JEFFERSON 1978

SCORING
138 POINTS / O.J. SIMPSON 1975

GAME HIGHS

RUSHING
275 YARDS / WALTER PAYTON 11/20/77

PASSING
496 YARDS / JOE NAMATH 9/24/72

RECEIVING
255 YARDS / JERRY BUTLER 9/23/79

SCORING
24 POINTS / WILBERT MONTGOMERY, 4 TDs 9/10/78 and 10/7/79; 19 OTHERS (once each)

> Time Capsule THE 80s

ERIC DICKERSON led the league in rushing four times, including his record-breaking 2,105-yard season in '84.

PETER READ MILLER; AL MESSERSCHMIDT/WIREIMAGE (PERRY)

> DR. Z's ALL DECADE TEAM

OFFENSE	WIDE RECEIVER **JERRY RICE** James Lofton Art Monk	RUNNING BACK **WALTER PAYTON** Eric Dickerson Marcus Allen	QUARTERBACK **JOE MONTANA** Dan Marino Dan Fouts	FULLBACK **EARL CAMPBELL** John Riggins Roger Craig	WIDE RECEIVER **STEVE LARGENT** Stanley Morgan Wes Chandler	KICKER **NICK LOWERY** Morten Andersen Gary Anderson
OFFENSE	GUARD **JOHN HANNAH** Russ Grimm Max Montoya	TACKLE **ANTHONY MUNOZ** Jackie Slater Luis Sharpe	CENTER **DWIGHT STEPHENSON** Mike Webster Jay Hilgenberg	TACKLE **MIKE KENN** Joe Jacoby Gary Zimmerman	GUARD **MIKE MUNCHAK** Bruce Matthews Bill Fralic	TIGHT END **MARK BAVARO** Ozzie Newsome Todd Christensen
DEFENSE	CORNERBACK **MIKE HAYNES** Frank Minnifield Ken Riley	END **REGGIE WHITE** Howie Long Richard Dent	TACKLE **JEROME BROWN** Joe Klecko Tim Krumrie	TACKLE **DAN HAMPTON** Randy White Gary Johnson	END **LEE ROY SELMON** Bruce Smith Fred Dean	CORNERBACK **DARRELL GREEN** Albert Lewis Lester Hayes
DEFENSE	STRONG SAFETY **JOEY BROWNER** Kenny Easley Nolan Cromwell	LINEBACKER **LAWRENCE TAYLOR** Clay Matthews Carl Banks	LINEBACKER **MIKE SINGLETARY** Sam Mills Harry Carson	LINEBACKER **TED HENDRICKS** Andre Tippett Rickey Jackson	FREE SAFETY **DERON CHERRY** Ronnie Lott Gary Fencik	PUNTER **REGGIE ROBY** Rohn Stark Sean Landeta

> NFL NEWS

ON JAN. 10, 1982, the 49ers upset the Cowboys in the NFC Championship game on a pass from Joe Montana to Dwight Clark in the corner of the Candlestick Park end zone with 58 seconds remaining. The Catch marks the start of San Francisco's dynasty.

THREE TEAMS RELOCATE during the 1980s:
• In 1982 the Raiders move from Oakland to Los Angeles after a successful suit against the NFL.
• Baltimore Colts owner Robert Irsay packs the team's equipment into trucks in the middle of the night of March 28, 1984, and moves to Indianapolis.
• Cardinals owner Bill Bidwill moves the NFL's oldest continuously operating franchise from St. Louis to Phoenix in 1988.

THE NFL PLAYERS strike for 57 days during the 1982 season. Seven of the scheduled 16 games are canceled.

WALTER PAYTON rushes for 154 yards against the Saints on Oct. 7, 1984, and passes Jim Brown as the NFL's alltime leading rusher.

ON NOV. 18, 1985, on *Monday Night Football*, Giants linebackers Lawrence Taylor and Gary Reasons tackle Redskins quarterback Joe Theismann, who suffers a gruesome compound fracture of his right tibia and fibula. Theismann will never play again.

ON JULY 29, 1986, the USFL is awarded $1 by the U.S. District Court in New York in its $1.7 billion antitrust suit against the NFL.

GEORGE (PAPA BEAR) HALAS, an original NFL member and the patriarch of the Chicago Bears, dies on October 31, 1988, at the age of 88.

IN MARCH 1989, commissioner Pete Rozelle announces his retirement.

> NICKNAMES <

John [Jumbo] Elliott
Norman [Boomer] Esiason
[Swervin'] Mervyn Fernandez
Howard [Hokie] Gajan
James [Jumpy] Geathers
Elvis [Toast] Patterson
^ William [Refrigerator] Perry
James [Tootie] Robbins
Willis [Weegie] Thompson
Andre [Dirty] Waters
Elbert [Ickey] Woods

RECORD OF THE DECADE

The Dolphins went an NFL record 19 games without giving up a sack. On Oct. 29, 1989, Bills nosetackle Jeff Wright broke the string when he sacked Dan Marino in the second quarter of Buffalo's 31–17 win.

> GO FIGURE

3 | Consecutive games in which the 1981 Raiders, the defending Super Bowl champions, were shut out. No team since the '43 Brooklyn Dodgers had been blanked in three straight games, and the Raiders hadn't been held scoreless in 15 years.

6 | Quarterbacks selected in the first round of the 1983 draft. John Elway went first, to the Baltimore Colts, and before Dan Marino went to the Dolphins with the 27th pick, four others were taken: Todd Blackledge (seventh, Chiefs), Jim Kelly (14th, Bills), Tony Eason (15th, Patriots) and Ken O'Brien (24th, Jets).

41 | Highest rank reached on the Billboard charts by *The Super Bowl Shuffle*, the video of which was released, along with the record, in the midst of the Chicago Bears' 1985 championship season.

68 | Years between the hiring of Fritz Pollard, the NFL's first African-American head coach, and that of the second, Art Shell, who was hired by the Raiders in 1989.

48 | Percentage of fans in a 1981 CBS–*New York Times* poll who considered football their favorite sport. Baseball was second at 31%.

454 | Regular season and playoff games, beginning with the advent of the Dallas Cowboys in 1960, coached by Tom Landry before he was replaced after the '88 season.

1,000 | Rushing and receiving totals surpassed in 1985 by 49ers running back Roger Craig, the first man to do so in a season.

0 | Number of backs who gained 1,000 rushing yards during the 1980s for the Dolphins and the Packers, the decade's only two teams without such a runner.

DECADE HIGHS

RUSHING
YARDS: 11,226 / ERIC DICKERSON
TDS: 82 / ERIC DICKERSON

PASSING
YARDS: 30,958 / JOE MONTANA
TDS: 220 / DAN MARINO

RECEIVING
YARDS: 9,465 / JAMES LOFTON
CATCHES: 662 / ART MONK
TDS: 69 / STEVE LARGENT

SCORING
1,006 POINTS / NICK LOWERY

SEASON HIGHS

RUSHING
YARDS: 2,150 / ERIC DICKERSON 1984
TDS: 24 / JOHN RIGGINS 1983

PASSING
YARDS: 5,084 / DAN MARINO 1984
TDS: 48 / DAN MARINO 1984

RECEIVING
CATCHES: 106 / ART MONK 1984
YARDS: 1,570 / JERRY RICE 1986
TDS: 22 / JERRY RICE 1987

SCORING
161 POINTS / MARK MOSELEY 1983

GAME HIGHS

RUSHING
YARDS: 221 / BO JACKSON 11/30/87
221 / GERALD RIGGS 9/17/89
221 / GREG BELL 9/24/89

PASSING
YARDS: 521 / DAN MARINO 10/23/88

RECEIVING
YARDS: 336 / WILLIE (FLIPPER) ANDERSON 11/26/89

SCORING
30 POINTS / KELLEN WINSLOW, 5 TDS 11/22/81

>Time Capsule THE 90s

1998 | REGGIE WHITE (92), the Minister of Defense, was one of the league's most fearsome pass rushers for more than a decade.

PATRICK FERRON/GREEN BAY PRESS-GAZETTE/AP/WIDE WORLD PHOTOS; ED ZURGA/AP (RISON)

> DR. Z's ALL DECADE TEAM

Unit	Position	Selection	Also	Also
OFFENSE	WIDE RECEIVER	**JERRY RICE**	Andre Reed	Irving Fryar
OFFENSE	RUNNING BACK	**EMMITT SMITH**	Barry Sanders	Thurman Thomas
OFFENSE	QUARTERBACK	**STEVE YOUNG**	John Elway	Troy Aikman
OFFENSE	FULLBACK	**DARYL JOHNSTON**	Mike Alstott	Larry Centers
OFFENSE	WIDE RECEIVER	**CRIS CARTER**	Sterling Sharpe	Michael Irvin
OFFENSE	KICKER	**MORTEN ANDERSEN**	Nick Lowery	John Carney
OFFENSE	GUARD	**LARRY ALLEN**	Dave Szott	Randall McDaniel
OFFENSE	TACKLE	**MIKE KENN**	Tony Boselli	Harris Barton
OFFENSE	CENTER	**DERMONTTI DAWSON**	Kent Hull	Tom Nalen
OFFENSE	TACKLE	**JACKIE SLATER**	Bruce Armstrong	Gary Zimmerman
OFFENSE	GUARD	**BRUCE MATTHEWS**	Will Shields	Steve Wisniewski
OFFENSE	TIGHT END	**SHANNON SHARPE**	Ben Coates	Jay Novacek
DEFENSE	CORNERBACK	**DEION SANDERS**	Rod Woodson	Aeneas Williams
DEFENSE	END	**REGGIE WHITE**	Charles Haley	Leslie O'Neal
DEFENSE	TACKLE	**BRYANT YOUNG**	Ray Childress	Michael Dean Perry
DEFENSE	TACKLE	**CORTEZ KENNEDY**	Warren Sapp	Dan Saleaumua
DEFENSE	END	**BRUCE SMITH**	Robert Porcher	Neil Smith
DEFENSE	CORNERBACK	**DARRELL GREEN**	Albert Lewis	Dwayne Harper
DEFENSE	STRONG SAFETY	**TIM McDONALD**	LeRoy Butler	Rodney Harrison
DEFENSE	LINEBACKER	**DERRICK BROOKS**	Junior Seau	Kevin Greene
DEFENSE	LINEBACKER	**RAY LEWIS**	Sam Mills	Chris Spielman
DEFENSE	LINEBACKER	**DERRICK THOMAS**	Seth Joyner	Rickey Jackson
DEFENSE	FREE SAFETY	**BRIAN DAWKINS**	Eugene Robinson	Merton Hanks
DEFENSE	PUNTER	**MATT TURK**	Darren Bennett	Rich Camarillo

> NFL NEWS

FOX OUTBIDS CBS for the NFC broadcast package and begins televising games in 1994. Four years later CBS takes the AFC from NBC with a staggering $17.6 billion, eight-year deal.

DON SHULA wins his 325th game, on Nov. 14, 1993, to surpass George Halas as the winningest NFL coach. The Dolphins coach would retire after the 1995 season with 347 wins.

IN 1994, a year before his induction into the Hall of Fame, former Seattle Seahawks wideout Steve Largent is elected to the U.S. Congress to represent the first district of Oklahoma.

THE NFL becomes the first major pro league with its own dedicated website when it launches NFLhome.com on April 10, 1995.

ON OCT. 3, 1995 Pro Football Hall of Famer O.J. Simpson is found not guilty of murdering his ex-wife, Nicole Brown Simpson, and her friend Ronald Goldman. Simpson is later found liable for the wrongful deaths in a civil suit filed by the victims' families and is ordered to pay $33.5 million.

FOUR TEAMS RELOCATE: the Rams (Anaheim to St. Louis), the Raiders (Los Angeles to Oakland), the Oilers (Houston to Nashville by way of Memphis) and the Browns/Ravens (Cleveland to Baltimore).

ON OCT. 25, 1998, Jason Elam of the Denver Broncos kicks a 63-yard field goal, tying the record set by Tom Dempsey of the New Orleans Saints in 1970.

THE NFL'S 29TH AND 30TH FRANCHISES, the Carolina Panthers and the Jacksonville Jaguars, begin play in 1995 and reach conference championship games in their second seasons. The expansion Browns begin play in 1999.

> NICKNAMES <

Jerome [the Bus] Bettis
Craig [Ironhead] Heyward
Qadry [the Missile] Ismail
Ragib [the Rocket] Ismail
Thomas [Pepper] Johnson
Nate [the Kitchen] Newton
^ Andre [Bad Moon] Rison
Deion [Prime Time] Sanders
Rick [Bootin'] Tuten
Reggie [the Minister of Defense] White

RECORD OF THE DECADE

No team had ever won its conference championship four years in a row or appeared in four straight Super Bowls—let alone *lost* all four—before the Buffalo Bills of 1990–93 were beaten by the Giants, the Redskins and the Cowboys (twice) in consecutive title games.

> GO FIGURE

1,457 Yards Barry Sanders needed to tie Walter Payton as the NFL's all-time leading rusher when the Lions running back abruptly retired before the 1999 season, at the age of 31.

22 Penalties (for a total of 178 yards) committed by the 49ers in their 26–21 loss to the Bills in 1998. That tied the single-game record set by the Brooklyn Dodgers and tied later by the Chicago Bears, both in 1944.

195 Players drafted in 1995 ahead of Terrell Davis, who becomes the lowest draft choice to rush for 1,000 yards in his first season with the Denver Broncos.

7 Rounds to which the NFL draft was reduced in 1994, down from eight the previous year and 12 from 1977 to 1992.

6 Consecutive 300-yard passing games by San Francisco 49ers quarterback Steve Young in 1999, breaking the NFL record of five by former teammate Joe Montana.

12 Rank at which *The Dark Side of the Game*, a 1996 novel by former Atlanta Falcons linebacker Tim Green, made its debut on *The New York Times* best sellers list.

51 Years between playoff wins for the Cardinals franchise after Arizona defeats the Dallas Cowboys, 20–7, in a 1998 NFC wild-card game.

15 Wins during the 1998 regular season by the Vikings, who joined the '84 49ers and '85 Bears as the only teams to win that many in a single year. Minnesota alone, however, failed to win the Super Bowl, losing the NFC title game in overtime to the Falcons.

DECADE HIGHS

RUSHING
YARDS: 13,963 / EMMITT SMITH
TDS: 136 / EMMITT SMITH

PASSING
YARDS: 33,508 / DAN MARINO
TDS: 235 / BRETT FAVRE

RECEIVING
CATCHES: 860 / JERRY RICE
YARDS: 12,078 / JERRY RICE
TDS: 103 / JERRY RICE

SCORING
1,130 POINTS / GARY ANDERSON

SEASON HIGHS

RUSHING
YARDS: 2,053 / BARRY SANDERS 1997
TDS: 25 / EMMITT SMITH 1995

PASSING
YARDS: 4,690 / WARREN MOON 1991
TDS: 41 / KURT WARNER 1999

RECEIVING
CATCHES: 123 / HERMAN MOORE 1995
YARDS: 1,848 / JERRY RICE 1995
TDS: 18 / STERLING SHARPE 1994

SCORING
164 POINTS / GARY ANDERSON 1998

GAME HIGHS

RUSHING
246 YARDS / COREY DILLON 12/4/97

PASSING
527 YARDS / WARREN MOON 12/16/90

RECEIVING
289 YARDS / JERRY RICE 12/18/95

SCORING
30 POINTS / JERRY RICE, 5 TDS 10/14/90
JAMES STEWART, 5 TDS 10/12/97

> Time Capsule THE 00S

2003 | CURTIS MARTIN (28) was still going strong in his 10th season, leading the league with 1,687 rushing yards for the Jets in '04.

KATHY WILLENS/AP; BILL FRAKES (JANIKOWSKI)

> DR. Z's ALL DECADE TEAM

OFFENSE

WIDE RECEIVER	RUNNING BACK	QUARTERBACK	FULLBACK	WIDE RECEIVER	KICKER
MARVIN HARRISON Hines Ward Derrick Mason	**CURTIS MARTIN** LaDainian Tomlinson Marshall Faulk	**TOM BRADY** Peyton Manning Brett Favre	**TONY RICHARDSON** Cory Schlesinger Mike Alstott	**RANDY MOSS** Torry Holt Jimmy Smith	**ADAM VINATIERI** David Akers Matt Stover
GUARD	**TACKLE**	**CENTER**	**TACKLE**	**GUARD**	**TIGHT END**
ALAN FANECA Bruce Matthews Marco Rivera	**WALTER JONES** Jonathan Ogden Brad Hopkins	**KEVIN MAWAE** Olin Kreutz Jeff Hartings	**WILLIE ROAF** Lomas Brown Orlando Pace	**WILL SHIELDS** Mike Wahle Steve Hutchinson	**TONY GONZALEZ** Jim Kleinsasser Frank Wycheck

DEFENSE

CORNERBACK	END	TACKLE	TACKLE	END	CORNERBACK
TY LAW Patrick Surtain Ronde Barber	**MICHAEL STRAHAN** Patrick Kerney Dwight Freeney	**LA'ROI GLOVER** Jamal Williams Kris Jenkins	**AARON SMITH** Richard Seymour Seth Payne	**JASON TAYLOR** Julius Peppers Aaron Kampman	**ANTOINE WINFIELD** Troy Vincent Nate Clements
STRONG SAFETY	**LINEBACKER**	**LINEBACKER**	**LINEBACKER**	**FREE SAFETY**	**PUNTER**
ED REED Darren Woodson John Lynch	**DERRICK BROOKS** Keith Bulluck Junior Seau	**RAY LEWIS** Zach Thomas Tedy Bruschi	**JULIAN PETERSON** Keith Brooking Chad Brown	**BRIAN DAWKINS** Mike Brown Darren Sharper	**SHANE LECHLER** Brian Moorman Craig Hentrich

> NFL NEWS

BALTIMORE RAVENS middle linebacker Ray Lewis pleads guilty to a misdemeanor charge of obstruction of justice in connection with the murder of two people in the early morning hours after Super Bowl XXXIV in Atlanta in January 2000. Lewis would be named the MVP of the Super Bowl the following season.

MINNESOTA VIKINGS offensive tackle Korey Stringer collapses from heatstroke during training camp, on July 31, 2001, and dies the next day.

IN THE FIRST NFL playoff game contested in February, Super Bowl XXXVI is decided on the final play. Adam Vinatieri's 48-yard field goal gives the Patriots a 20–17 win over the Rams.

THE EXPANSION Houston Texans join the NFL in 2002. The Seattle Seahawks move from the AFC to the NFC as the league realigns into eight four-team divisions.

RETURN SPECIALIST CHAD MORTON takes the overtime kickoff 96 yards for a touchdown, as the Jets defeat the Bills on Sept. 8, 2002. It takes Morton—who also returned a second-quarter kickoff 98 yards for a touchdown—just 14 seconds to reach the end zone, making this the shortest overtime game since the extra period was introduced in 1974.

COWBOYS RUNNING BACK Emmitt Smith becomes the NFL's alltime leading rusher, surpassing Walter Payton's career record on Oct. 27, 2002.

NFL NETWORK, a 24-hour cable channel, is launched on Nov. 4, 2003.

AFTER 35 SEASONS on ABC, the league announces on April 18, 2005, that *Monday Night Football* will move to ESPN in 2006.

> NICKNAMES <

Ronald [7-Eleven] Curry
Robert [Mountain] Gallery
Scott [Lurch] Gragg
^ Sebastian [Sea Bass] Janikowski
Adam [Pacman] Jones
Freddie [Fred-Ex] Mitchell
Julius [the Matrix] Peppers
John [Turnstile] St. Clair
James [King Tut] Tuthill
Floyd [Pork Chop] Womack

RECORD OF THE DECADE

Vikings kicker Morten Andersen extended his NFL record scoring streak to 332 games by producing at least one point in each of the Vikings 16 games during the 2004 season. Next on the list: the Broncos' Jason Elam, who is 144 games behind him.

> GO FIGURE

165 Points allowed by the 2000 Super Bowl champion Baltimore Ravens, the fewest ever by an NFL team in a 16-game season.

22½ Sacks in 2001 by New York Giants defensive end Michael Strahan, breaking Mark Gastineau's NFL record of 22. The final sack was disputed by some, who contended that Packers quarterback Brett Favre set up Strahan for the record-breaker.

0 NFL games played on Sept. 16–17, Week 2 of the 2001 season, in the wake of the 9/11 terrorist attacks in New York City and Washington, D.C.

1 Career completions by New England Patriots quarterback Tom Brady before he replaced an injured Drew Bledsoe in the second week of 2001. Brady would lead the Pats to three Super Bowl titles in four seasons.

107 Length, in yards, of an NFL-record return for a touchdown by Ravens cornerback Chris McAlister after a missed 57-yard field goal during a 2002 game against the Denver Broncos.

76 Number of times Houston Texans quarterback David Carr was sacked in 2002, an NFL record.

27 Touchdowns by Priest Holmes of the Kansas City Chiefs in 2003, which set the NFL record for rushing TDs in a season.

500 Hours of community service required of Ravens running back Jamal Lewis as part of a 2005 plea bargain for his involvment with a cocaine distribution ring in his hometown of Atlanta. Lewis also served four months in jail and two months in a halfway house and paid a $20,000 fine.

DECADE HIGHS

RUSHING
YARDS: 6,848 / AHMAN GREEN
TDS: 72 / PRIEST HOLMES

PASSING
YARDS: 21,568 / PEYTON MANNING
TDS: 164 / PEYTON MANNING

RECEIVING
CATCHES: 534 / MARVIN HARRISON
YARDS: 7,368 / TORRY HOLT
TDS: 65 / TERRELL OWENS

SCORING
625 POINTS / MIKE VANDERJAGT

SEASON HIGHS

RUSHING
YARDS: 2,066 / JAMAL LEWIS 2003
TDS: 27 / PRIEST HOLMES 2003

PASSING
YARDS: 4,830 / KURT WARNER 2001
TDS: 49 / PEYTON MANNING 2004

RECEIVING
CATCHES: 143 / MARVIN HARRISON 2002
YARDS: 1,722 / MARVIN HARRISON 2002
TDS: 17 / RANDY MOSS 2003

SCORING
163 POINTS / JEFF WILKINS 2003

GAME HIGHS

RUSHING
295 YARDS / JAMAL LEWIS 9/14/03

PASSING
504 YARDS / ELVIS GRBAC 11/5/00

RECEIVING
291 YARDS / JIMMY SMITH 9/10/00

SCORING
30 POINTS / SHAUN ALEXANDER, 5 TDS 9/29/02
CLINTON PORTIS, 5 TDS 12/7/03

COURTESY OF THE PRO FOOTBALL HALL OF FAME

HELMETS BEAR the battle scars of two Hall of Famers: Billy Shaw, the Bills' guard (1961–69), and Bobby Layne, the Steelers' quarterback during the last five years of his career (1958–62) | *Photographs by* DAVID N. BERKWITZ

Acknowledgments

THE WORDS AND PICTURES COLLECTED HERE REPRESENT THE WORK OF SEVERAL GENERATIONS OF SPORTS ILLUSTRATED WRITERS, PHOTOGRAPHERS AND EDITORS. BUT THIS BOOK WOULD NOT HAVE BEEN POSSIBLE WITHOUT THE IMMEDIATE CONTRIBUTIONS OF MANY CURRENT MEMBERS OF THE SI STAFF: LINDA VERIGAN, ED TRUSCIO, CHRIS HERCIK, LINDA ROOT, MICHELE BREA, STEVE FINE, DAN LARKIN, BOB THOMPSON, MARY MOREL, GEOFF MICHAUD, JOY BIRDSONG, HELEN STAUDER, NATASHA SIMON, LINDA LEVINE, GEORGE AMORES, LARRY GALLOP, ANN MCCARTHY, KAREN CARPENTER, GABE MILLER, BRIAN CLAVELL AND BARBARA FOX. INVALUABLE ASSISTANCE WAS PROVIDED BY THE PRO FOOTBALL HALL OF FAME, ESPECIALLY BY SALEEM CHOUDHRY, JASON AIKENS AND REUBEN CANALES OF NFL/WIREIMAGE. MITCH SHOSTAK AND CORIN HIRSCH DID PAINSTAKING WORK ON THE GATEFOLD. AND SPECIAL THANKS TO TERRY MCDONELL, THE MANAGING EDITOR OF SI, FOR HIS CONSTANT AND UNSTINTING SUPPORT.

COURTESY OF THE PRO FOOTBALL HALL OF FAME

Photo Credits

HALL OF FAME PHOTOGRAPHY BY DAVID N. BERKWITZ: P. 1, 28, 44, 68, 69, 84, 160, 161, 170, 171, 199, 205, 218, 230, 294 ARTIFACTS COURTESY OF THE PRO FOOTBALL HALL OF FAME

TABLE OF CONTENTS (TOP TO BOTTOM, FROM LEFT): JOHN G. ZIMMERMAN, NEIL LEIFER, NEIL LEIFER, DAMIAN STROHMEYER; NEIL LEIFER, HY PESKIN, JERRY WACHTER; RICHARD MACKSON, WALTER IOOSS JR., AL TIELEMANS; JOHN W. MCDONOUGH, TONY TOMSIC, ANDY HAYT, NEIL LEIFER

COVER CREDITS: AP/WWP 1, JOHN BIEVER 5, TODD BIGELOW/AURORA 1, GEORGE BRIDGES/KRT/ABACA 1, PETER BROUILLET/NFL/WIREIMAGE 1, SIMON BRUTY 1, ANTHONY J. CAUSI/ICON SMI 1, JEROME DAVIS/ICON SMI 1, ALBERT DICKSON/TSN/ICON SMI 1, TOM DIPACE 4, MIKE EHRMANN/WIREIMAGE 1, JAMES FLORES/WIREIMAGE 1, GREG FOSTER 1, BILL FRAKES 2, RICH FRISHMAN 1, JOHN D. HANLON 1, ANDY HAYT 1, HOF/WIREIMAGE 1, KENT HORNER/AP/WWP 1, GEORGE GOJKOVICH/GETTY IMAGES 1, NFL/WIREIMAGE 1, JOHN IACONO 1, ICON SMI 2, WALTER IOOSS JR. 3, LAWRENCE JACKSON/AP/WWP 1, GLENN JAMES/WIREIMGE 1, STEVE JACOBSON 1, ALLEN KEE/WIREIMAGE 1, HEINZ KLUETMEIER 2, DAVID E. KLUTHO 1, KIRBY LEE/WIREIMAGE 1, NEIL LEIFER 8, FRED LYON 1, BRAD MANGIN 1, AL MESSERSCHMIDT/WIREIMAGE 3, MANNY MILLAN 2, PETER READ MILLER 1, ANTHONY NESTE 1, MICHAEL O'NEILL 1, KEN REGAN/CAMERA 5 2, ROBERT ROGERS 1, BOB ROSATO 2, RON SCHWANE/ICON SMI 1, MARK SEROTA/REUTERS 1, SPORTSCHROME 1, RICH SUGG/THE KANSAS CITY STAR/AP/WWP 1, KEVIN TERRELL/WIREIMAGE 1, TONY TOMSIC 5, TONY TOMSIC/US PRESSWIRE 2, JOE TRAVER/REUTERS 1, ROB TRINGALI/SPORTSCHROME 1, STEVE WEWERKA 1, FRANK WHITE 1, JOHN G. ZIMMERMAN 3

GATEFOLD: COURTESY OF PRO FOOTBALL HALL OF FAME (2), NFL/WIREIMAGE (7)

AP/WIDE WORLD PHOTOS: P. 29, 58, 80, 81, 114, 115, 138, 144, 145, 193, 198, 212 (2), 219, 250, 251, 254, 263 CAMERA 5: P. 58 COLORADO SPRINGS GAZETTE/KRT/ABACA: P. 148 CORBIS: P. 94, 95, 181, 214, 215 GT IMAGES: P. 20, 21, 236, 238 GETTY IMAGES: P. 72, 116, 194, 265 ICON SMI: P. 59, 125, 231 MILWAUKEE JOURNAL SENTINEL/AP/WWP: P. 195 NFL/WIREIMAGE: P. 116, 138, 139, 174, 194, 195, 212, 270 REUTERS: P. 149, 174 SPORTSCHROME: P. 117 TIME & LIFE PICTURES/GETTY IMAGES: P. 2, 8, 9, 10, 11, 140 TOPEKA CAPITAL-JOURNAL: P. 200, 201 TOPEKA CAPITAL-JOURNAL/AP/WWP: P. 174 TSN/ZUMA PRESS/ICON SMI: P. 139, 194 (2) TSN/ZUMA PRESS/US PRESSWIRE: P. 81, 194 US PRESSWIRE: P. 117, 213 (2), 239 WIREIMAGE: P. 59, 80, 116 (2), 138, 139, 175, 195, 212

TIME INC. HOME ENTERTAINMENT

Publisher.................................Richard Fraiman
Executive Director, Marketing Services......Carol Pittard
Director, Retail & Special Sales.................Tom Mifsud
Marketing Director, Branded Businesses..........Swati Rao
Director, New Product Development.........Peter Harper
Assistant Financial Director............Steven Sandonato
Prepress Manager...............................Emily Rabin
Book Production Manager.................Jonathan Polsky
Marketing Manager...........................Kristin Rivela
Associate Prepress Manager.......Anne-Michelle Gallero
Assistant Marketing Manager.............Calandria Wells
SI Director, New Product Development....Bruce Kaufman

Published by Sports Illustrated Books

Time Inc.
1271 Avenue of the Americas
New York, New York 10020

ISBN: 1-932994-74-2
Library of Congress Control Number: 2005906437

A piece of the goalpost from the NFL's first sudden-death championship game resides in the Hall of Fame, in Canton.